D0504098

Gothic Painting I

To Anke, my wife

Gothic Painting I

The New World

Michel Hérubel

Edito-Service S.A.

Collection directed by Claude Schaeffner
Artistic Consultant:
Jean-Clarence Lambert
Art Director: André Held
Assistant: Martine Caputo
Cartographer: Jacques Ricci
Translated by Pamela Marwood

Illustration on cover:

The Limbourg Brothers
Late 14th-early 15th century
The Very Rich Hours of the Duke of Berry
c. 1416
Calendar for January (detail)
Condé Museum, Chantilly

Title-page illustration:

The Limbourg Brothers
Late 14th-early 15th century
The Very Rich Hours of the Duke of Berry
c. 1416
Calendar for April
Dourdan Castle
Condé Museum, Chantilly

The colour reproductions illustrating the first section were supplied by André Held of Lausanne, with the exception of:

Giraudon, Paris: cover, pages 3, 13, 16, 17, 23 right, 38, 39, 48, 58, 65, 79 and 83;
Scala, Florence: pages 50, 74, 76, 82 and 93;
La Photothèque Giraudon, Paris: pages 10, 66 and 68.

The black-and-white illustrations in the Dictionary were supplied by:
André Held, Lausanne: pages 146, 150, 151, 153 left, 162, 163, 164, 166, 167, 169, 170, 172, 173, 180, 181, 182, 184, 186, 188, 190, 191, 195 left, 196, 197 right, 201, 202 and 203;
Giraudon, Paris: pages 147, 148, 149, 153 right, 157, 161, 175, 176, 177, 178, 189, 193 and 200;
Brogi-Giraudon, Paris: pages 152, 185 and 195 right;
Anderson-Giraudon, Paris: pages 159 and 197 left;
Alinari-Giraudon, Paris: page 156.

Contents

Story of the Holy Virgin
Lower section of a 13th century stained-glass window
Chartres Cathedral

It is difficult to imagine two scenes more sharply contrasted than those which form the beginning and the end of the " Gothic " period. In the pictorial field, these contrasts are among the most striking in all history, whether of facts, ideas, thought or institutions. The term " Gothic " is traditionally linked to the pointed arch and the ribbed vault, which typify the architectural movement of the 13th century. In fact, the ribbed vault dates back even to the 12th century, and it is known that as early as 1144, when the choir of St. Denis was consecrated, it was an innovation recognised by contemporaries for its strength. It may seem more advisable to keep to its first great realisations —Notre-Dame de Paris, for example—but we still find ourselves in the 12th century there, as the first stone was laid in 1163. So, encircling the royal domain, arose a " crown" of cathedrals beginning with Sens, Noyon and Senlis, which continued around the Ile de France and culminated in the great vault of Beauvais.

During this period (it is known that the Beauvais vault collapsed in 1284 and was not completed until about 1324) occurred the whole era of splendour and prosperity which distinguished the reigns of Philip-August, Louis VIII and St. Louis, followed by the uncertain times of the two Philips (the Bold and the Fair), then their sons, foreshadowing already the great disasters which marked the latter part of the Middle Ages. Throughout the Gothic period, the feudal world achieved its full flowering, from chivalry, personified by men like Joinville and St. Louis, to the " Orders of Chivalry", pretexts for ostentatious banquets, tournaments and processions, in the course of which the participants displayed the most sumptuous extravagance.

The Gothic period at its height was one of great international trade, which in the 13th century created a continuous exchange between the wool-producing countries of the West and the silk-producing countries of the East. The trade routes converged on the Fairs of Champagne, where Russian furs and Flemish fabrics appeared alongside sachets of musk, sandalwood and bresel wood from India or Asia Minor. In the 14th century a series of bankruptcies brought about the decline of the Champagne Fairs; trade passed into the hands of the great silver merchants, who possessed warehouses and branch establishments, and its axis moved eastwards, while Flanders became the focal point of the West. Also, this was the time when the trades organised themselves into guilds. Free-lance work, subject only to local regulations that guaranteed finish and quality, was the general system of all trades in feudal times: there was a danger of its becoming a monopoly. Trades began to set themselves up in categories on which public authority soon imposed its regulations, while confirming them in the form they themselves had taken. Furthermore, the industrial towns, both in Flanders and Italy, were theatres of strong social upheaval—in the course of which the French cavalry tasted its first defeat on the battlefield of Courtai; economic and social upheavals became associated with the great dynastic quarrel which divided France and England and paralysed the West for over a hundred years, by the end of which the towns in the Hanseatic League, the Flemish ports and the Italian cities, had channelled a large part of the commercial movement to their own profit. If the 13th century was the century of St. Louis, those which mark the end of the Gothic era are the century of the Medicis, and the century of the Függers; bankers and traders dominated an epoch when the idea of nationhood entailed the idea of conquest, and when the monarch tried to conform to earlier precedents, which formerly commanded the admiration of the élite, by holding as his ambition the conqueror's wreath and triumphal arch; his thirst for conquest necessarily entailed recourse to the financiers, the brokers (the two functions are as yet hardly distinct) who, in their own good time, allowed military demands to be considered. It is a very significant anecdote which Jacob Függer recounts of receiving in his princely Augsburg home the Emperor Charles V after his election and lighting a log of cinnamon in his hearth in acknowledgement of the debt the latter had pledged himself to. And this ascendance of the financiers, whose commercial openings and monetary transactions were associated with war and conquest, had direct repercussions in the field of art; from the 15th century artists might equally well work for Etienne Chevalier, the Duke of Berry, a Medici, or the papal court. With the Dukes of Burgundy the lordly heyday experienced its most ostentatious splendours, but they were also its last: Charles VII and Louis XI forged the instruments of the monarchial splendour which only reigned at Versailles, and the castles that embellish the Loire Valley were mostly built by financiers in the service of the Monarch.

As for the Church, it has undeniably never affirmed its vitality more than by the series of great Gothic cathedrals which began with Notre-Dame de Paris and was completed with those of Milan, Seville and Cologne. But can one speak of completion? The power and fascination of Gothic architecture are such that, having fired the whole of Europe, from Westminster to Bologna, from Belem in Portugal to Mechlin in the Low Countries or Trondheim in Norway, having stretched as far East as the cathedrals of Sebastopol, or of Famagusta in Cyprus, Gothic was to survive even itself with the Cathedral of Orleans in the 18th century, and with innumerable edifices, churches and castles, in the 19th and even the 20th century, on the old and on the new Continent.

It has long been recognised that the great epoch of cathedrals was also the great epoch of doctrines. Both sculpted decoration and stained glass borrowed their themes from university teaching, which tended to group the various learnings according to logical systems: that of Vincent de Beauvais for science, that of Thomas Aquinas for theology. For example, the rose-window of the Cathedral of Lausanne is designed to evoke the liberal arts. But this encyclopaedic vision of the world gradually faded, replaced by the process of animating the allegories in " Le Roman de la Rose ", which had an immense vogue in the 14th and 15th centuries. The hero evoked in turn Courtesy, Danger, Idleness and Mirth, and his looks were bent on one ideal: not Woman, but The Rose. This same hero was to span two centuries and become the Heart of Smitten Love. Meanwhile, he was the subject of countless tedious descriptions, assuming the shield of Righteousness, and the spurs of Zeal; and the echoes of these refinements were to be heard later still in the literary salons where women bent over the chart of love. Meanwhile, the allegory inspired painters, particularly Italians, and gave them, among other things, a theme perfectly attuned to the period, that of the triumph of

Death, contemporary of the danses macabres *in which the Middle Ages seemed to celebrate their own funeral.*

Here, then, is the period background against which the figures described in the following text stand out. This historical survey concentrates principally on the themes used by the painters, whose stories can be followed by studying their works. Whatever the contribution of their individual genius may have been, each of them was involved in the spirit of an epoch which he would not have known how to avoid even had it been possible. And though their differences in style and their individual forms of awareness permit the art historian to differentiate and classify the works, of which many are still anonymous, the historian himself is often struck by what links the works to one another, common features determined by the main streams of thought, religion, war and peace.

Régine Pernoud.

Melchior Broederlam
Born c. 1388
Reredos of the Crucifixion
from the Carthusian Convent, Champmol
Detail of the *Flight into Egypt*
Fine-Arts Museum, Dijon

Colours of the Middle Ages

Gothic art is the infancy of a civilisation, a fresh relationship between man and God, the revelation which formed a whole miscellany in itself. The people of Europe created Gothic art. Even though the image of faith was always inscribed on the tympanum of cathedral doors, though philosophy was only a branch of theology, drama half composed of passion plays, and though miniatures, stained glass and frescoes* usually illustrated the Bible and moral scenes, it is none the less true that, under this moral, dogmatic and theological exterior, a whole hidden world of passions, dreams, desires and needs stirred and flourished in the 13th century.

Gothic art expressed man's liberty and intelligence, in their most profound sense. It was a journey towards the absolute, through the abysses of the soul, in both past and future. It was the journey of each man and every man, of the privileged and the peasant. Though there can be found in the cathedral the very symbol of the Druidical* forest, of the mystic universe constructed according to the initiate rules handed on from master craftsman to master craftsman, from mason to mason, from glazier to glazier; though it is also the high seat of the bishop representing the Pope, the temple of divinity, the fortress of the Christian Order; nevertheless it is also the house of God built by the people. The Gothic cathedral is first and foremost a popular monument erected by the common people; it is the very mirror of their faith in God, but also in themselves, of their despairs, their hopes, and their fortitude.

Gothic painting is a flower with petals of infinitely varied colours. It emerged in the West after almost ten centuries of darkness, during which ancient thought had taken exclusive refuge in the monasteries. Romanesque art was at the same time cosmic and mystic; it was inaccessible to the masses and the common people; peasant art and that of embryonic communities stayed outside its spirit. Gothic art was a popular revelation.

Drawn from man's conscience in the face of God, from nature, and from himself, it is what we find carved on the capitals of churches in a form still simple, tender, sometimes brutal and often fearful; it is what the glazier poured between the leads, where the daylight plays and sunbeams penetrate the depths of the colours as if the sky itself responded to the urgent demands of man and matter; it is the miniature in whose new haven of colours tentatively appears the look which already shows the disquietude of the human condition, the tenuous liberty of heart and mind. St. Bernard* expresses his dilemma when, on the brink of the Gothic age, he writes: "So numerous, so astonishing appears everywhere the variety of forms that a monk is tempted rather to study marbles than books and to meditate on these figures rather than the law of God". But St. Bernard belonged to a revolutionary age; he was the mystic in the fustian habit that hid the coat of mail, the adversary of the public spirit which, in the name of a terrible God, condemned equally the

* An asterisk after a word refers to the alphabetical glossary at the end of the book. This word forms the subject of a note or explanation.

first intellectual liberties of Abelard* and the first sensual visions of a people crossed by misfortune and hope.

Colour was paramount. In the walls of the churches blossomed the rose windows, from whose corolli, in rhythm with the daylight hours, beams of multi-coloured light swept the pillars and ogival vaults; colours drawn from nature and embroidered in cloth (cloths that draped the choir on feast days, castles, and rich mansions); colours in the oriflammes of war, the gonfolans of the tournament, and the curtains at the windows of town houses; colours of frescoes revealing man's rediscovered face, emerging from the obscurity of Italian churches; colours applied delicately to praying lips among the last Romanesque flourishes and the metallic Byzantine golds. Everywhere man stood up; everywhere his finger pointed to the sky as in a gesture of conquest or appeasement; everywhere nature half opened and the last robust Romanesque shrines* gave way to pillared houses.

It was an epoch of instinct and ardour combined with the birth of reason. Already a balance was established in men's relations, one philosophy was set against another, Duns Scotus* against St. Thomas*, and the human body was displayed side by side with Christ-in-Glory on west door pediments*. From the most mysterious depths of the West, where Celtic* superstitions were founded in the new light of semitic thought introduced by St. Paul*, and where the Latin order extended by papal authority modified, diluted and fertilised Viking ardour, German temerity, the infinite thoughtfulness of Gaul and the lyrical emotionalism of the Slavs, sprang an enormous movement which brought to ascetic* Europe a new sensuality and a new desire to live. Rare are the periods in human history that witness such an outburst of life. Gothic art in all its forms is, above all, a sign of life.

Even after six centuries of penitences, brutalities and convulsions, which the Church sought to check by asceticism, and which Charlemagne tried to contain within an order copied from that of Ancient Rome, even though heavy Romanesque basilicas still conserved Cistercian* mentality enshrined in their sombre stones and palely lit through colourless windows, and though the last feudal castles still sheltered peasants whose greatest desire was for emancipation, the first rumbles of the Gothic eruption could already be heard. Suger* raised the vaults of Saint-Denis*; Durham* in England and, some time later, Morienval on the borders of Picardy saw the first ribbed vaulting; Chartres* lit up as though astonished by colour. In the reign of St. Louis*, in spite of endemic friction, heresies, still barbarous passions, superstitions and badly-formed ideas, we perceive the launching of a new man, who carved, painted, wove, and wrote. And, alongside an aristocracy which had already lost its *raison d'être*, alongside a clergy fettered by strict dogmas (which three centuries later the Council of Trent* would fail to liberate), the spirit of the people took shape, and stamped new creations with its genius.

The Renaissance* did not so much return to the ancient spirit as resuscitate exhausted medieval energy, for the Gothic revolution, rather than being a radical change of form, was a birth, an impetus. All these flames of stone, these

The Limbourg Brothers
Late 14th-early 15th century
The Very Rich Hours of the Duke of Berry
c. 1416
Calendar for January
Condé Museum, Chantilly

fires, these gleams, all these modest and anonymous images of collective man at his birth, all these brocades and all this gold attests an advent, a profound originality, a sort of dynamism which the still embryonic thought of the time would try to control. Surely there is a prototype "Renaissance" in the plastic realism of the crowd of the damned and the blessed on the West Door of Bourges*, and in the rediscovery of woman in the tender lines which make the Virgin in Simone Martini's* *Annunciation* so precious to us, and in the reality of objects which introduces a sort of profane gravity into the illustrations of the manuscript of King René of Anjou, the *Book of the Heart of Smitten Love*. In this great æsthetic enterprise the art of the miniature was to progress through two centuries and arrive at a synthesis of thought and feelings which would be illustrated by easel paintings in the 15th century.

The Gothic epoch is a mirror of the universe, a "reflection of the world" as Vincent de Beauvais* already described it at the beginning of the 13th century; a complete universe equipped with its own economy, its sciences, and its æsthetic. But if we wish to grasp the medieval spirit in its entirety, we must look behind the mirror. There appear the moral and intellectual exigencies which made the contrasting art of the 13th and 14th centuries some of the most comprehensible and also the most puzzling. There has rarely been a phase of humanity combining such faith and superstition, tenderness and cruelty, most intransigent authority and intellectual liberty (even the propagation of heresies, or the resistance of universities to theologians), the severity of monastic rules and alchemists' research for the Absolute, morality and dissolute behaviour, crime and saintliness. Of all that, Gothic art is the reflection, and the reverse of the mirror reveals the mechanism. So the cathedral's forest of stone sheltered at the same time petrified nature, dogma, faith, pagan myths, eroticism and infernal rites, while above the roofs and the weathercocks grimaced demons brooding from proud heights over the sleep of right-thinking townspeople; so too the alchemists' manuscripts where the naïve appearance of a devil provokes an uneasy impression; so too the mysterious symbols in the tapestry* of the Apocalypse at Angers, or the secret, flower-bordered pages in certain books of hours. Mystery suspended from the skies over the Ile de France, Lincolnshire, the Rhineland, the Low Countries, Florence, Salamanca, mystery emanating from the Latin, Celtic and German soils, such was Gothic, the style which conquered one world and ushered in another.

If Gothic art were only mystery and spiritual quest, we would still be overwhelmed, but it is more, it is omnipresence, universality. By means of new techniques and oriental influences brought back from the Crusades*, it was all mankind which expressed itself, from the peasant to the lord, from the soldier to the citizen, the scientist to the priest. The cathedral was built to receive the whole town within its walls; the stained-glass windows of Chartres or Mons* or Canterbury* are like films which unrolled in sacred or profane sequence for the entertainment or instruction of the people; the statuary was not the privilege of private parks, as it was three or four centuries later on the banks of the Loire and at Versailles; it was displayed for the admiration of all on the portals of monuments, fixed to towers where it caught the fires of sunset, perched like a bird on entablatures; it rested like a flower among leaves of stone, leant over the bowed backs of pilgrims entering the churches, joined hands in formal prayer, or, in contrast, displayed its nakedness. Illumination* illustrated favourite books: all their characters seem to leap from the page to express a new world, to give themselves; it was no longer restricted by the dictates of the convent folios*, it was the auxiliary of the modest books of popular piety, but also of fabliaux, love stories, and medieval epics, besides university text books, esoteric books, and medical books.

Europe on the threshold of the 13th century shone with a thousand colours; colours from the oldest dawns in Flanders, from the deepest twilights of Armorica and Ireland, the freshest springtimes of the Loire, and the most vibrant afternoons of Tuscany; colours culled from the countryside of the West and enlivened by the breath of Eastern genius brought by the Crusaders.

Miniatures before the Gothic Period

Paleo-Christian illumination was located round the fringes of the Mediterranean: the Merovingian and the Carolingian in France, particularly in the East. We possess numerous manuscripts of this last period, including the *Echternach Gospels*, in which the best-known picture is that of the Lion of St. Mark the Evangelist. German miniatures always retained the Ottonian style, and for long after the height of the Middle Ages this was perpetuated within the Romanesque style, giving it a hard and over-refined flavour. Anglo-Saxon manuscripts between the 9th and 11th centuries were often associated with Winchester*, which was an old political capital and one of the chief centres of artistic and literary work on this side of the Channel. After the Norman Conquest, Continental influences, especially Parisian and Burgundian, eclipsed for a time the originality of Anglo-Irish genius.

The Romanesque miniature was basically mystic and abstract, being the result of long maturing in European monasteries, where, throughout the Paleo-Christian era, the various styles were established: Greek, Latin, Byzantine, Celtic and German. Illumination at this time was monks' work. The monasteries preserved the heritages of Rome, Greece and the Middle East throughout all the invasions. The Romanesque miniature was primarily ornamental, decorative, intentionally humble (even when it displayed genius, as in that hell closed by the angel in the *Psalter of Henri de Blois*—last quarter of the 12th century—or the *Annunciation* in the *Albany Psalter* of about 1125), and was auxiliary to the liturgy. It illustrated the missals, which were placed on the altars, the evangeliaries, or the books of Gregorian* chant set up in the centre of the choir as antiphonaries*. Though controlled by Cistercian severity, it already in many places heralded the Gothic style by its riot of colours and a positive naturalism.

Jean Fouquet (c. 1420-c. 1480)
Etienne Chevalier and St. Stephen, surrounded by angels, doing homage to the Virgin and Child.
Parchment extracted from the *Hours of Etienne Chevalier*
Condé Museum, Chantilly

Jean Fouquet
Birth of St. John the Baptist
Parchment extracted from the *Hours of Etienne Chevalier*
Condé Museum, Chantilly

Attributed to René of Anjou, 15th century
Book of the Heart of Smitten Love (about 1455)
Heart reads the inscription on the enchanted spring
National Library, Vienna

The Gothic Miniature

Thirteenth-century society

In the reign of St. Louis, especially towards the end, the whole of society was shifting and beginning to change its structure. It was a revolution of manners, silent and profound. The arts and literature* were becoming secularised. So were books, which were already in the hands of most nobles, some of the middle class and a few peasants. Jean Porcher* writes: "There is a phenomenon of 'laicisation' of art".[1] The common people had achieved emancipation. Towns, having gained their independence, enlarged and improved, especially in Germany and Flanders. The nobleman equipped himself at great expense for lavish hunts, feasts and tournaments; he fell into debt to merchants, Jewish and Lombardy banks, and lost a great deal of the moral and material credit granted him by the Church under a contract patiently worked out all through the great years of the Middle Ages. The nobility started to become the aristocracy. In the 13th century the first suggestion of functionalism appeared. The nobility, newly idle, grew refined. The masses no longer learnt solely by word of mouth, and there were even peasants' sons who could read. Laymen learnt to paint and calligraphers*, who were also illuminators, gathered into corporations.

Under the influence of prudent government French society settled down and began to develop new impetus. Thanks to the patronage of princes and lords, now on the verge of becoming a clientele of aesthetes, thanks also to his profession being officially recognised and protected by its corporative laws, the painter-illuminator was able to define and develop the art of the miniature in secular as well as religious paintings. From then on his work was addressed to very different classes, much more numerous and certainly less refined. Painting was more often for pleasure. Towards the middle of the 14th century hints of mannerism appeared. The difference is plain if we compare the *Ascension of Christ* in the *Evangeliary of Frantz von Erthal* (Mainz, about 1260) with the *Magnificat* in the *Book of Hours of Gian Galeazzo Visconti*, painted by Giovannino de Grassi* about 1385. It took the genius of Jacquemart de Hesdin* and the Limbourg* brothers with their *Very Rich Hours of the Duke of Berry* to restore to the miniature temporarily the honest intention and the power of the illuminators of the great epoch of the *St. Louis* and *Ingeborg Psalters*.

Gothic illumination

The qualities that characterised Gothic illumination from the first and made it thoroughly original were freshness, a naturalism that rejected Romanesque and Irish abstractions, and realism developed with an almost naïve care for precision.

[1] Jean Porcher, *Exposition des Miniatures gothiques*, Bibliothèque Nationale, Paris, 1957.

There was also deliberate *naïveté*, for the lack of perspective in Gothic miniatures is not a mistake, but a convention imposed by the design, and an intention dictated by the mood: why lead the spirit towards the horizon when it need only alight on a clever play of colours? Afterwards perspective clearly marked a decadence in painting and came into conflict with the realism of the scenes.

The miniature was now free of the yoke of the Romanesque initial letter. The first capital letter still provided opportunity for figures and allegorical or realistic scenes, but the subjects henceforth took prominence in number and importance. We often find pages ornamented with elaborate illuminated capitals*, but in this case the artist's deliberate intention was to make a complete work of the whole page. To define it more precisely, the 13th century miniature became more human and the art of painting for the first time in centuries was no longer simply the tool of morality, but actually a science. It is, moreover, moving to watch this tender young science evolving in the illuminators' first studios and springing up spontaneously here and there in Europe. The almost secret symbolism of the Romanesque manuscript (consider the *Apocalyse of Saint-Sever**) is reduced to more idealistic, yet more concrete proportions. One might say there was a "yielding" in faith; not heresy, but already some æsthetic, in place of ethical, or more precisely mystic, consideration. It was an era of research, of contradictions and misunderstandings, but full of life and movement. It is difficult to pinpoint the date of the metamorphosis from Romanesque to Gothic. The form of the *St. Louis Psalter*, for example, is still near to the Romanesque style and the mystic; by contrast, the miniatures of the *Creed* commissioned by the Master of Joinville* derive from the new naturalistic style, where movement is displayed in an interplay of colour and gesture.

Portraiture, in the sense of a picture designed to represent a recognisable person or object, appeared for the first time in the miniatures of St. Louis' reign. The Marquis of Laborde*, authority on medieval art, described it as follows: "The great French renaissance of the 13th century, original in conception, national in origin, created portraiture".[1] Lecoy de la Marche* defines even more closely the situation of French painting at this period: "The miniature, at first stiff and dry, gradually acquires a truly admirable delicacy and finish, particularly in facial expression, and soon reaches its zenith. It is thus that the French school, at whose head shines the brilliant name of Jean Fouquet, will later on make its greatest impact".[2] Less idealistic than the Italian school, less idiosyncratic than the English, less sentimental than the German, the French miniature, although perhaps lacking in imagination, is superior on many points of composition, balance and clarity. French portrait style was already being established, and there can be recognised in a look of Fouquet*, a trait of Clouet*, a dimension of Poussin*, a colour choice of

[1] L. de Laborde, *Les Ducs de Bourgogne*, Paris, 1849-1852.
[2] A. Lecoy de la Marche, *Les Manuscrits et la Miniature*, Paris, 1884.

Beatus uir qui non abiit
in consilio impiorum et
in uia peccatorum non
stetit: et in cathedra pesti
lencie non sedit.
Sed in lege domini uolū
tas eius: ⁊ in lege eius meditabitur die ac nocte.
Et erit tanquam lignum quod plantatū ē

Psalter
King David in his Palace
Quiriniana Library, Brescia

Renoir*, this same balance, this same restraint in colouring that first saw the light of day in the 13th century in the scriptoria* of the Rue de la Parcheminerie.

Realism

Gothic miniaturists rapidly established the new characteristics of their art, their approach to reality. The French National Archives possess the *Portrait of St. Louis*, painted about 1320 and the oldest picture of this king that has come down to us; it comes from the *Register of Ordinances of the Royal Mansion*. We notice that the artist (anonymous, of course, like nearly all medieval artists) has closely observed the folds of the garments, particularly the one decorated with fleurs-de-lys. The exploration of the shadows made by the folds of the robe separates us at one stroke from the almost abstract art of the Romanesque monks, who clothed a figure with only a few lines.

This heralded studies of a rigorous reality, later defined in Italy by Giotto* and Masaccio* and in Flanders by the brothers Van Eyck*. The portrait of the saint-king is posthumous, we are sure, and no doubt carried out by reference to the Archives of Canonisation* from which the artist drew his inspiration. Nevertheless, we have a "reality"—perhaps the first; posthumous, admittedly, but marked with the first ephemeral traces of human life, the first look that identifies the spirit of an age. The painter was able to portray in a moving way, by a masterly harmony of facial lines, the nobility, the generosity and the ascetic spirit that characterised the illustrious crusader. In this way, the portrait tallies with the written description by the Master of Joinville.

Altar facing, known as the Narbonne Frontal
Detail of the centre section:
Calvary c. 1375
Louvre, Paris

The realism and naturalism of the new style was also expressed in religious art. The figures in the missals seem to come down to earth and a play of light creates for the first time a duality between the kingdom of heaven and the transitory world of men. The earth seems to reclaim all the characters and set them inside the cardboard doorways, within a delicate vaulted framework. They live, and are no longer related simply to eternity. It, also, seems to come down from the sky. We can place in this period the *Pontifical* of the Châlons-sur-Marne library.

The Paris school

It is not easy to identify the different styles and schools. In France there was the Paris* school. It lasted during a large part of the Hundred Years War*, but the English invasion and the Burgundian succession destroyed it. Among the political and economic ruin, the art of the miniature was rescued, not by monks, but by painters, such as Jean Bourdichon*, André Beauneveu*, Jean de Bandol*, Girard d'Orléans* (creator of the famous *Portrait of John the Good*, painted on wood) and, greatest of all, Jean Fouquet, who illustrated the famous *Hours of Etienne Chevalier*. These painters are, however, no longer specialists in illumination, like Master Honoré*, who lived in the latter half of the 13th century. The miniatures of the Paris school were mostly created in the scriptoria of the rue Boutebrie, the rue de la Parcheminerie and around the church of Saint-Severin in Paris, by anonymous artists (like the one who signed himself with the couplet: "Henry is the illustrator's name, God guard him from dishonour"), and were swept away by the powerful movement from Flanders.

Breviary of the Grand Master Leon
The Blessed Agnes , Foundress of the Order, presents the Church of the Order to the Second Grand Master Conrad
National and University Library, Prague

Psalter of Ingeborg of Denmark
c. 1210
The Burning Bush; Moses and the Commandment Tablets
Condé Museum, Chantilly

Girard d'Orléans
Portrait of John the Good, King of France
c. 1360
Louvre, Paris

Jean Pucelle and his period

After the *Great Chronicles of France** (one of the most beautiful and accomplished works from the Saint-Denis scriptorium, dedicated to Philip III the Bold*), other illuminated manuscripts by masters such as Richard of Verdun* (son-in-law of Honoré, to whom is attributed one illustration in a manuscript of *The Decrees of Gratian*), are landmarks in this whole period, which straddled the 13th and 14th centuries. It occurred between the height of an art and the beginning of an imperceptible decline: realism wasted away for lack of new dimensions and technique. From this period, around 1325, arose the great miniaturist Jean Pucelle*, whose genius brought together the purity of early 13th century realism, and the refinement of the century which followed. Jean Pucelle and his school left a marked impression on the pictorial art of the later Middle Ages and had a profound influence on French painting generally.

Jean Pucelle was a "head of studio", which does not mean much today, but at that time a head of studio was recognised as an undisputed artist, a master; usually he held an honourable position at Court: first gentleman of the bedchamber, etc. In many of Pucelle's works we find the names of his principal collaborators: Anciau de Cens*, Jacquet Maci*, Jean Chevrier*. He was appointed painter to Charles IV (the Fair)*, and this discerning monarch commissioned many works from him, including the *Bible of Robert de Billyng*, the *Belleville Breviary*, and the *Little Hours*.

Pucelle started a new style in miniatures. He gave imagination free rein and Gothic flowered again. Moreover, he confirmed the master craftsman's independence of contemporary thought, scholarship and conventional style. The manuscript was now an illuminated entity, not only combining flourishes and folioles* entwined with many delightful beasts, but in which the text itself was given its full weight, written within a new, more flexible, framework, freed from traditional rules. In the 14th century the humble Romanesque manuscript, with backgrounds of flat colour, became a book of art, and it is difficult to decide which to admire more, illumination or portraiture, both of which reached their maturity. Soon, the brothers Van Eyck and others took advantage of the rift between the two incompatible disciplines, and the art of portraiture left its cradle. Pucelle gave such great freedom to the two styles that the miniature survived more or less successfully according to its own rules for much of the 15th and 16th centuries. There were in this period a few rare exceptions that heralded the coming decadence: the work of Bourdichon for example, six manuscripts of whom, or whose pupils, are known, including the *Hours of Anne of Brittany*, the *Tours Missal* and a book of hours in the collection of Baron Edmund Rothschild. Like Fouquet, Bourdichon was not a miniaturist in the tradition of the scriptoria. The style of the Master of the *Belleville Breviary* was elegant, full of imagery and innovations, but sometimes weakened by a certain preciousness, which in other artists became a mannerism. Pucelle's school

Jehan Roy de france

15th century miniature attributed to René of Anjou
Boccaccio: *Theseid*
Entry of Theseus into Athens
National Library, Vienna

was no exception, and after the master's death his ideas were so little understood by other illuminators that a formal mannerism was established in the workshops of the Paris school.

The miniature in France during the Hundred Years War

The French background became poorer. "From 1316 to 1350", writes Jacques Dupont*, "of ninety-two recorded copyists or booksellers in Paris, fifteen or perhaps nineteen are English. Master Honoré's *Decree of Gratian* is finished by Thomas of Wymonduswold in 1323, and Pucelle's *Bible* is written by another English calligrapher, Robert de Billyng. The artistic rapport between France and England has become very strong and typifies this community of civilisation which explains the political events of the 14th century."[1] These fatal events, brought about by the Hundred Years War, tolled the knell of the Paris school. For a time Flemish sap transfusing through Burgundy revived the flagging body, but not for long and the results were always limited.

Between 1350 and 1380, a respite in that interminable war, France rallied, and Charles V* succeeded in surrounding himself with painters of real talent, such as the Master of the Copses*, who illustrated the *Bible of Jean de Sy*, the *Poems* of Guillaume de Machaut*, the *Golden Legend* by Jacques de Voragine* and the famous *Great Chronicles of France*. During the reign of this cultured king, the depiction of living persons was extended to painting on vellum. Blanche of Navarre*, second wife of Philip of Valois*, is shown with her husband and her daughter, Jeanne, in a luminous and delicate miniature, in which she kneels before Christ and several saints, including St. Denis holding his severed head, offering to them a small building, representing a foundation she had just made. The execution is still sometimes naïve, but the artist has caught the psychology of the characters with a certain felicity.

Towards the end of the Middle Ages, between 1460 and 1470, a rarely talented artist, known as the Master of the Heart of Smitten Love*, illustrated the romance of the *Heart of Smitten Love*. There have been many attempts to identify the artist. Certain critics maintain that it was King René* himself; he would have had the opportunity to study painting and practise it during his years in captivity at Dijon when he was the prisoner of Philip the Good*, Duke of Burgundy. Sixteen miniatures were carried out of the forty-one planned. This work, full of premature "romantic" mystery and bathed in a sometimes disturbing surrealism, was the first to place realistic human beings in a setting of realistic objects and nature. Incontestably it marks a new step towards easel-painting.

[1] Jacques Dupont and Cesare Gnudi, *La Peinture gothique*, Skira, 1954.

The Scourging
13th century or early 14th century stained glass
From the church of St. Fargeau (Yonne)
Geneva Museum

The decadence of illumination

The mixture of lively colours and contrasting tones in the portraits and their surrounding borders is the general rule in Gothic miniatures. But, as if the illuminators decided to give the reader's eye a rest from this riot of colour, they resorted occasionally to cameo-painting*, especially towards the end of the great miniature period, after Pucelle. This often complicated style provides clear and definite origins for the decadence of this art. In this later, almost colourless, style, there are several *tours de force* that announce the Renaissance, rather than the renaissance of the art of illumination. The cameo was not always in monochrome; skin was sometimes painted in natural tones, gold bands enriched the folds of garments. Sometimes two tones of the same colour were used: a pale red on a bright red, sky blue on royal blue. But the cameo quickly degenerated into grisaille* (whose name it kept) and looked like an imitation of bas-relief. Jean Fouquet has left us several examples in the manuscripts he decorated, and our admiration is divided between the art of the master and the last bursts of Gothic energy.

From this period dates a piece of white silk painted about 1375 in the "grisaille" style: it is the *Narbonne Frontal*, which is in the Louvre. This drapery, which used to decorate the altar of the old Cathedral of Saint-Just in Narbonne, is a unique example of its genre. Designed for the Easter ceremony, it strikingly illustrates the crucifixion. Christ on the cross dominates the scene; to the left as one faces the picture are the holy women; on the right, gazing at his Master, stands an affecting St. John, undeterred by the bullying of grimacing guards. On either side of the cross are the two thieves and, further from the central scene, on the left, the arrest in the Garden of Olives, the scourging, the carrying of the cross, the deposition in the tomb, and the descent into hell. In the middle, portraits of Charles V and Queen Jeanne de Bourdon* are interpolated. It was a revolutionary work, not only in its style of composition, but also in its psychological effect and "modern" feeling. Confronted by the *Frontal* one is reminded of Grünewald*, or Bosch*, by the ravaged, torn and triturated features of the characters.

The end of the miraculous and the introduction of printing

The European wars, which were such vehicles for ideas and new techniques during the final Middle Ages, brought, with a transformation of custom, the rapid decline of the miniature. But the death blow was only dealt by the discovery of printing*, which put books within the reach of most, and relegated the miniature to the rank of an Epinal* print: as the number of pictures increased, the value of each one dropped. Towards the end, the religious spirit was progressively displaced by a new conception of life, which was to blossom later in the humanism of the Renaissance and take shape with the spirit of the Reformation* in the northern countries. The disappearance of the miniature can be considered as one sign of the eradication of the miraculous-realist in the spirit of men at the end of the 15th century. Spontaneity was replaced by a desire to please, and imagination by the frivolities of the Courts. Additionally, in France, the influence of neighbouring countries, particularly Quattrocento* Italy, completely submerged local traditions.

Stained Glass, Frescoes and Tapestry

To this cascade of colours poured on to parchment in the Middle Ages, were added the colours of tapestry, fresco, enamel and stained glass. There were powerful works in all these four means of harnessing light, though the fresco was least well represented in Northern Europe where glass windows took the place of stone walls. So, in a multicoloured symphony the vast waves of thought of a new civilisation arose out of the night.

Stained glass

Suger, Abbot of Saint-Denis (died 1151), did not hide his admiration of stained glass. In the record book of his administration he adds, after defining the teaching role of stained glass ("which directs thought", writes Marcel Aubert*): "through tangible means towards the intangible".[1] Thus, one of the greatest minds of his time defined the role of stained glass in town life in the Middle Ages. Today, we can compare certain stained-glass windows to a kind of film, in that the various stages of one event are shown following each other in the same window. One example is the late 13th century window depicting the legend of St. Nicasius and St. Eutropia, which is now in the Louvre. In fact, stained glass may be considered specifically French in origin, and even the forerunner of French Primitive art. (England and Germany produced some fine glaziers, but they were later.) Jacquemart de Hesdin, Nicolas Froment* and many other miniaturists also worked in stained glass. It should be remembered that the popular, common and often anonymous art of the Middle Ages was also polyvalent. We have already seen that the painters Fouquet and Bourdichon were also miniaturists, and that similarly a master mason was a sculptor and sometimes an architect. An artist was a "journeyman" who became, if his talent warranted, a head of studio. Strongly protected by their guilds*, artists were able to spend some time expressing themselves through different media before they specialised. This was a good training, in which their style became flexible and their imagination free.

To start our study of stained glass here, however, would take us a long way round. We can best proceed by a basic survey of some great collections.

[1] Marcel Aubert: *Le Vitrail en France*, Larousse, 1946.

The stained glass of Chartres

At the end of the 12th century and the beginning of the 13th the predominant colours were red and blue. Great compositions like the *Story of the Virgin* in Chartres Cathedral and the slightly restored windows of Saint-Remi of Reims belong to this period. The colourless, greenish and bluish glass of the Romanesque style disappeared to make room for the first intangible gleams mentioned by Suger, who was one of the promoters of stained glass in France. The several restored windows of the apse of Saint-Denis were commissioned by him, and are the last remnants of an astonishing number of stained-glass windows which lit that famous abbey.

Towards the middle of the 13th century, the ogives were extended and the rose windows enlarged. Like the miniature, the art of stained glass took a century to come to full flowering. The drawing was perfected; the art of clothing the figures became surer; the proportions followed the same natural course as those of the miniature. There was the same tendency towards naturalism and realistic representation of people and things. Windows were embellished with tall, slim, noble figures; their expressions became enlightened, their gestures seemed more effective; circling doves appeared. The borders were set with medallions, which often enclosed secondary characters surrounding the principal person, as in the late 12th and early 13th century glass of *Our-Lady-of-the-Beautiful-Window* in Chartres.

All these windows, contemporary with St. Louis, Frederick II* of Germany, Richard the Lionheart*, up to Philip the Fair* and Edward III*, share common features of composition and technique. Just as the art is collective, so the work too is universal and European. A working glazier would often perfect his craft by making a sort of journeyman tour of France, and could then settle in Flanders, Germany, or Sweden. He paid for what he learned with what he had learned elsewhere. For instance, a German master glazier might work in England. From that time on a uniformity in the art of glasswork was found in the workshops of Chartres, Laon*, Bourges, Notre Dame*, and Cologne. We only know the name of one 13th century French painter-glazier; he was called Clément*, worked in Rouen, and came originally from Chartres.

The stained glass of Sainte-Chapelle

Towards the end of the 13th century, we sometimes find works in which badly-conceived subjects are represented in terms of naïve realism. The colours are always lovely, but the harmony of shades lacks the early inspiration: the blues tend towards violet; the reds have lost the fieriness they had in the Chartres window of the *Good Samaritan*, the Saint-Remi of Reims *Crucifixion*, or Notre-Dame's west rose window, in the centre of which rises the Virgin in majesty holding the Infant Jesus.

Clement IV ▶
12th century mural painting
Ferrande Tower, Pernes (Vaucluse)

Battle Scene ▼
Fresco, c. 1364-70
Chapel of the Knights Templar,
Saint-Floret Castle (Puy-de-Dôme)

It is, however, the windows of Sainte-Chapelle* that form one of the loveliest collections of medieval stained glass. They were completed in time for the consecration on 25th April, 1248. The fifteen windows with medallions in the high chapel form the most beautiful example of man's handiwork to the glory of light. The story of the windows of Sainte-Chapelle has handed down to us two names: Etienne de Mortagne, master craftsman, and Richard de Montreuil, painter-glazier. The work of the architect of Sainte-Chapelle, and the master glaziers who lit it justifies this remark of Vincent de Beauvais, reported by Emile Mâle*: "In labour and in skill man begins the work of his redemption"[1].

The fresco

Cathedrals opened to the light like stone polyptychs*; windows grew longer and more numerous; ogival vaulting reduced the surfaces that had been like stretches of desert in the Romanesque-Byzantine cupolas. Gothic style acquired a measureless upwards aspiration, opposing its verticality to Romanesque horizontality. It goes without saying that all these transformations displaced wall painting. Secular art left it a place in the castles. Thanks to its cupolas, Cahors* Cathedral offers us several excellent sets in elegant tonalities. But most of the masterworks have almost disappeared. We shall never know the 14th century frescoes illustrating the life of St. Louis, which decorated the cloister of the Franciscan nunnery at Lourcines; the murals tracing the life of Caesar, which John the Good had carried out in his castle at Baudreuil, and the legends which decorated most of the rooms of the Saint-Pol mansion and the old Louvre; only through manuscripts have we an echo of all these vanished works. All this play of medieval history, all this intense, rich, ardent, obscure, luminous life, this poem of gesture which illustrated with day-to-day details the walls of castles, manors, churches, and mansions, all is utterly lost to us. Here and there a colour, a gesture, a line comes back to us in a poem by Rutebeuf* or Villon*. In the church of Petit-Quevilly*, near to Rouen, there remains a beautiful fresco with medallions inserted between the ribs of a sexpartite vault in the chapel of Saint-Julien. It traces the story of Christ. At Avignon*, at Puy, at Etigny*, and at Asnières-sur-Vègre, various religious sets attest the zenith of Gothic mural painting. But frescoes were progressively reduced to isolated examples, as in the Cathedral of Clermont-Ferrand*. Mural painting was reduced to features of decoration. It lightened the places that stayed in shadow or enriched the keystones of vaults, the angles of ribbed vaulting, and certain spandrels* as can still be seen in the Jacobin church in Toulouse. But, with Gothic frescoes, as Mâle[1] adds: "all was subservient to the art of stained glass".

[1] Emile Mâle: *L'Art religieux du XIIIe Siècle en France*, Armand Colin, 1931 (7th edition).

CLEMENS: P: IIII

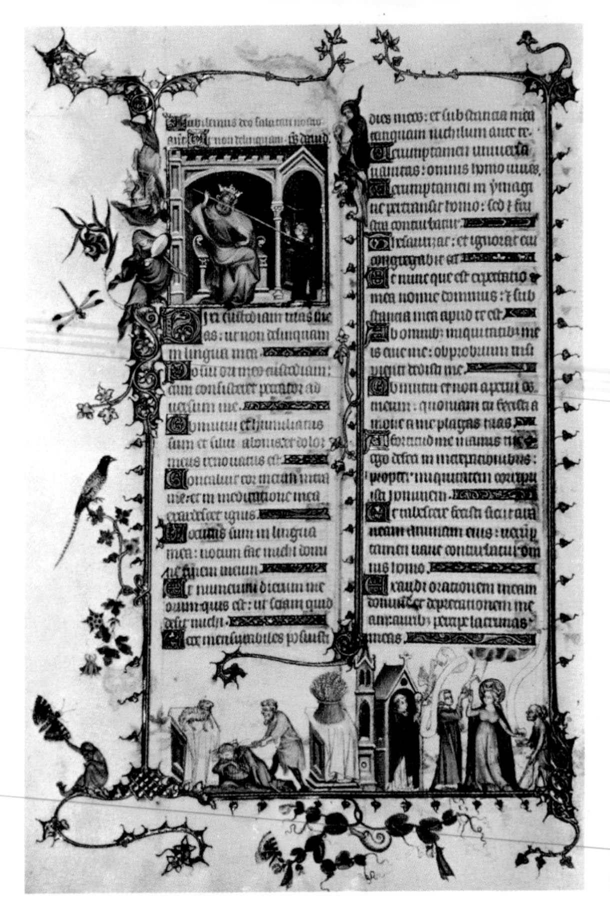

Shrines and reliquaries

Gothic was a time of light and colour. The least restoration dazzles us today. We have only to imagine the processions fluttering with multicoloured banners, entering cathedrals hung with draperies and lit through rose windows, the painted statues on the west doors beating on golden drums (see the colours that still remain on the west door of Saint-Germain-l'Auxerrois), the long decorated corridors of the Château des Loches, the fine gilded wainscoting in the Cluny Museum, the simple houses with brown and white scantling in the Saint-Maclou district in Rouen, to perceive how much colour was reverenced in the Middle Ages. All the ways of using it were good. The 13th century vellum parchments glowed, stained-glass windows grew larger, and on the smallest scale the most delicate enamels added a joyous note. From the 12th to the 14th century Limoges was the important centre of enamel. Many shrines and reliquaries* have survived, in particular the silver-gilt reliquary from the Sainte-Chapelle (1261), which is now in the Cluny* Museum. The simplified lines of its figures show an exquisite grace and masterly technique. In the same museum the 15th century reliquary statuette of the Virgin clearly shows the difference between the simplicity of the style's beginning and the delicate mannered carving of its end. Let us notice in passing the 13th century shrine in the church of Ally, at Cantal, consecrated to the martyrdom of St. Vincent, alive with raised scenes in red, light blue, yellow, green and black enamels on a blue ground; the charming shrine of Bellac, 1200 (Haute-Vienne), decorated with enamelled medallions and precious stones; the late 13th century shrine of St. Romain, a scale model of a church with no transept, in copper-gilt and repoussé and decorated with grooved enamel plaques;

◂◂ Jean Pucelle
Belleville Breviary
Below: *Cain, Abel, The Eucharist, Charity*
National Library, Paris

◂ St. Louis' Psalter
Destruction of Sodom and Gomorrah; Lot's Wife Turned Into a Pillar of Salt
National Library, Paris

also, the Mosan and Rhenish shrines and the reliquaries where light plays through the cornelians, jades and amethysts. The covers of holy books were also often decorated with enamels and precious stones.

Tapestry

The year 1377 was among the most famous in the annals of tapestry; it was then that Nicolas Bataille* began the famous cloth of the *Apocalypse*, based on the drawings by Jean de Bruges*, in honour of the Duke of Anjou*; this cloth was kept for a long time in the treasury of Angers Cathedral. It is exhibited today in a room specially set aside for it within the walls of King René's castle. We should also mention the very beautiful tapestries in the Basle Museum, executed towards the end of the Middle Ages, among which are the 15th century *Squire* and *The Symbolic Animal;* the *Resurrection* and *The Oblation of the Heart*, two beautiful products of the Arras workshops in the 14th and 15th centuries. Cathedral treasuries, particularly Sens, Paris, and Reims, also have the embroidered colours of altar cloths, chasubles and mitres of very typical design.

Interior decoration

Paris had a great influence on tapestry as on the miniature. The art of the weaving trade in Flanders followed the Parisian style. In 1330, a certain Pierre de Bruxelles* collaborated with Evrard d'Orléans* to decorate the Castle of Conflans-lès-Paris with large scenes illustrating the maritime exploits of Count Robert on the Sicilian coast. When history failed them they had recourse to mythology or imagination: "The knights of our time have imaginary battles painted in their rooms", writes the author of *The Verger's Dream*. In Paris, the luxury of a prince's or great citizen's house was judged by his tapestries and often just by their number. Take the king, for example: John the Good owned no less than two hundred and twenty-nine for the decoration of his own and his sons' apartments in the Louvre Palace, two hundred for Charles V alone, who occupied "a very lovely green chamber, figured in red, with tapestries of a green background strewn with foliage". Most Parisians owned one or more small tapestries.

From the Arras* workrooms, one surviving tapestry illustrates a romance, full of flowers and songbirds (about 1420), and another dated 1402 depicts the lives of St. Piat and St. Eleuthère, the work of Pierrot Féré, presented by the Canon Toussaint Prier, chaplain to the Duke of Berry*, to the Cathedral of Tournai.

Michel Bernard* of Arras wove the *Battle of Roosebeke* for Philip the Bold in 1382. The *Life of Du Guesclin* was treated by Jacques Dourdin*, Pierre Beaumetz* and Nicholas Bataille. Lastly, we have the sets that trace the legendary lives of knights and ladies, of Ivinail and the Queen of Ireland, of Jason, and the story of the Holy Grail. There were also many woven poems and medieval epics, of which more than three-quarters have been lost.

St. Stephen
Mural painting
Puy-en-Velay Cathedral

Burgundian Art

Burgundian art flourished independently for quite a long time between the French art of Paris at its zenith and Flemish art at the beginning of its vigour, serving as a catalyst between the two and a melting-pot from which the new styles spread to Germany, Avignon, Italy and England.

The Princes of Burgundy (both of Valois and Anjou) had a taste for luxury, refinement and proportion; and proportion and balance are the predominant qualities of French art. It was not until after the assassination in 1419 of John the Fearless* on Montereau Bridge that the state affairs of Burgundy were identified with those of England and Flemish art with Van Eyck supplanted that of Paris.

Jean Malouel and Henri Bellechose

Philip the Bold, Duke of Burgundy and brother of John of Berry*, another famous art patron, attracted such artists as Jean d'Orléans*, Jean d'Arbois*, Jean Petit de Troyes* and Jean de Beaumetz*. When Beaumetz died in 1396, Jean Malouel* succeeded him as chief painter to the ducal court. He undertook *The Last Communion and Martyrdom of St. Denis*, which was finished by another great painter from Brabant, Henri Bellechose*, who worked in the ducal palace from 1415 onwards. It is now fairly certain that Bellechose or his workroom executed the round *Pietà* in the Louvre and the one in Troyes Museum. He also painted the charming little panel of the *Virgin and Child* in the Bestegui collection.

Melchior Broederlam

Melchior Broederlam*, another poet in colour, came originally from Ypres and worked in Burgundy; he was introduced to Parisian painting by Jean d'Arbois. He was appointed painter and valet to Philip the Bold, who in 1395 commissioned him to paint the wings of the reredos carved by Jacques de Baërze. These two panels, *The Presentation in the Temple*, and *The Flight into Egypt*, were painted at Ypres between 1392 and 1399. The work is full of vigour, delicacy and realism, which displays the painter's excellent mastery of his art. Broederlam was an artist with typically Burgundian qualities—a synthesis between the very controlled execution of the Parisian school, the perspective technique of Siena, and the lyricism of the North. An unknown artist of the same era and the same school produced, in the Broederlam style, the little polyptych whose panels are distributed between the Mayer Van der Bergh Museum in Antwerp and the Walter's Art Gallery in Baltimore.

Apocalypse of Angers
Tapestry, 14th century
Blessed are they who die in the Lord (detail)
Tapestry Museum, Angers

Apocalypse of Angers
Tapestry 14th century
The angel bringing the Gospel to men (detail)
Tapestry Museum, Angers

Burgundian Art and the Low Countries

The rich production of the Low Countries miniaturists should be included in the scope of Burgundian art. The workrooms were numerous, and focussed the various influences from Germany, Flanders and France; they were active throughout the Gothic period and produced some remarkable manuscripts. The Archbishop of Utrecht used his temporal power to become one of those mainly responsible for establishing the art in the northern provinces across the Rhine. After that, an exchange of artists took place through family ties which linked the nobility of that country with France. It was the same with the high nobility of the province of Guelders, which through its French relations introduced the style of the Parisian school.

Low Countries manuscripts

The royal museum of the Science Academy in Amsterdam, the museum of the Archbishopric of Utrecht, of the bishopric of Haarlem, and the museums of Bois-le-Duc, Leyden, Bruges and Ghent all possess valuable collections of illuminated manuscripts. Among the most important (not counting the *Utrecht Psalter*, which

Jean Malouel
Great round Pietà painted for the Duke of Burgundy
Louvre, Paris

dates from the Carolingian period) are the *Rhymed Bible of Jacob Van Maerlant**, carried out in 1332 by Michel Van der Borch*, and the rich manuscripts of the abbey of the Marienwerde Premonstratensians (province of Guelders), which are all in the Groningen University Library. The Guennol collection in New York houses, from the Utrecht school, the *Book of Hours of Catherine of Cleves*, illustrated in 1435: it has given its name to its illuminator, the Master of Catherine of Cleves*, who must have known Roger Van der Weyden* and been influenced by him. The older manuscript *On the Flowers of Nature by Van Maerlant* was probably illustrated between 1350 and 1370 and is at present in Leyden University Library. The library of the town of Haarlem owns numerous manuscripts of great interest, among them the *Missal of the Haarlem Weavers Guild*, of which the binding and a short text inserted at the beginning date from the 16th century, but the illustrations and the text were certainly done in Utrecht shortly before 1400. The borders and the letters are similar to those in the *Table of Christian Faith*, illustrated by Dierck Van Delft* (Pierpoint Morgan Library). The same artist was probably also the author of the *Weavers' Missal*. The manuscript of the school of the province of Guelders is a precious book of hours carried out for Maria Van Gelre, about 1415, by the Master of Otto Van Moerdrecht*. This artist took his name from a canon of Utrecht for whom he worked.

Flemish manuscripts

The Royal Brussels Library houses a very well-known collection of illuminated books from the end of the Middle Ages, including the works of Simon Marmion*.

Other rarities include the famous *Black Prayer Book*, written and illuminated at Bruges between 1466 and 1476 (Austrian National Library, Vienna). It was carried out in the workshop of the Master of Anthony of Burgundy*, "written in gold and silver letters on black parchment". The town of Bruges presented this sombre and foreboding book to Charles the Rash* in 1467.

The English Miniature

From its very beginning around the 7th century, Anglo-Irish illumination expressed its poetic nature in continuous interlacing* and fine convoluted arabesques. Ireland was the initiator of the movement, and its monasteries filled up with monk-copyists, who produced one of the West's greatest manuscript works, under a leaden Atlantic sky and interminable rain—ideal weather for embroidery or lettering. *The Kildare Gospels*, unique monument of its genre, which legend claims to have been executed by an angel in answer to St. Bridgit's prayer, contain a mystic representation of the four Evangelists.

Missal of Zweder Van Culemborch ►
c. 1440
Crucifixion
Seminary Library, Bressanone

Letter B with stem of Jesse from an English Psalter ►►
(St. Albans Abbey)
c. 1200
Municipal Library, Imola

In the Romanesque era, the initial letters were still very rich, but the texts were surrounded by fine interlaced borders; the interlacings are the most striking characteristic of the Celtic style, and they can be found engraved on certain chromlechs in Morbihan and Wales. The borders are designed in the form of Barrel* arches, as in *Aethelwold's Benedictional* and the *Missal of Robert of Jumièges*, which may be seen in the Rouen Library. Afterwards, this sort of border became important and formed various series, as seen in the Leyden University Psalter, executed in England at the end of the 12th century. This manuscript is considered to be halfway between the Romanesque and the Gothic style.

Portraiture in miniatures

In the 13th century portraiture was introduced into the English art of miniature—the Irish, after its apotheosis from about the 7th to the 10th century, was extinct. It was the captured likeness of the race. Thus, in the *Hours of Isabelle of Castille*, the *Psalter of the Capucins of Boulogne* and that of Sir H. Lawrence, we perceive, as Shaw* points out (in his *Handbook of the Art of Illumination*), virgins with pure features and thick fair hair, apostles who all already have the phlegmatic expression of an officer of the Crown. The landscapes, the buildings and the costumes were rendered with equal fidelity, and certain Oxford or Cambridge colleges would not look out of place in an English miniature of the 13th century.

The Latinised English miniature

From the 13th to the end of the 14th century English miniatures suffered a long eclipse. Winchester continued to produce, but had lost its inventive originality. Just as the Paris school absorbed the impact of the Hundred Years War by submitting to the assault of Flemish art, so illumination on this side of the Channel, because of the victories of English troops on the Continent, was very strongly influenced at this period by the art of the vanquished. English painters worked in the French style, with not altogether happy results. Bohemian influences of Germanic nature can also be traced. They can be explained by the marriage in 1382 of Richard II* to Anne of Bohemia, daughter of the Emperor Charles IV. The National Gallery, London, possesses the *Wilton Diptych* of this period. It shows King Richard II kneeling and surrounded by his patron saints: St. Edward the Confessor, St. Edmund and St. John the Baptist. This work, executed around 1395, unites the art of the miniaturist and, by the brilliance of its gold background, that of the goldsmith. There may have been French influence. The name of Beauneveu has been suggested as one of the authors of the work. But the open debate as to whether the *Wilton Diptych* is by English or French hands is of little importance when one

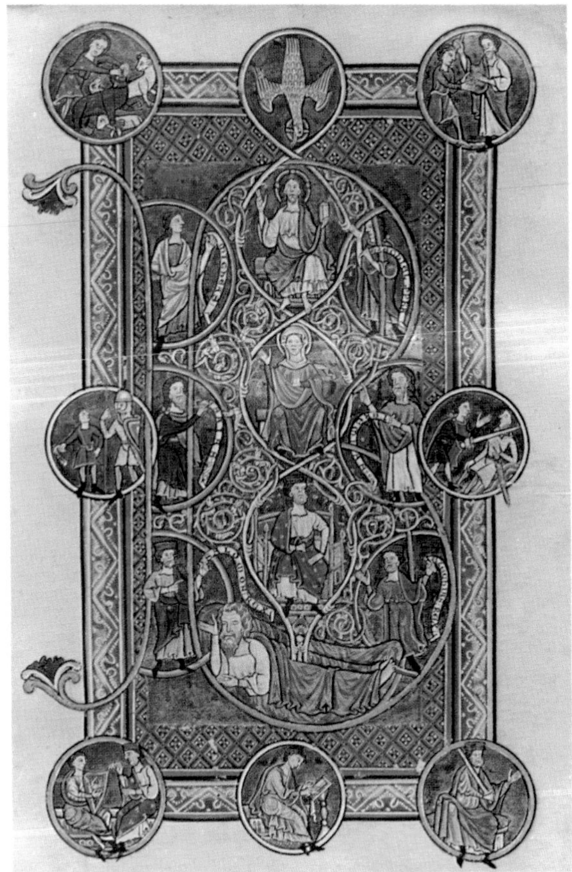

considers the state of Anglo-French rapport during the Hundred Years War. English troops occupied Paris for a long time and an artistic current formed over the years between Paris and London.

If French and even German artists crossed the Channel, as we have seen, English miniaturists worked under the influence of Parisian style. Corpus Christi College, Cambridge, preserves a copy of Chaucer's *Troilus and Cressida*, which clearly shows unmistakable French influence. The queen and her followers come out of a castle while an audience grouped round a prince bedizened with gold listens abstractedly to Geoffrey Chaucer* expounding his poem. The castle shown at the top right recalls a building on the banks of the Loire; the figures are drawn with a grace which would not have been disowned by a miniaturist of the Parisian school. The composition represents all that is most accomplished in the courtly style of illumination at the time of Gothic decadence. It is a beautiful piece, with lively colours and didactic poetry.

Spanish Painting

Barcelona and Valencia, by their strategic positions, were to take an important place in Iberian art. At the end of the Carolingian period, the most famous Spanish miniature was the *Commentary on the Apocalypse* by Beatus Liebana. From the 10th century, the work is enriched by boldly drawn characters. Hispano-Catalan art is already manifested there.

French and Flemish influences

The naturalistic period produced several valuable manuscripts such as the *Regulation of the Household of the King of Majorca*, in which the details of the ceremonies are minutely carried out and already herald the prevailing etiquette of the Escorial* court under Charles V and Philip II*. French influence can be seen in other subsequent works and, later, Flemish influence.

In the 14th century, Roussillon* introduced the first elements of the Gothic style, which were to replace the local Romanesque in the Kingdom of Catalonia. The reredos of Serdinya is an example of a Catalan work inspired by the French—the reredos apparently dates from 1342. Eight sections surround the *Crucifixion;* they trace the childhood of Christ and the life of the Virgin. Figures, draperies and architectural details are painted in opaque colour on a silver ground which glimmers delicately between the subjects. This is an irreproachable alliance between the taste for French drawing, and the Catalan painters' brilliant and contrasting use of colour.

The school of Barcelona and Bassa Ferrer

The end of French influence came with the collapse of the Kingdom of Majorca. The King of Aragon* extended his authority into Catalonia and imposed a new style, that of the Barcelona school, determined by King Pedro IV's* numerous commissions: a reredos for the chapel royal at Perpignan and others at Saragossa, Lerida, Majorca, and Barcelona attest the popularity of the painter Bassa Ferrer* who in 1345 decorated the St. Michael's chapel of the Clarissans of Pedralbes in the region of Barcelona.

15th century Book of Hours (in Dutch)
Pentecost

Ramón Destorrent

Ramón Destorrent* succeeded Bassa Ferrer. We owe to him the Iravalls reredos dedicated to Martha and Mary. It is a traditional composition of Catalan art, in a fairly conventional style but with a naïve brilliance. Certain traits peculiar to Destorrent save it from banality. His realism is more developed than that of contemporary painters, though he does not attain Ferrer's mastery. Characteristic of his style are: lowered eyes, pointed nose, tiny mouth.

Italian influence

The Serra* brothers were very influenced by Siennese painting, like the two preceding painters, and were even more inspired by French iconography. They were the creators of the standard Virgin and Child surrounded by angels, the inspiration of which was doubtless the *Virgin* painted by Simone Martini on the tympanum of Notre-Dame-des-Doms at Avignon.

Luis Borrassa

In 1389 the Minorites of Tarragona commissioned a reredos from Luis Borrassa*. He was rapidly promoted to official painter to the court of Juan I of Aragon, set up his workroom at Barcelona and lived in that town until his death in 1424. After the Tarragona reredos, Borrassa continued to perfect his style, based primarily on

Luis Borrassa (c. 1380-1424)
St. Dominic Rescuing the Shipwrecked Mariners
Episcopal Museum, Vich

Bernado Martorell (died c. 1453)
Death of St. Vincent
From a reredos dedicated to St. Vincent
From Monarguens (Lérida)
National Museum, Barcelona

freedom and flexibility allied to an accomplished technique. Borrassa's figures make natural gestures, and appear familiar to us because the painter showed them in day-to-day surroundings, eliminating all clumsiness from the drawing. The figures are always draped in rich costumes and placed in settings which were sumptuous though too often rigid and cold. The polyptych in the Museum of Decorative Arts in Paris is attributed to him. This is a splendid reredos recounting the life of St. John the Baptist; at the top is a crucifixion which crowns the hermit-saint's life; below left, the principal early events of his life: his birth, the appearance of the angel, the visitation; to the right the events of his sojourn on the banks of Jordan: the baptism of Christ, the preaching in the desert, and finally Herod's feast.

Bernado Martorell

After Borrassa, Bernado Martorell* ended the line of great Catalan Gothic painters. His work already expressed the tortured and magnificent spirit of Spain. He painted a *St. George* and had no hesitation in reproducing down to the last detail a French miniature of 1410-15, the *Boucicaut Hours*, preserved in the Jacquemart-André Museum, Paris. He had the same concern for details and familiar things as Borrassa. He knew how to pose his figures, bring them to life, give bold touches to certain characters, such as the Samaritan woman in the reredos of *The Transfiguration* in Barcelona Cathedral. After 1432 Luis Dalmau*, returning from Flanders, brought to Barcelona a new teaching from the Van Eyck brothers, and a page was turned on a short, but fertile, period of Spanish painting.

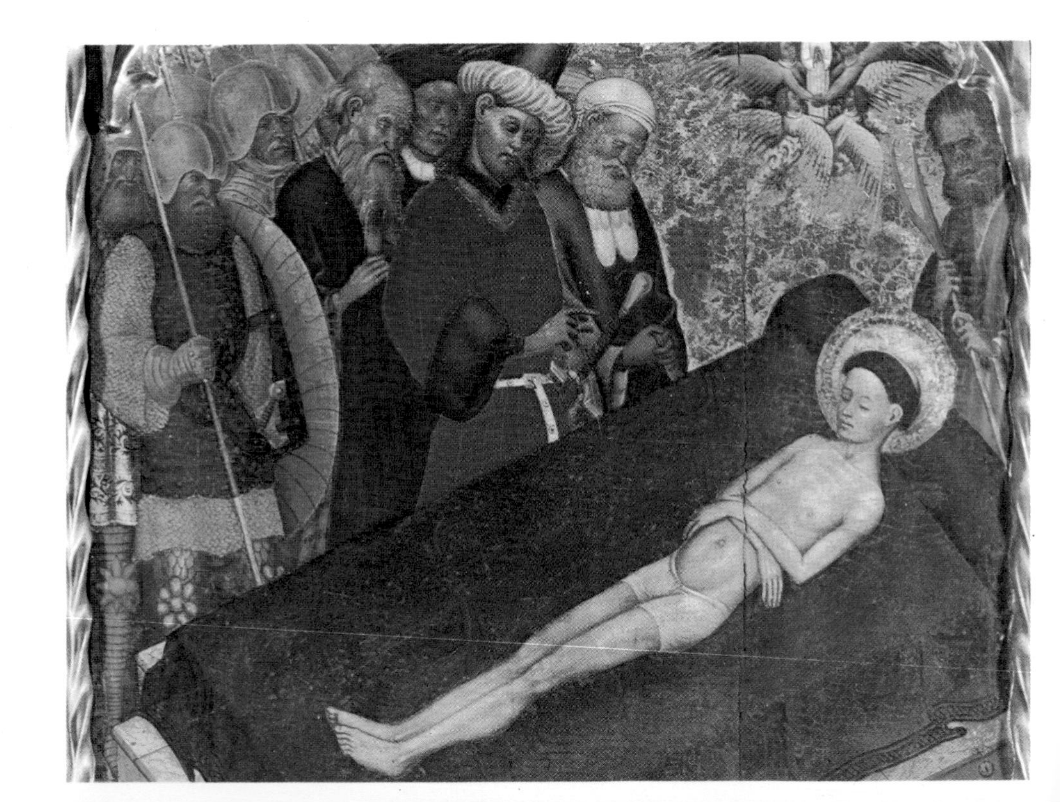

Resurrection
From the reredos of the main altar in the Cistercian
Monastery of Santa Cruz
Early 15th century
Museum of Catalan Art, Barcelona

Master of Westphalia
14th century
Christ in Purgatory (detail)
Wallraf-Richartz Museum, Cologne

The Valencia school

The Valencia school, rich in glowing colour and movement, was composed of many painters whose names we know: Gerardo Gener*, Antonio Guerau*, and Gonzalo Perez*, to whom is attributed the reredos presented by Berenguer Marti de Torres in 1443 to the Carthusian convent of Protacoeli, and now in the San Carlos Museum, Valencia. It is a monumental work composed of three panels on a gold background; to the right is St. Ursula holding the arrows of her martyrdom; in the centre St. Martin, on horseback, dressed in French style with a pearl-embroidered hood, is dividing his cloak; to the left is the abbot St. Anthony. It is a painting full of gold, darkness and severe lines.

Marsal de Sax*, of German origin, painted the reredos of *St. George* in the Victoria and Albert Museum. It is a large ex-voto* work in honour of Pedro I's* victory at Albocacer near Huesca. The work is full of passion and enlivened by the movements of the warriors, contrasting with the calm celestial figures which adorn the upper part of the picture.

German Art

Despite a certain perfection of detail and the importation of Greek and Roman models, German art from the 11th century fell behind that of the Latin countries. As we said earlier, Germanic artists at the start of the 13th century always produced work of Romanesque character, including the *Hortus Deliciarum*, by the abbess Herrad von Landsberg. Several parts show that the artist worked from life; for example, in the *Massacre of the Innocents*, the dress of the soldiers, who are really contemporary knights, and the typically German figures in the *Burial of Moses*. Here we plunge to the roots of the German genius, powerful, mystic, dreamy, sometimes depressive. Care for realism has not, however, prevented the artist from showing the Muses in Byzantine dress! This remarkable manuscript, begun at the end of the 12th century, is unfortunately not known to us except by some texts which describe it and 19th century engravings which reproduce certain illuminations: it was burned along with other precious volumes in the Strasbourg Library fire of 1870. All these paintings have common features, a crudity of movement and expression, and a sometimes aggressive richness of decoration and colour, betraying a civilisation which had not yet found its point of equilibrium. The German miniaturists, their minds full of dreams of Valhalla, followed from afar, throughout a great part of the Middle Ages (in particular during the 13th and early 14th centuries, which saw in France the golden age of illumination and stained glass), the progress inaugurated by the other schools, both Italian and French. They produced some beautiful books of hours in the Flemish manner, but more idealised and laboured in execution. A certain Thomas von Hoemmerlein particularly distinguished himself in decorating the *Book of Hours of the Duchess of Guelders*.

The development of German art

With the evolution of society and the increasing preponderance of large towns on the east side of the Rhine in the late 14th century, we witness a revival of the art of illumination in Germany. But the works were always inspired by outside stimuli. Master Bertram*, born in Westphalia about 1345, worked in Hamburg, where he died in 1415. His work was influenced by Bohemian painters at the court of Charles IV. He was the author of several altar screens in St. Peter's, Hamburg. Master Francke* continued Bertram's work.

Conrad von Soest*, moving away from Romanesque-Byzantine influences, sought to create a style more national in character, if one may apply the term to such a disturbed epoch in the history of the Holy Roman Empire, when the efforts of artists were associated with the spirits of their own provinces: Westphalia, Suabia, Bavaria, etc. South-German painting absorbed the influences of Bohemia, France, and Italy.

Painters of Cologne and the Master of Middle Rhine

At Cologne, a school of painters broke away for a time; towards the end of the 14th century the fashion in that town was for altar screens, many of which were painted. The most significant was that for Cologne Cathedral executed about 1380. The Master of the Middle Rhine* painted *The Garden of Paradise*, which is exhibited today in the Staedel Institute, Frankfurt. The colours are bright and sharply contrasting, and the technique is rather reminiscent of enamel painting. But, as with the miniature, this style was to become precious and mannered. The great painter Stephen Lochner*, half a century later, was still working in it.

Martinus Opifex c. 1445 Guido Colonna:
History of the Sack of Troy
Battle Scenes
National Library, Vienna

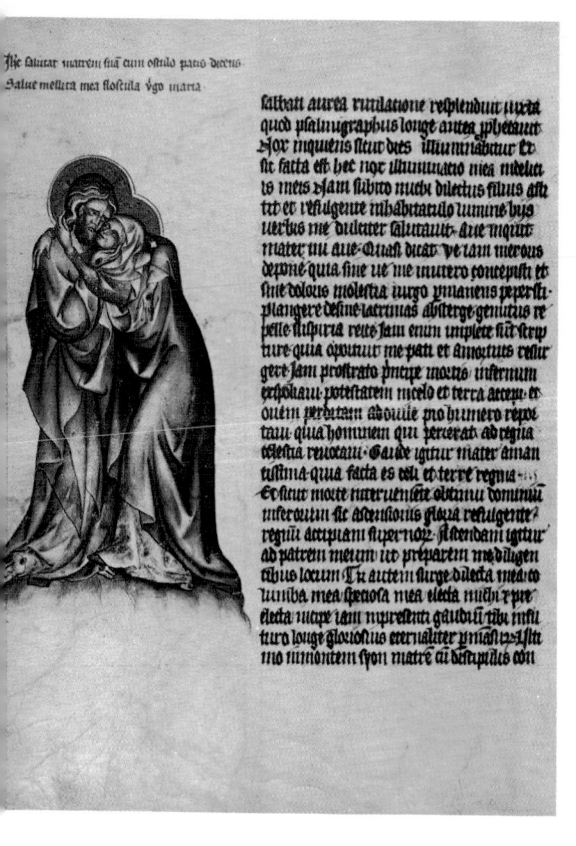

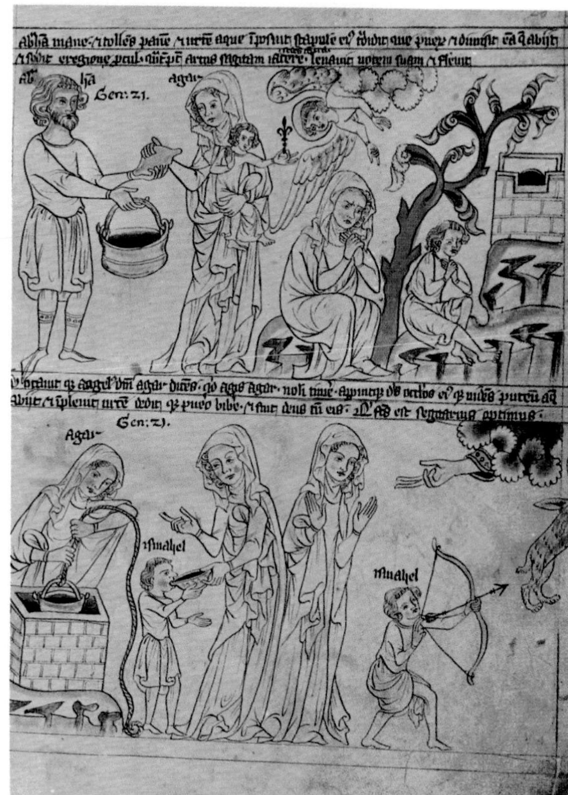

Austrian Art

In Austria, too, the Gothic period, or more precisely that of the 13th century—for Gothic art had infinite nuances of style and thought—was a time of near exhaustion. After the defeat of the Ghibelline* party at the beginning of the 13th century, artistic activity in Austria diminished. Certain convents continued to decorate manuscripts according to foreign influence, in the case of Zwettl, near to Bohemia, for example, under that of Prague. For others illumination was only an exercise in style around a traditional theme. They merely repeated, without any care for refinement or development.

Italian influences

There is no doubt that between 1270 and 1290 an Italian school of illuminators was working in Austria. The monk Engelbert von Admont, who later became father abbot of his convent, studied at Padua University—renowned for the arts among other disciplines—with the famous illuminator Giovanni Gaibana*. In the *Missal for Abbot Admont* one of the most beautiful pages is that of *The Crucifixion*. From other manuscripts illuminated for other Austrian convents influenced slightly by Gaibana and his pupils we would mention the original and curious figure of the wheel surmounted by a king of very Capetian appearance. To this same school also belong the frescoes to be seen in the church of St. Nicholas near to Martrie in the eastern Tyrol.

At Klosterneubourg*, near to Vienna, the Augustine convent possesses a Bible illuminated with miniatures in the Italian style, full of verve and invention. But, owing to the barrier of the Alps, Italian influence in Austria was less strong than the French or the Flemish in Germany.

Passionale of the Abbess Cunegunda
Christ and His Mother Embracing
c. 1320
National and University Library, Prague

Picture Bible attributed to Velislav
Agar and Ishmael in the Desert of Beersheba
c. 1340
National and University Library, Prague

Manuscripts and monasteries

Decorated works in the 14th century display a certain attempt to be original, but, unfortunately, there are not many of them. These are missals in which the pages of the canon form a harmonious entity in the purest, but too often most formal, Gothic style.

At Saint-Florian, in Upper Austria, and at Klosterneubourg, besides Bibles and missals, the great scholastic doctrines were illustrated, as were other "typological" studies, such as Biblical concordances*, the works of erudite monks who weighted the comparisons between Old and New Testaments. The most famous work in this genre is the *Biblia Pauperum* (The Bible of the Illiterates). Several illuminated manuscripts of it exist; the most typical being the *Vienna Manuscript*, certain pictures from which have been repeated in the windows of St. Stephen's Cathedral. This manuscript is an example of Gothic style, elegant in its "mannerisms", the colour harmony of which indicates French influence. The pen drawings are so many, and their colours so varied, that they constitute a rich picture book, of which the text, unlike classical manuscripts, serves rather as captions to the illustrations. Of the same period, and certainly from a monastic workroom, the *Speculum Humanae Salvationis* is a work of scholastic erudition written in verse. A good copy has been preserved by a convent in Upper Austria. In the 14th century, the illuminators of the Waldhausen convent decorated a *Life of Mary*, which remains to us as a precious example of the popular art of that century.

Several artists were employed in decorating the German version of the *Rationale Divinorum Officiorum* by Guillaume Durand. This manuscript, written by the chaplain to Duke Albert III, was begun around 1384 and finished in 1406. As for the illumination, certain medallions in the first part belong to the Verona school, while the others follow Bohemian influence.

The later manuscripts

Finally, some important works from the end of Austrian Gothic: the manuscripts written by Henri Aurhaym for Ernest of Styria, the Iron Duke; the Book of Hours begun for Barbara of Cilli, the widow of the Emperor Sigismund*, and later finished for the Emperor Frederick III*; Guido Colonna's masterpiece *The Trojan War*, decorated by the man who signed himself Martinus Opifex*. These are very clearly influenced by the German schools, some of them giving the impression particularly that Master Martin*, when he abandoned the Bohemian tradition and introduced idyllic landscapes, must have been familiar with the contemporary art of the Upper Rhine. Apart from illumination, Austrian art produced the Master of Heiligenkreuz*, whose style was both precise and naïve, and very influenced by the German painters.

Corpus Juris Civilis
Law and Punishment
14th century
National Library, Turin

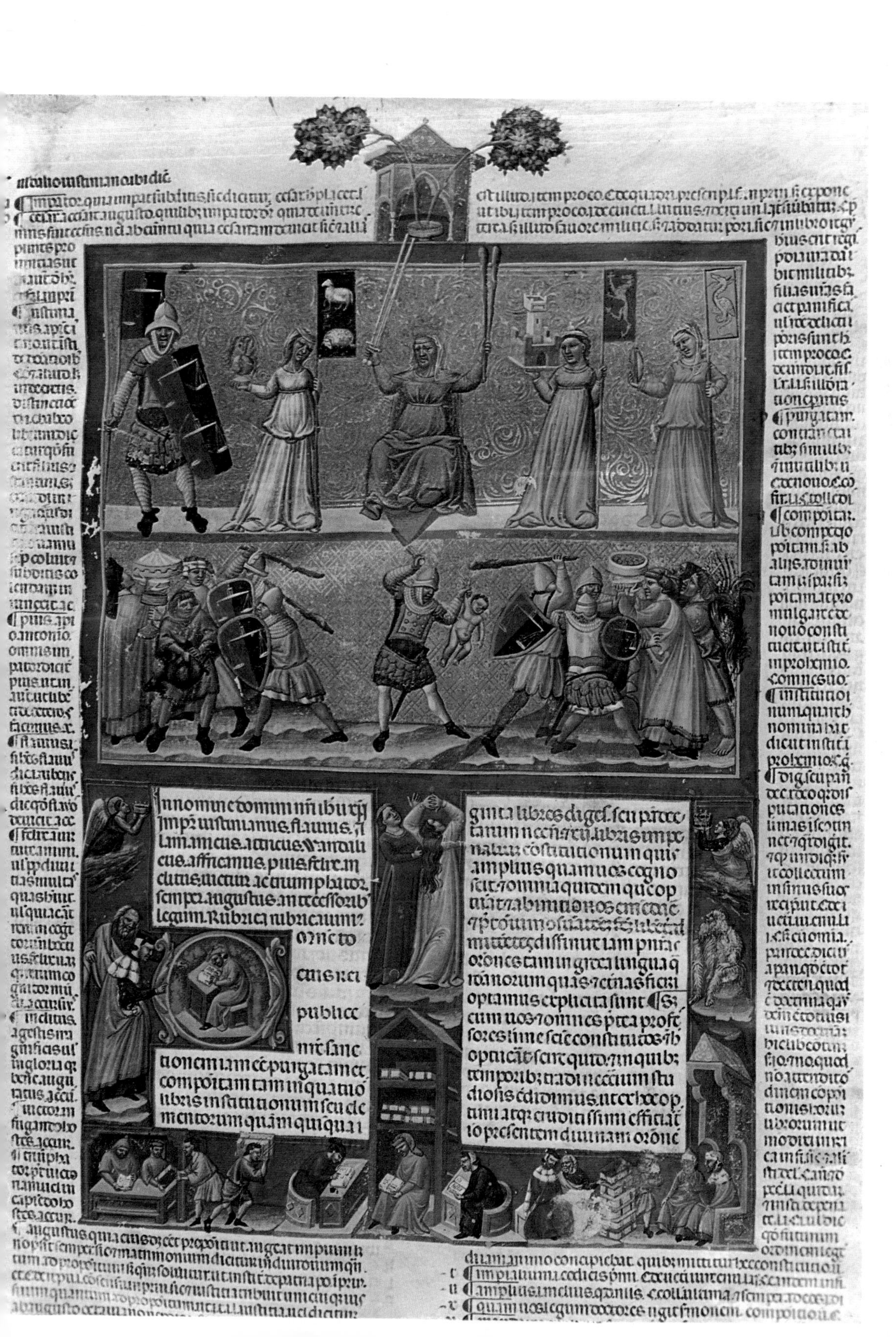

Painting in Bohemia

Bohemia, situated on the border between the Slav countries and the West, for ages the ultimate barricade against Mongolian attacks, inevitably became, by virtue of this very position, a meeting-place for Byzantine, Romanesque and Western arts.

Illumination

All through the Middle Ages the art of illumination flourished vigorously. As in painting, foreign influence determined its direction. Italian-Byzantine imports were significant right up to the Gothic period. From the 13th century onwards, the style of Padua was brought to Prague by the Franciscans. At the end of the 13th century, the *Franciscan Bible* displays practically all the attributes of Gothic illumination. In the course of the 14th century, one can observe the formation of an interesting synthesis of Italian and West European influences. The *Passionale of the Abbess Cunegunda*, carried out about 1320, is the most typical example of early Bohemian Gothic illumination. Religious and mystic meanings are interpreted there in a

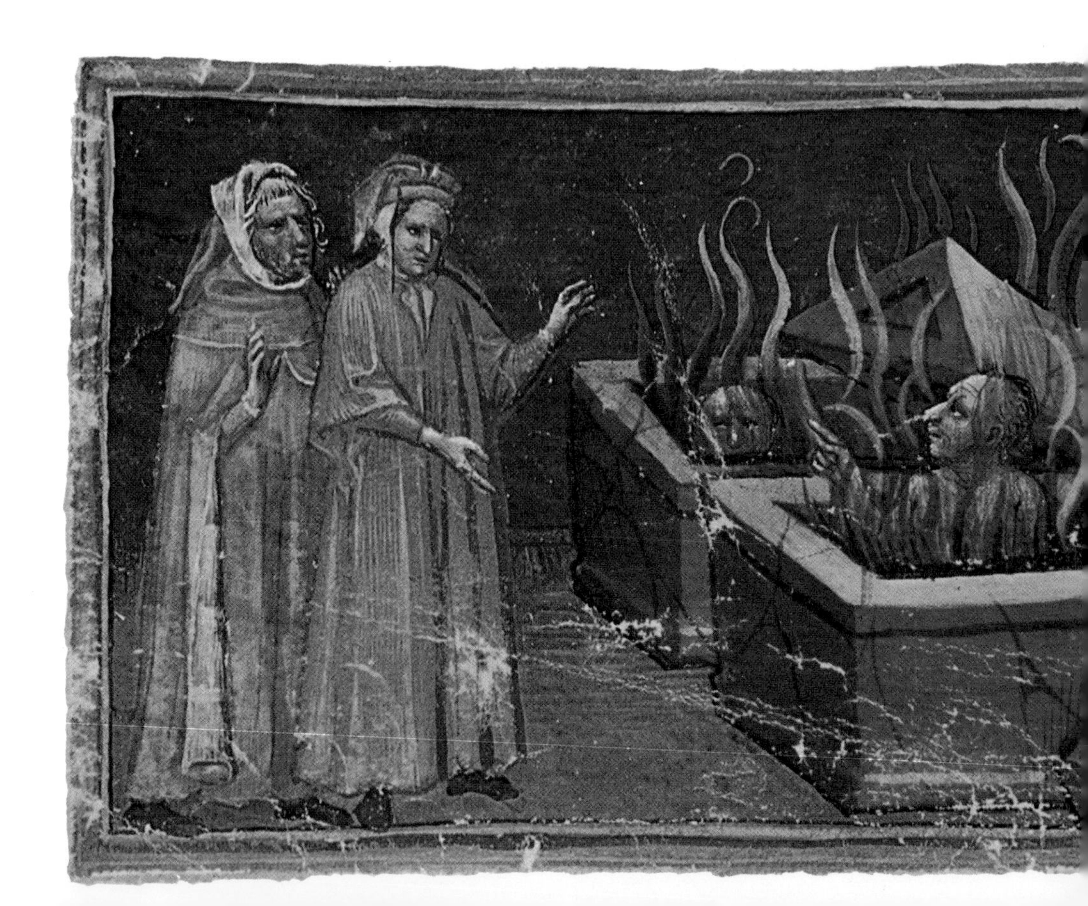

Dante: *The Divine Comedy* (1405)
Trivulziana Library, Milan

remarkably original style. The beautiful *Velislav Picture Bible*, dated 1340, should also be mentioned.

French art had spread to Prague by about 1320, with the arrival of the Premonstratensians and Dominicans, and inspired the *Antiphonary of Queen Elisabeth Rejcka*. French influence was later counterbalanced by Italian. Works from the height of Gothic illumination in Bohemia are: the *Liber Viaticus*, of Bishop Jean de Streda, and the *Breviary* of the great Master Leo, from the monastery of the Crusaders, Prague, and the *Laus Mariae*, by Konrad von Haimburg.

Panel Painting

From the 14th century Bohemia assumed a more definite political role. At the death in 1346 of John the Blind*, his son Charles IV, descendant of the Luxembourg family, and educated in France, gathered round him both French and Flemish artists. Charles IV became Emperor of Germany on the death of his father.

The art of panel painting soon became celebrated. Saint Guy's Cathedral, Prague, begun in 1344 by a French architect, Mathieu d'Arras*, had no less than sixty altar screens, and the Vyšši Brod Cathedral chapterhouse thirty-two.

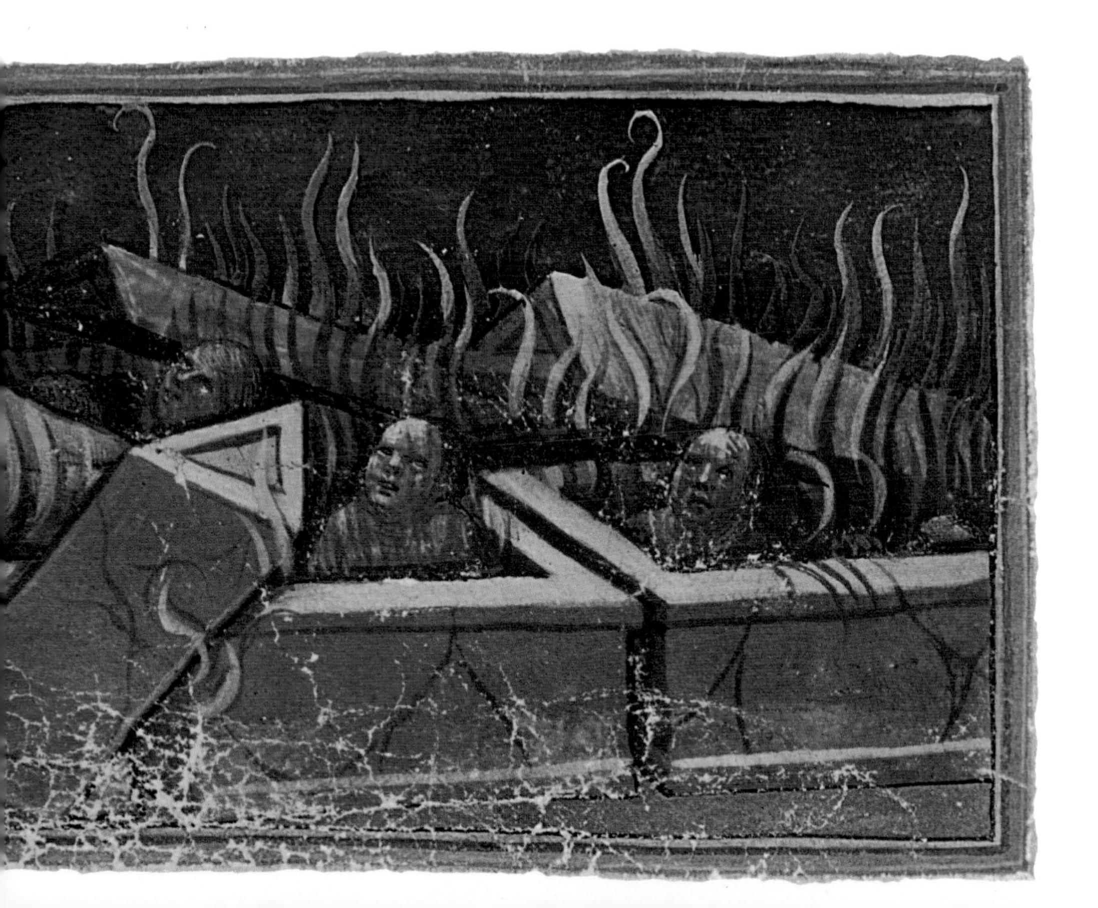

Master of the Vyšši Brod Cycle
c. 1350
Christ on the Mount of Olives
National Gallery, Prague

The Master of the Vyšši Brod Cycle

It is sometimes difficult to draw the line between what is truly Bohemian and that which is French or Italian influenced. For example, the panels of the *Life of Christ* in the Hohenfurth Collegiate Church, the Glatz *Madonna*, and the Roudnice predella (1340-1350) are works very affected by the art of Duccio*. A true synthesis of the three styles is found in the tempera* paintings of Vyšši Brod. The nine panels of the *Life of Christ* are largely influenced by Giotto's style of composition and convey a poetic delicacy and a profound, even disturbing, mystery.

When Tomaso da Modena* settled in Prague during the second half of the 14th century Italian art became preponderant in Bohemia. The Italian master's teaching was amply followed by the first president of the painters' corporation in

Prague, Theoderich*, himself a painter, whose style was composed of heavy lines, dull faces and short bodies. The volumes are embossed, which causes the movement and the inspiration to suffer a little. Theoderich decorated the chapel of Saint-Croix, which was intended to house a relic of the Holy Thorn.

The Master of Trebon

The Master of Trebon*, on the other hand, was more independent of foreign influence. His three panels, particularly the *Mount of Olives* and *The Resurrection of Christ*, which form part of the Trebon reredos (about 1380) express profound spirituality and accomplishment in drawing, colour and chiaroscuro effects that create a sort of mystic aura.

The Florentine Miniature

In the time of Dante*, Italian illuminators acknowledged that France was superior in the art of the miniature. In this field Italy did not produce anything very original after the height of the Middle Ages. The play of light drew the Italian aesthetic nearer to frescoes and statuary than to chamber work. Italy was content to express its genius in several beautiful, but all-too-rare, manuscripts. Of such are an 8th-century missal according to the usage of the Church of Florence, preserved at Rome, and the evangeliary of the same period, which now belongs to the Saint-Geneviève Library, Paris. Italian decoration of this period maintained an easily recognisable uniformity: wide scroll patterns, heavy foliage copied from the country's rich flora—but there ends the debt to the Italian countryside—and a characteristic mixture of showy colours, principally yellow and green, which later formed the dominant note in church decoration.

The Italian miniature at the time of Giotto

These were the principal elements of the art of the peninsula until studies of antiquity brought about a metamorphosis during the Middle Ages. It needed all the genius of Giotto to save the Italian miniature from foundering in its own mediocrity well before the first early signs of the Renaissance: not that this artist himself definitely did illumination—that remains to be proved—but his revolutionary style had a strong influence on the illuminators of his country. They began then to differentiate themselves from other schools and their individual taste became recognised as far as France, primarily by the agency of the Papal Court of Avignon*, which attracted the Lombardians and Florentines, among other foreign artists. Books painted by Italian illuminators were reaching France from the beginning of the 14th century; one of them, acquired about this time by the chapter of Laon Cathedral, contains an elaborately designed miniature in which the pope and cardinals (of Avignon,

Master of the Vyšši Brod Cycle
c. 1350
Nativity
National Gallery, Prague

of course) form an important scene. But generally the art of the Italian miniature is often monotonous or grandiloquent.

At Florence the illuminators were influenced by the Cimabue* school. Most early 14th-century work, both sacred and secular, remained anonymous. Two interesting miniatures of that era are those dated 1317 which decorate the manuscript of the *Capitoli della Confraternita della Misericordia di San Giovanni Battista.*

The influence of Giotto

We must turn to the work of the great painter and illuminator Pacino di Bonaguida* to appreciate the influence Giotto had on his contemporaries and find examples of its two essential features: plasticity and monumentality. The Pierpoint Morgan Library, New York, owns an interesting series of *Scenes from the Life of Christ*, illustrated by Bonaguida. In spite of very personal touches, the style appears affected by the revolutionary innovations of the Florentine master.

"The Divine Comedy"—best-seller

Dante, nearly a century after his death, was one of the authors whose work was most popular with illuminators, especially *The Divine Comedy*, of which there were very many illustrations. But the Florentine miniaturists were not concerned to create a very personal work in decorating the *New Life*, or the *Purgatory*. They devoted themselves principally to making a sort of film in episodes without troubling to interpret the spirit of Dante's poems. For example, he is shown facing the three fierce beasts at the gate of hell, on the barge which takes him to Purgatory, in a golden auriole with Beatrice in the highest heaven, but the figures, as the Italian critic Sandra Vagaggini* comments, rarely move us.

Pre-Renaissance manuscripts

After a period of simplicity, even *naïveté* (apart from a few rare exceptions, such as Pacino di Bonaguida mentioned above), Florentine illumination took on an appearance more in keeping with the 14th century. The Lombardian and Venetian workrooms were influenced by it. The first school that has left us signed manuscripts was the Camaldolese school of the Convent of the Angels, with a series of books of hours, breviaries and antiphonaries bearing the signature of Don Simone Camaldolese*. Here, the first tentative originals were formulated of an art which was shaking off both the last Byzantine influences and the strong personalities of Cimabue, Giotto, and Duccio di Boninsegna, which weighed on the art of the miniaturist at the end of the Trecento*.

The new forms of illumination were primarily architectonic—at first perhaps reminiscent of early Siennese style. They were defined by a solid, concrete touch and heavily worked design as in the work of Bernado Daddi*, or Jacopo del Casentino*. The motifs were more contrasting, sometimes slightly to the detriment of the general harmony, as in the antiphonary of Santa Croce, Florence, signed by Don Simone Camaldolese, where we notice, incidentally, the first signs of a Baroque form. But the Italian art of illumination always found it hard to escape from the page which imprisoned it, and at the time when it was living an independent, though monotonous, life, there took place in the country one of the greatest pictorial revolutions of all time. Perhaps it suffered as a result.

Lorenzo Monaco, miniaturist and painter

In Siena, Florentine influence allied to experimental work in the new forms brought to the fore several painters who gave a lustre to the declining Sienese school. Among them was the painter Lorenzo Monaco*, of whom more later. When he left his native Florence he brought with him a transcendence in composition and colours. Round about 1409 illumination in Italy passed smoothly from the medieval vision of the world to the Renaissance. From that time dates the *Chorale 3* (Laurentiana Library, Florence), where the plastic art of Lorenzo Monaco announces this transition from Trecento to Quattrocento, while his vision and technique, doubtless through the influence of the great sculptor Ghiberti*, reveal a compromise between Florence and Siena. Moving slowly away from his earlier fluid style, Lorenzo Monaco approached towards the end of his life the diaphanous and ecstatic conceptions of Fra Angelico*.

A New Dimension

Thirteenth-century Italian painting was first " light " and then " man " and, as though connecting these two—the earth and the sky—there was Francis of Assisi and freedom of expression.

To understand the aesthetic revolution accomplished there seven centuries ago, one really needs to know the Tuscan countryside, the undulating hills of Umbria, the broken enclosure-like relief of Emilia, the changing shades of the soil, the coincidental irregularities of the ground, the clustered fortified towns, the individuality which seems to emanate from the Italian landscape, and the vibrant transparency of the air which impregnates the vines and fields hedged with vigilant cypresses. There, and there only, man rediscovers himself after a thousand years of disorder. We shall always be indebted to the Florentines and the Sienese for having taught us what we are.

At first, then, there was the light, with the ground and the birds; then men appeared like gods or saints who prayed as men. The story of early Gothic Italian painting could well be a legend, or even a tale where fairies assumed the brilliance of the colours, and magicians appeared in the guise of painters. Thus rose from obscurity the square churches of Tuscany, the blind chapels of Umbria, the flattened monasteries of Emilia, with flexible shapes that moved on the walls, astonished faces, eyes dazzled as by the light of the first day: a look curbed by knowledge and already full of curiosity and anguish. So these fancies group, spread, overlap: nocturnal characters, beings with hesitant, cautious, modest gestures. They come out of the night from the naves and vaults and seem to mount towards the sky. It is a metamorphosis half-human, half-divine, a miraculous balance between soul and body. These men and women, still drawn in schematic lines, with garments as transparent as aquatic colours, ivory complexions, and arms arrested in initiatory gestures, remain mysteries as impenetrable as the coloured silhouettes in Egyptian temples.

This individuality of Italian art was in the image of its cities. There they were, proud, luminous, perched on their hillocks or nestling in their lagoons, such as Giotto and Ambrogio Lorenzetti* have given us. There was no collective art, as in the North, no "fancy cathedrals", no anonymous sublime stained glass, few manuscripts directed to the people—the *minores*—and to students: the masses were dispersed into castes, the spirit of a cathedral was embodied in a fresco, the stained glass took the form of a man's portrait signed by a painter, and the Flemish guilds changed under the Latin sky into scattered workrooms, in each of which a master reigned over several pupils. These parcelled-out terrains, these jigsaws of small states, these passionate lives enclosed in young cities, a sun which heated the thoughts and emotions and induced everyone to react to the moral precepts of the Church according to his own instincts: such was, broadly, the setting from which a new world was to emerge.

To light, sensualism and individuality should be added money and knowledge; without patronage, or philosophy—all the better if the two coincide—there can be no painting. All the Italian towns: Florence, Bologna, Siena, Ferrara, Pisa, Parma, Mantua, Lucca, Cremona, Assisi; the larger ones to the north: Milan, Bergamo, Verona, Brescia; those more to the East: Venice and Padua, and the smaller ones such as Rimini, Imola and Pistoia—formed in the Middle Ages a mosaic of tiny states, principalities and republics governed by sages or despots, who gained and protected their independence through often complicated systems of alliances. There were short and not very bloody battles, crimes for reasons of state, long and subtle diplomatic negotiations, overthrown alliances, feuds between Guelphs* (partisans of the Pope) and Ghibellines (partisans of the German emperor). But this intense, passionate, sometimes cruel political life did not hinder the economy. The soil was cultivated, and enriched peasants, nobles and townsmen, as contemporary writings and painting testify. The geographical position of these little republics at the crossroads between the pontifical states in the South, and Venetia with Austria and

Germany beyond in the East, between the Orient and Spain, France and England, enabled them to develop a capitalist economy. The financiers controlled politics and often ecclesiastic domains; the Lombardy banks were rich and lent to all Europe. It is not surprising therefore that the modern spirit crystallised in the northern and central part of Italy, rich, expanding, forming a link between East and West, complex and extended by constant effort.

Tuscany, formerly Etruria, played an important part. Florence, Pisa, Siena and Lucca rapidly became active cultural and artistic centres. From the end of the 12th century the first painters were confronted by Byzantine art. Greek, Serbian and Macedonian monasteries and churches, as well as Ravenna and Monreale in Sicily, had reliably preserved and transmitted the heritage of Antiquity. The frescoes in the church of Peribleptos at Mistra in Greece, and later (11th and 12th centuries) those in the churches of Macedonia, Serbia, Nerezi, Mileseva, and above all the admirable series at Sopocani (especially *The Annunciation* and *The Sleep of the Virgin*) inspired the first Italian frescoists of the Gothic period, Conxolus* and Bonaventura Berlinghieri*. The latter painted a moving portrait of St. Francis of Assisi at present in the Church of St. Francis at Pescia.

It is difficult to dissociate this new world, with its first collective consciousness of the human being and the sun, from the Christian thought which to a certain extent suffused it. Often in the past there has been a tendency to overlook the richness of ideas and the originality of the arts in Medieval Gothic and see only the darkness which hid superstition, barbarity and confusion. There was that, it is true, but

Ambrogio Lorenzetti (d. 1348), attributed to
View of a Town
Siena Picture Gallery

Gothic in Europe generally was an advent, an emergence of new ideas, a combination of geniuses of different races where the liberty of aesthetic expression had taken free rein. In all this, the Church acted as a regulator. It would be difficult to grasp the genius of, say, Duccio, Giotto, Gentile da Fabriano*, or even Ambrogio Lorenzetti, without understanding the paramount influence of the Franciscan ideology. St. Francis of Assisi had fired the Western World with not only the spirit of charity, but also the love of nature:

Blessed be Thou, O God, for all thy creatures,
especially for our brother, the Sun,
who gives us the day, and by whom Thou lightest us.
He is beautiful; he beams with great splendour,
he is Thy symbol, O Thou Most-High.
Blessed be Thou, O God, for our sister
the Moon and for the stars,
which thou hast set in the sky
clear, precious and beautiful . . .[1]

Also love of animals: " My very dear brother birds, you owe much to God . . ."[2] Medieval art would certainly seem very obscure if one failed to recognise this

[1] *The Canticle of the Sun.*
[2] *The Sermon to the Birds.*

Ambrogio Bondone, called Giotto (1266-1336)
Upper part of triumphal arch
Fresco, c. 1305
Scrovegni Chapel, Padua

efflorescence of life, this herbarium, this vivarium, this cosmogony which are to be found on the west doors of cathedrals, in the illuminations and in the frescoes of the Sienese and the Florentines.

To this predilection for nature, to this need to express themselves in light, was added the amorous lyricism which was expressed in the courtly novel, and a growing necessity to define an idea which was forming between Heaven and Earth, represented by the theological doctrine of St. Thomas Aquinas, the *Fides quaerum Intellectum:* the faith which seeks to comprehend.

One must picture medieval life in the imagination in order to grasp its vitality, its religiosity, and at the same time its hostility to the Church; its depraved tastes, but also the asceticism of its religious orders. There had never been so much travel since the fall of the Roman Empire. The Norwegians landed in Greenland; navigators visited Africa; the crusades made Jewish and Arab ideas and the philosophies of Maïmonides*, Avicenna* and Averroès* known in Europe; St. Louis sent an ambassador to Mongolia, and Marco Polo* returned to Europe from his first voyage to China in 1269. As that date Cimabue began his work; St. Thomas completed his theological doctrine; Roger Bacon* in England had just published his *Opus Majus*.

There was fruitful interchange of ideas, interpenetration of different branches of the arts: painting, sculpture, architecture, letters and philosophy. All the medieval creators compared points of view and inspired each other. Fifty years later Dante produced his *Divine Comedy*, through which, in the abysses and heights he described, he formulated a critical appraisal of clerics, politicians and artists of all time, but mainly of his own era. The great theologian and mystic Ruysbroek* was contemporary with the first humanist, Petrarch, who sang of his love for Laura di Noves; Master Eckhart* was condemned by the Pope for his audacious theology. In all the realms of the spirit, the Gothic age was a kind of revolution, an accession to liberty, a realisation of man's responsibility. This revolution was never aesthetically incarnated with as much frankness and lucidity as in Italy during the Trecento.

The Art of the Duecento and the Trecento

The renown of Giovanni Cimabue was so great that Dante paid him the honour, along with Giotto, of a line in his Divine Comedy; towards Cimabue it was biting:

> *Cimabue thought himself, in painting,*
> *Master of the field; Giotto thought so too,*
> *Although his fame eclipsed the earlier man's.*[1]

[1] *Purgatory*, XI, 94.

Giotto, workshop of
St. Francis Receiving the Stigmata
Predella (detail):
St. Francis Preaching to the Birds
Louvre, Paris

Sometimes attributed to Cimabue
Virgin with Angels
Louvre, Paris

Giotto, workshop of
St. Francis Receiving the Stigmata
Louvre, Paris

Giotto, workshop of
Crucifixion
Fine Arts Museum, Strasbourg

Dante always had a preference for Giotto, whose humanity, rationality and balance suited him better than Cimabue's entirely Byzantine ecstasy, but Cimabue is earlier and therefore does merit the respect due to the pioneer of a new art.

Last Byzantine, First Gothic

The new aspirations of Italian painting towards the middle of the Duecento* were revealed in Cimabue, who paved the way for Giotto, yet did not break too drastically with Byzantine tradition. The "orthodox" spirit of his form can be seen in the *Virgin with Angels* in the Louvre; only the attention to the equilibrium of masses, and to the study of light, and the fixity of the expressions, are new.

This serious Florentine painter would have known how to set the blues, reds and golds of a more monumental design. In his composition *The Virgin Surrounded by Angels with St. Francis*, part of the frescoes with which he decorated the church of St. Francis at Assisi, he has used the Byzantine style on a more terrestial scale. Already perceptible signs of feelings and an attention to psychology can be read in the faces; the drama of man unfolds. For example, Mary Magdalene's two raised arms in the Assisi *Crucifixion* bestow on the composition a dramatic power never before equalled.

Twenty years after the Assisi frescoes, Cimabue finished the *St. John* of the Pisa Cathedral mosaic, which displays new attention to plasticity and distribution of masses.

Duccio: realist and mystic

Duccio was about twenty years younger than Cimabue, and six years older than Giotto. With Simone Martini, and the brothers Pietro and Ambrogio Lorenzetti*, Duccio is the greatest Sienese painter. He can be considered to a great extent the founder of the Sienese school, which for more than a century rivalled the Florentine painters of whom the uncontested master, who had no immediate successor, was Giotto.

To define Duccio is to make an instant synthesis of Gothic realism, Byzantine symbolism, and Mysticism. This great artist, who painted in a state of mind close to that of St. Francis of Assisi when he preached to the birds, with that tenderness and spiritual abandon so characteristic of religious minds, expressed his entire self in the naïve and passionate phrase which he wrote in gold above his *Madonna:* "Holy Mother of God, give peace to Siena; be the life of Duccio since he has painted thee thus."

Giotto, workshop of ▼
St. Francis Receiving the Stigmata
Predella (detail):
Innocent III approving the Franciscan Rule
Louvre, Paris

Duccio di Buoninsegna ▶
The Franciscan Madonna
Siena Picture Gallery

Traditional and visionary

Duccio's art, despite its static appearance, is a poetic unity where movement is imperceptibly incorporated as a slight tremor. Still permeated with Byzantine influence (recognisable in his treatment of hands and use of contrasting colours) yet influenced by French Gothic, the artist stood at the junction of two worlds. He ushered in the Quattrocento by his "transfigured tradition". His style—harmonious, always solemn and majestic, but stamped with a deep sense of religion, linked to a refined form of composition and a delicacy of facial expression—is a long way from the misunderstandings, sometimes rather violent, through which western ideas and spirituality were passing at the end of the 13th century. With Duccio, all is calmness, serenity, delicate vibration of colour allied to an undulating, balanced linear form. He could translate the least reflections of spirituality resting in a human face, particularly in the Virgin Mary's—that transfigured expression radiating infinite goodness. It is really the work of a son who has painted his mother as he cherished her. In a most dramatic tableau, *The Denial of St. Peter*, the upper part of which shows Jesus before the High Priest Annas (Cathedral Museum, Siena), one is scarcely convinced by the tragic scene, preliminary to the Passion, Duccio has so transcendentalised it.

The Franciscan Madonna in the Siena Picture Gallery is one of Duccio's most characteristic works. In composition and design, it is still very influenced by Byzantine principles. But the rhythms repeated in the colour harmony, the Virgin's expression, where the desire for truth is evident, and the elegant placing of the arm and hand on the knee signify the innovator. A lyrical feeling appears in the warm colours, which seem to melt against the background of little green squares vibrating intensely in their geometric structure. We are in the presence not only of a great colourist and poet, but also of a great visionary.

In *La Maestà*, Duccio's last work, which is in the Cathedral Museum, Siena, the artist, illustrating the episodes of the New Testament, definitively established the characteristics of his style. All is harmony, peace, and optimism in human destiny, redeemed by the sacrifice of the Divine Master. Neither the gravity of the subject, however, nor the tragic scenes of that redemption have been manipulated. Rather, they are transfigured. There is none of that dramatic tension seen in the fatigued and attentive faces presented by Giotto, nor the transparent realism which haloes Simone Martini's monks, but rather a translation of human feelings on to a higher plane, human feelings moulded by divinity and already relieved of many terrestrial circumstances which deform them and cause them to grimace. The characters of Duccio must be studied closely, especially those in the scene depicting the Adoration of the Magi in the *Maestà* predella. Each expresses his feelings with an economy of gesture and remarkable facial movement. Nothing is left to chance, nothing is done to excess; the inclination of the heads is judiciously controlled, the slightest features of the face carry their full weight in a simple, one might almost say unobtrusive,

Giotto
The Entry into Jerusalem
Fresco, c. 1305
Scrovegni Chapel, Padua

harmony, where the drama taking place is completely transferred to the divine plane. In this sense Duccio appears to be still in the mystic period of the Romanesque Middle Ages.

A modern

Very different from each other, the two styles of Giotto at Padua and Duccio at Siena are both expressive examples of timeless Christian art. The serious rhythm, the intense spirituality in the faces, create for the first time in the history of painting a link between divine revelation and human expression. Never has such a transformation manifested itself in so tangible a form as in the scenes of the *Maestà*. Divine poetry melts before our eyes in a language which is still traditional but which holds the echoes of man's first utterance when he questioned himself about his own destiny

Giotto
Noli me Tangere
Fresco, c. 1305
Scrovegni Chapel, Padua

and the insoluble mysteries of God. On the other hand, Duccio does not aim solely at objectivity in his painting, but offers and analyses his own soul.

In that respect, Duccio is a modern. Through the genius of the great Sienese all the tested ingredients of old medieval art acquired a new significance: it heralded the metamorphoses of western thought which were to take place throughout the next two centuries.

Giotto

The miracle of Giotto was the revelation of the human face. Certainly, since Byzantium man had had his place in iconography, but very quickly his features were frozen for eternity and were repeated indefinitely during the high Middle Ages and the Romanesque period. From the appearance of Gothic with the French miniaturists,

Giotto, sometimes attributed to
The Expulsion of the Demons from Arezzo
Before 1300
Fresco in the Upper Basilica, Assisi

Giotto
The Kiss of Judas (large detail)
Fresco, c. 1305
Scrovegni Chapel, Padua

Giotto, sometimes attributed to
Innocent III Approving the Franciscan Rule
Fresco in the Upper Church, Assisi

movement ran through the body with a long tremor. The face came to life and the lips relaxed in a smile. The renewal of forms stimulated a harmony of movement, where gestures, looks and body seemed to communicate in a new rhythm.

To understand the miracle of Giotto we must also remember the smiles of characters in the psalters and books of hours. To the angelic vision of the Byzantines, inherited by the illuminators of St. Louis, to the revolution in form, let us add the knowing eyes, with lids like a pharaoh, that seem to split open the faces drawn by the master of Padua and Assisi.

We are struck immediately by the realism of Giotto's faces. He penetrated life very easily. After many centuries of hieraticism the subjects he painted resemble living creatures, and not mere rudimentary characters (the French miniaturists were the first to try with success to humanise man's divine life). Giotto's revolutionary naturalism had incalculable consequences for the destiny of western art. What strikes us about the Florentine master is intelligence—human intelligence. Unlike Duccio, who conveyed a sort of divine intelligence, Giotto presents, one might say, a portrait of man's intelligence purged of his weakness, stripped of superfluous and over-candid feelings. In Giotto there are both the monastic ascetic and real man exposed to the contradictions of existence. He too is modern, but unlike Duccio, who is modern in form, Giotto is modern in spirit. It would be pointless to write about Giotto without mentioning his religious side, for though he was not a religious man at least he had a religious sense, like Dante; otherwise the study of the Assisi or Padua frescoes would become a brilliant, but quickly exhausted intellectual exercise. But we must always bear in mind the mystic, compassionate, idealistic and superstitious nature of medieval thought. The interest of Giotto, moreover, lies principally in his contradictions.

An aesthetic, ascetic doctrine

There is a sober harmony which repeats the colours at intervals, as a symphony recalls its original theme. This intense reflection of reality only stopped when Giotto worked out the archetype once for all. Most of the characters seem to bear a common resemblance. The line of the drawing, carefully studied and stripped of all unnecessary detail (we can even say of all details), indicates a kind of aesthetic ascetic doctrine which projects an expression of the soul mixed with the materialist thinking of individual man. The deliberate accentuation of the "doe-eyes" gives to all Giotto's characters an other-worldly look only recalled by the eyes painted on Egyptian sarcophagi. Restraint in each movement, voluntary omission of the effects which can distract the attention of the spectator who here becomes rather a reader of the human soul than a lover of objective paintings, all this confers on Giotto's art a quality of profound spirituality, both embellished and torn by human contradictions.

Giotto's realism is fixed on only one subject reproduced apparently over and over again; the facial expressions are set once for all; very painstaking, they have become formulas for expressing an intense vibration of the soul rather than a reflection of thought. Giotto's character do not live; they love and they meditate. All is intensity in a transcended realism. Rarely has such an expression of profound life been achieved with such economical means. We must turn to Egypt to find similar concentration in form and conception.

The solitary

Giotto imitated nobody. He left no theory and very few disciples: the miracle was not repeated. He communed with life in private. He devoted himself to painting as a monk devotes himself to prayer and anonymous work. Giotto was a visionary and the realisation of the frescoes marked one of the summits of his fervour—his joy in painting and expressing the vision he carried within him. But Giotto was also in touch with all human emotions, the most simple and the most devastating. The hands which are folded or stretched out, the despair conveyed by a gesture of a sobriety accessible only to the mind and the heart, the feelings which spring from a mysterious and cosmic harmony, make the realism of the Renaissance by comparison seem too often theatrical or even desperate.

Simone di Memmi, called Simone Martini
(1284-1344)
The Blow with the Lance
Detail: Group with Mary Magdalene
After 1339
Royal Fine-Arts Museum, Antwerp

The Church of St. Francis

Here is what the critic Cesare Gnudi* says about the earlier frescoes in the Upper Church of St. Francis at Assisi: "When there appears, after the *Sacrifice of Isaac* (ascribed to the brushes of Cimabue's pupils), under the grandiose and colourful upper lunettes of still-Byzantine inspiration, the two last scenes of the *Life of Isaac* and those of the *Life of Joseph*, one realises that architecture has at last found its painter. Take for example the representation of the room where Isaac is lying in the two last scenes in the *Life of Isaac*. There is an evident attempt at perspective. In the space bounded by the gradation of the different planes the figures settle with ease into their frame, move and adjust to the mood which surrounds them. The dramatic and human story is conveyed by an absolutely clear image which determines the plastic and spatial structure of the scene. From this point of view, perhaps, no painting in the church at Assisi is nearer Giotto's mature phase. The poetic revelation of reality which was Giotto's is already there in its entirety."[1]

In the Assisi frescoes Giotto showed himself in full possession of his powers. The church of St. Francis, the Upper Church, contains another series of more recent frescoes which are, in places, less beautiful than the earlier ones: they trace the life of St. Francis.

Despite weaknesses inherent in Giotto's assistants who could not grasp their master's colour combinations and harmonies of light and shade, the *Life of St. Francis* marks one of the peaks of Florentine inspiration. Firstly, the setting, which is in itself a harmony within the harmony of the church. The vast wall of the monument is divided into twenty-eight large panels. Between each part a pictorial motif is inscribed in the geometric space edged by columns rising from a basement and supporting an architrave* on corbels in perspective. Framed thus, each scene blends with the harmonious architectonic equilibrium of the long nave.

We witness the unfolding of a rarely balanced whole, It is the master's most "Gothic" work, in which his psychological exploration was concentrated on the faces by means of a new process, accentuating a detail (he who was so sparing of them), improving it, and integrating it into his poetic universe. There is not yet the mastery which presides over the execution of the Padua frescoes, where the detail is more completely defined and succeeds in giving his later works a more absolute finish. But even there at Assisi the embodiment of a new vision and a developing style appear with an incomparable freshness of feeling. The scene of *St. Francis Renouncing the World* is a good example of this new approach, where Giotto's art expresses more subtle and complex feelings in the faces of his characters.

Here are the scenes depicting the chamber where Pope Innocent III* is dreaming, and the throne-room where he receives and sanctions the Rule; then the vision of the fiery chariot which envelops St. Francis with its electric green light

[1] Jacques Dupont and Cesare Gnudi: *La Peinture gothique*, Skira, 1954.

S P

Simone Martini, follower of
Virgin and Child
National Museum of Ancient Art,
Barberini Palace, Rome

while Brother Pacificio crouches, with his head on his knees, his eyes closed, his soul invaded by the vision. Lastly, among many other panels bursting with the new expression and the new vision of the world which Giotto works out before our eyes, there is the panorama depicting the town of Arezzo freed from demons. It is an extraordinary picture of a town suddenly restored to calm by the Saint's exorcism. The town of Arezzo, like a cloud of dew, seems to rise from behind the ramparts, made buoyant by the void created by the departure of the demons. They are seen flying above the town, black and heavy, across a royal-blue sky against which the newly purified houses stand out in pure bold colours of pink, white, grey, and orange. Moreover, in the astonishingly true detail of the inclined cross in *The Christmas Miracle at Greccio* one is impressed by this incursion of an object into an apparently new space. Here Giotto, breaking in a revolutionary manner with the tested formuli of medieval illuminators, delivers figure and object from that formal rigidity to place it in the new-found space. In the same scene of *The Christmas Miracle at Greccio*, the different groups of people who advance from all directions create for the first time in western painting a new spatial reality—a reality with a dramatic and decorative content, with passionate feelings sanctified also by piety, filled with divine longings and unutterable tenderness and, behind those calm faces, a strong restlessness which betokens man's suffering. Further on, the panel depicting Jerome of Assisi examining the miracle of the stigmata* shows us one of the achievements of Giotto's art: the cross and the images of the Virgin and the angel in a perspective which raises them in space above the altar; in the foreground lamps hang from an invisible ceiling.

The Arena Chapel

Giotto finished the Assisi frescoes between 1290 and 1300. Several years later, between 1304 and 1306, he decorated the Arena Chapel, which was formerly part of the Scrovegni Palace at Padua. It was there that his style was crystallised and defined. At Assisi there was a pictorial harmony precisely integrated with the architectural harmony of the church and more particularly of the nave. At Padua, the frescoes harmonise with the Arena Chapel because Giotto managed to strike an admirable balance between colour and stone. This is one of the rarest examples of fresco, whose poetic tenor is firmly maintained from start to finish.

The frescoes start with a kind of prelude: *The Stories of Anna and Joachim*. The theme—human representation—appears straightaway in ample, simple and solemn movement. Each gesture, each expression is made concrete, shown for its own intrinsic value and plastic power, a range of expressions and feelings hitherto unequalled in amplitude. It is a continuous harmony of linking motifs over which is imposed a meditation, an intense religious silence, the pared-down details of each face rigorously expressing all the high spirituality a mystic character can reveal. The movement of Mary's forearm, for example, in *The Meeting of Mary and Elizabeth*

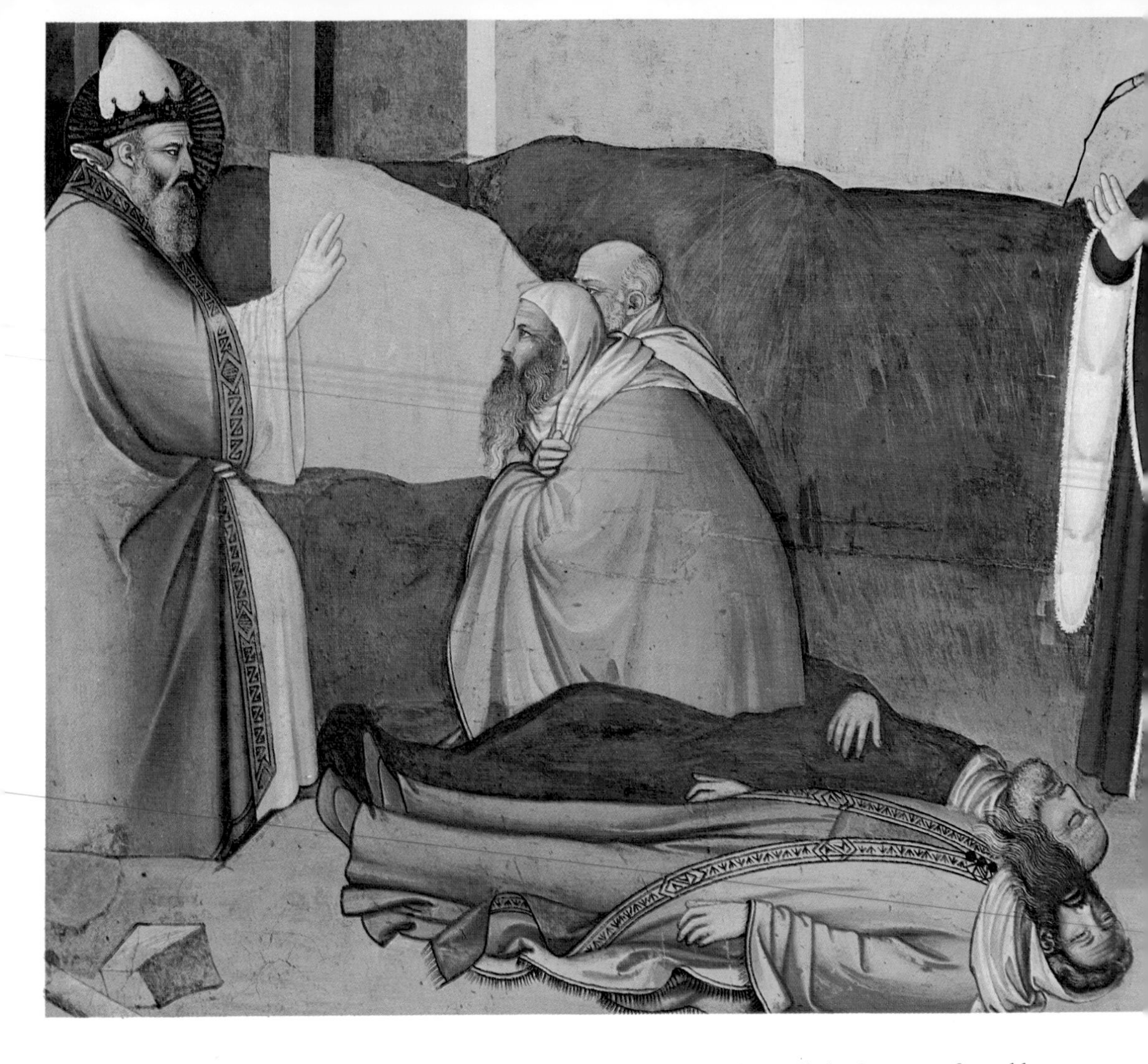

is a movement full of gravity, and firm, noble modesty, linked to a profound harmony indicating internal life. Elizabeth's face appears as in a mirror, and her eyes, on the same level as Mary's, seem to hold those of her companion in tacit admiration. There is a mysterious rhythm governing their expressions, which carry their destinies, their controlled movements and their hieratic bodies clothed in a light swirl of fabric that seems to have a life of its own, like the pinkish ochre tunic draping in a single sweep the body of Joachim during his vision. It is not one of Giotto's least achievements to have given to all these people a human expression contained within their own divine contemplation. The face three-quarters hidden by a black cloak of the woman at the Golden Gate *(The Meeting at the Golden Gate)*, who regards Anna's followers with a grave joy, could equally well be that of an angel or a common woman, so far has Giotto's genius succeeded in maintaining the human and the angelic in vertiginous equilibrium.

In the scenes of *The Marriage Procession of Mary*, and *The Meeting of Mary and Elizabeth* we discover statuesque characters nevertheless animated by a vibrant internal life, and acutely questioning expressions that seem to exchange a set of mysterious conventions for eternity by means of short clear gestures. Power in the portrayal of *The Resurrection of Lazarus;* intensity of feeling, strong, close contrast of masses, concentration of the three troubled and anxious looks which waver before that of our Lord in *The Kiss of Judas:* these are the impressions we get from

Maso
St. Sylvester Reviving two Magicians
Santa Croce, Florence

Simone Martini
Annunciation
1333
Uffizi, Florence

the scenes of the life and death of Christ linked in a sequence of clear-coloured panels, simplified almost to the point of coldness.

The Church of Santa Croce, Florence

After the evocation of Padua, the frescoes in the church of Santa Croce, Florence, seem like a return to the naturalism of Assisi. Analysis of space at Assisi, hieraticism at Padua, and the *Obsequies of St. Francis* at Florence are a synthesis between conquered space and balanced masses, still imbued with reasoned spirituality expressed in simple lines and transparent colour. Perhaps they do not transmit the noble familiarity to which Giotto has accustomed us by the delicacy of his colours, but never has any legend of a saint given rise to such sublime scenes.

Simone Martini: realist and psychologist

To a certain extent, the art of Simone Martini is indebted to, and does approach, French culture. His style, more refined than that of his compatriots, the very Gothic composition of most of his works, and his stay at Avignon are facts which contribute to giving him a special place beside Duccio, Giotto, and the Lorenzetti brothers.

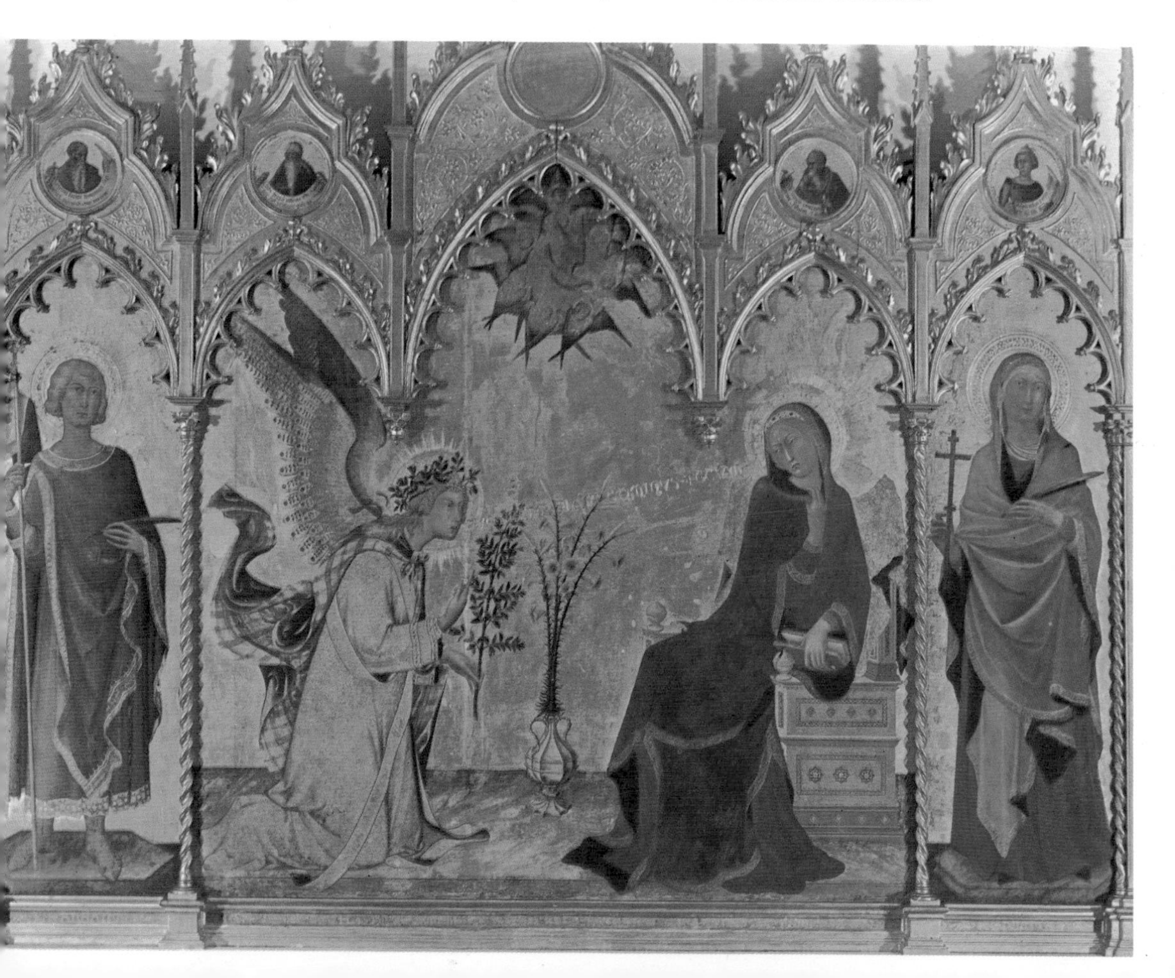

The style of Simone is close to the French illuminators by a very linear design; he had more incorporeal colours than Giotto, but a less mystic inspiration; and his greater care for details was allied to more optimism than serenity: this sums up his basic approach. In detail, we distinguish a deeper and more deliberate investigation of perspective. (Giotto knew all about it but avoided it as much as possible in his works; in that respect he came nearer to the illuminators and Martini moved away.) Martini tried to make the face more expressive, sometimes not hesitating to accentuate the facial features, as in certain characters in the scene depicting the raising of a child by St. Martin (fresco—*The Life of St. Martin*, Church of St. Francis, Assisi). To Duccio's transcended realism, and Giotto's spirituality (stripped as it is of vain ornaments and leaving only internal tension), Simone Martini added a finesse of composition, and transparency of expression which characterises his people. Giotto's spirituality may be defined as the force and tension of internal life showing clearly in the face; mysticism and nobility reside in a face painted by Duccio; similarly it is a reflection of the soul's transparency, a psychological analysis, that appears in the eyes of those monks who chant in front of the trefoiled Gothic windows at the obsequies of St. Martin.

The symphony

Simone Martini looked at men, he observed and scrutinised them; but he also noticed objects, walls and crenelated towers in the Tuscan towns. He brought nature into his compositions. His art is a marvellous assembly of men's expressions, stained glass legends and celestial echoes. We have been caught in the waves of an increasingly vast symphony ever since Duccio, and now mysticism joins with realism, feelings and objects. The face of man set by Martini is calm and tranquil, as tranquil as his panoramas with limpid skies and castles cut out sharply like the setting for a children's

Pietro Lorenzetti (first half of 14th century)
Story of the Blessed Umiltà 1341
Panel of a polyptych
Uffizi, Florence

Pietro Lorenzetti (first half of 14th century)
Story of the Blessed Umiltà 1341
Panel of a polyptych
Uffizi, Florence

play, such as that in which a sumptuously caparisoned knight makes his progress (*Equestrian Portrait of Guidoriccio da Fogliano*, Town Hall, Siena). His finesse often tends towards a certain preciousness, but this he succeeds in neutralising by his technique. But a meditative expression, a magic charm, surrounds all the people of Simone Martini, who gives to each work an incomparable effect of contemplative ravishment.

The legacy

With the polyptych of the Virgin, certainly painted at Avignon, the Master of *The Life of St. Martin* attained recognition in France. Unfortunately, the panels have been dispersed, and only *The Virgin and the Angel of the Annunciation* remain in the Royal Art Museum at Antwerp; the other parts were acquired by the museums of Paris and Berlin. Cesare Gnudi finds in them numerous elements of international Gothic and a " quasi-aerial lyricism in the motifs, a poetic, almost fairy-like, imagination revealing itself by a quite musical shape of line ".[1]

Several beautiful sections of the frescoes painted by Martini and his pupils are maintained in the Papal palace, in the Wardrobe and elsewhere.

Simone Martini played a major role in artistic relations between France and Italy. His stay in Avignon from 1340 till the year of his death in 1344, the profound influence he left behind him in that town, and his bold technique in fresco composition were factors which persuaded both French and Italian artists into new ways at the beginning of the 14th century. He contributed largely to the formation in Europe of the " International Gothic Style " and introduced into Gothic painting an attention to psychology still very much involved with traditionalism and contemplation.

[1] Jacques Dupont and Cesare Gnudi, *La Peinture gothique*, Skira, 1954.

Giovanni (da Rimini) Baronzio (died before 1362)
Scenes from the Life of Christ (detail) Pietà
National Museum of Ancient Art,
Barberini Palace, Rome

Ambrogio Lorenzetti
The Effects of Good Government (detail)
1337-40
Town Hall, Siena

The End of Italian Gothic Painting

The last breath of the Trecento is a heavy evanescent perfume, pervading one to the heart. At that time, decadence touched the stained glass of France (the Paris school that the Hundred Years War succeeded in ruining), and the tapestries which then foreshadowed the bold convolutions of Baroque. In sculpture there was already some flamboyance, and the pure verities of Chartres disappeared to make room for the occult and delirium. But a prestigious style rose out of the decadence, hollowed out the space in confused perspective and closed up the void again with bell-tower and acanthus leaf. So, this period of the new world, begun with Cimabue, metamorphosed into its autumn; its leaves fell to enrich the ground from which were to spring the great pre-Renaissance painters of the Quattrocento, and later the symphonists of the Renaissance itself. An idea ebbed and flowed in the space of two centuries, enriched and fertilised a soil and then retired. In this slow decline of Italian Gothic primitive painting of the Trecento some powerful and original painters appeared to form a bridge between the Trecento and the Quattrocento, between Giotto and Fra Angelico. Sano di Pietro*, Bartolo di Fredi* and Lorenzo di Pietro*, among others, continued to apply, often with grace and inspiration, the formuli of the early time of Cimabue and Duccio.

Ambrogio Lorenzetti
The Effects of Good Government (detail)
1337-40
Municipal Palace, Siena

Pietro Lorenzetti: a new approach

Anguish, continuous experimenting, a way of projecting himself in numerous manners, an affirmation of man and at the same time an underlying despair—these are the windows through which Pietro Lorenzetti gives a glimpse of Renaissance and modern painting.

Of all his illustrious predecessors—Duccio, Giotto, and Martini—he is certainly the painter who, with his younger brother Ambrogio, is more representative of the metamorphosis in Italian painting over that period. The Lorenzetti brothers slightly raise the veil which hides the revolutionary workmanship of the great painters of the Quattrocento: Masaccio, Fra Angelico, Ucello*, Piero della Francesca*, Ghirlandaio*, and Bellini*.

The style of Pietro Lorenzetti conveys intense ideas and feelings. His palette still remains within a certain tradition of medieval illumination, and his dualist morality recalls dogmatic intransigence, but the accuracy of his touch and the development of geometric methods allowed him deeper studies of landscape and character. Thus, the faces of the people who surround *The Crucifixion* (fresco in the Lower Church of St. Francis, Assisi) especially the faces of the knights, are remarkable models of psychological portraits. Paintings as dissimilar as *The Dream of*

Sobac in the Carmelite altar screen at Siena, and *The Crucifixion*, or *The Blessed Umiltà* in the Uffizi at Florence (this last is nearer to the Carmelite screen though composed twelve years later) show that introspective research is a common denominator in all Pietro Lorenzetti's works despite their diversity.

Giotto concentrated the passions, Cimabue hid them but let them be guessed, Duccio drew them out, Simone Martini refined them, but Pietro Lorenzetti brought them into the full light of day. In that way he was a modern: in our phrase he "relaxed, let himself go."

All the expressions are noticed, grasped and reproduced with a realism which, despite his occasional exaggerations, is always sharpened by the medieval clarity that still surrounded the great Sienese painters, who were at the same time the last witnesses of the far-off influence of Byzantium and prophets of the new age.

A subtle idiom

Pietro was a painter in a difficult idiom, continually changing his style and his inspirations, sensitive to everything new; he seems out of period. He attained the summit of his art in the Assisi *Crucifixion*, which reveals a cruel beauty mingled with love, tenderness, hatred, anger and scorn. This simple range of emotions is developed by subtle nuances into a harmony entirely subordinate to the passions. When we contemplate the crucified Christ who dominates the perverse, arrogant, indifferent crowd, we think forward to Breughel*. Pietro was a great innovator, and his enlarged vision of the surrounding world enabled him to introduce new values into a divine poetry that was rapidly tending to become humanised.

Paolo Veneziano, or Paolo da Venezia
Madonna and Child
Academy, Venice

Ambrogio Lorenzetti: visionary and geometrician

While Pietro innovated in the field of passion, his brother Ambrogio discovered a new vision of society and a way of treating it from unprecedented angles. Spirituality being always in the domain of Pietro's passionate investigations, Ambrogio may be defined as a "social" painter with a wider psychological range.

Ambrogio was a profound psychologist and also a poet of town and country. He described the activities of the people, the little townsmen; he revealed the hills and the rivers, the thatched cottages and the harvests being stored. He presented a new world, a humanity which seemed to come out of its original gangue before his eyes. He scrutinised faces and reproduced them in stark lines and flat colours which occasionally recall Japanese portraits. The force of his touch, the geometric composition of his works, a sober and severe interpretation of the world, already pave the way for Uccello, del Castagno* and Signorelli*.

Though a great part of Ambrogio's work still had religious inspiration —which applied to all artists of his time—he was one of the first to give a social and secular touch to a work. The fresco *The Effects of Good and Bad Government* (Town Hall, Siena) is the typical example.

In 1319, Ambrogio painted the *Madonna of Vico l'Abate*, which is the first work he dated. A comparison is inevitable with his brother's *Virgin and Child:* Ambrogio's style is much more monumental, more abstract with, still, a neo-Byzantine design.

The *Madonna of Vico l'Abate* anticipates Ambrogio's later style, and the sculptural moulding of his figures, which vibrate with profound expression, already heralds Piero della Francesca.

Ambriogio never attained Giotto's indication of internal life, but he retained his noble and direct intentions. His universe had the Florentine's breadth and grace, but there ends the comparison. Like his brother, Pietro, he devoted himself to a close study of faces, but whereas Pietro let his concern be obvious, Ambrogio was restrained, and limited himself to indicating a character by a single stroke. Shades of feeling were always registered in an apparently uniform way, and a certain monotony would be apparent in his work were it not that the consummate art of the colourist and the analyst outweighs this weakness.

Innovation in the field of perspective, new experiment in the balance between masses, harmony of unprecedented ranges of colours, depiction of a world more fabulous and legendary than real—all this can be seen in most of Ambrogio's work.

The reredos depicting episodes in the life of St. Nicholas (Uffizi) executed at Florence about 1332, the Frankfurt polyptych, the little *Madonna* surrounded by saints and angels (Siena Picture Gallery) and *The Presentation in the Temple* are only some of the works in which Ambrogio introduced his own developments of light and shade, clarity and original choice of colour, and refinement of perspective.

But it is in the fresco *The Effects of Good and Bad Government*, 1337 to 1340, that the painter most happily expressed his poetic vision of the world. It is a work of already very secular tone (which is a little surprising after Giotto), but in Ambrogio Lorenzetti it is the fruit of profound meditation on the nature of life detached from all mystic preoccupation. Thus, the rustic scenes turn out rather like the Limbourg brothers'; an apparently long-lasting peace, in a serene natural setting where animals mix with men working calmly in the fields; towns illuminated by a limpid joy which seems to invade and inundate the least alley—there is no trace of a shadow in Ambrogio's towns.

All this enchantment, more magic than religious, more poetic than moral, this everlasting daily round of work and leisure (even a fatalism is faintly discernible among these slightly indifferent people and too-luminous buildings) form a most beautiful union of lyricism, restraint, fantasy and reality.

Italian Painting after Giotto

The Lorenzetti brothers were able to capture and combine all the qualities of Cimabue, Duccio, Giotto and Martini; after they died, Italian art, at the end of the Trecento, produced the great Sienese and Florentine masters. Not counting a few minimal foreign influences, most 14th century Italian painters followed the influences of their illustrious predecessors. In the unstable period which preceded the great dawn of the Quattrocento, at that junction between two worlds, we witness the decline of the Gothic spirit. Sienese art contrived to die in a formalism which blinded it to the new horizons, the Tuscan towns withdrew into their narrow independence, while Florence prepared to take the leading place during the next century. There were, however, still some great painters who brought a whole new range of poetry and colours into a traditional framework. Among the artists of the new generation was Maso*, one of Giotto's pupils, who painted the frescoes depicting episodes in the life of St. Sylvester in the Church of Santa Croce, Florence.

Maso and Giottino

Maso absorbed the teaching of Giotto. His painting is direct and simple, the expressions of his people are supported by a strong internal vitality. He retained Giotto's economical manner of presenting his subjects but his composition is different, more monumental; decor became more important, and consequently his points of interest were dispersed. In *The Miracle of St. Sylvester* the planes have been clearly differentiated: the colonnade and the broken arch mark the first, the people are in the second, the wall and a meadow in the third, the fourth consists of two houses, one white and ruined, the other pink and apparently unfinished, and,

Bernado Daddi
Martyrdom of St. Cecilia
Tempera, c. 1335
Civic Museum, Pisa

behind, an enclosure wall hides the horizon of a night-blue sky. This work conveys an effect of depth never surpassed by any Italian painter of the Trecento. Maso's artistry was perfect and through his geometry and economy he attained a high peak of spirituality.

Giottino was another of Giotto's pupils, perhaps his favourite. He had a firm technique, and his sincere art was served by a good colour sense, but he did not shine with originality, and was inhibited by his master's influence. According to Vasari, he was the author of the San Remigio *Pietà*. He may have painted the inside of the pendentives of the vault above the main altar in the lower church at Assisi. These very lifelike paintings illustrate the Franciscan vows of poverty, chastity and obedience.

The last painters of the Trecento

Influenced alternately by Florence and Siena, the new painters like Nardo di Cione*, who decorated the Strozzi chapel in the Church of Santa Maria Novella, Florence, his brother Andrea Orcagna*, Taddeo Gaddi*, Bernado Daddi*, Angelo Daddi* and Spinello Aretino* formed an important group in the second half of the 14th century.

In 1365, Andrea Bonaiuti da Firenze* decorated the Spanish Chapel in Florence with a fresco composed of allegorical motifs full of freshness and grace. His was a primarily descriptive, even courtly, art portraying a sensual form of existence and a taste for luxury which was moving away from the spirituality and anxious realism of the Middle Ages. Nevertheless, Andrea Bonaiuti was close in design and colour to the great Sienese artists of the early part of the century, particularly Ambrogio Lorenzetti. Barna* was another painter who dominated the second period of Sienese "traditional" art, a period "which seems to be confined within more restrained and more provincial limits"[1], writes Cesari Gnudi. Mentioned by Ghiberti, Barna, a pupil of Simone Martini, painted the frescoes in the Collegiate Church of San Gimignano, representing scenes from the New Testament. Also ascribed to him, the *Madonna* of Asciano has a delicate workmanship which recalls the technique of Martini.

The Campo Santo of Pisa

About 1360 a set of frescoes was carried out by an anonymous painter in the Campo Santo of Pisa; they are among the most significant of the 14th century. Was it a Tuscan or Bolognese master who painted *The Triumph of Death*, *The Last Judgement* and *The Life of the Hermits*? The question remains unanswered, but the Tuscan influences seem decisive. It is a work of powerful and tragic lyricism, essentially full of movement. The sorrowful faces already have "extrovert" rather than "introvert" expressions. We are with death and its contradictions. This fresco, still in the medieval tradition, nevertheless reveals, in form and background, the decline of Gothic art.

The Rimini school and the Bologna school

Several great artists, among them Cavallini*, gave a quite individual brilliance to what we may call the Rimini school, which owed its style to the profound influences of Tuscan culture and to the art of Giotto. It was one of Giotto's pupils who decorated the Campanile Chapel of the Church of St. Augustine, Rimini. A disciple of Cavallini decorated the back of the apse with three frescoes: Christ enthroned, flanked by the two St. Johns, the Virgin in glory, and the triumphal arch. The Rimini school, still paralysed by the distant Byzantine influences, subsequently left behind by the rapid soaring of the Sienese and Florentines, was to keep its archaic flavour for a long time.

In connection with this Byzantine taste, let us notice in passing the scenes from the life of St. John the Evangelist and, in a scheme of pale blue, pink and watery grey, the fresco which depicts the Ephesus earthquake.

The Rimini school, like the Bolognese school, was of great importance in the development of Italian painting all through the 14th century. At Rimini we find the names of Neri da Rimini*, the illuminator; Pietro da Rimini*, author of the frescoes in the Church of Santa Chiara, Ravenna, and of the *Deposition* in the Louvre; and Giovanni Baronzio*, who painted the polyptych in the Urbino gallery.

[1] Jacques Dupont and Cesare Gnudi, *La Peinture gothique*, Skira, 1954.

Altichiero (1330-85)
Beheading of St. George
Oratory of St. George, Padua

Gentile da Fabriano (1370-1427)
Adoration of the Magi
1423
Detail of a predella painted for the Palla Strozzi Chapel, Santa Trinità
Uffizi, Florence

Though the Bolognese painters moved away from the severity of the Tuscans, certain of their great artists, such as Vitale*, or Jacopino da Bologna*, always kept the direct style in which their fantasies were expressed within a very Latin structure. The Bologna Picture Gallery possesses several beautiful fragments of frescoes by Mezzaratta depicting the Nativity. The Bologna school also came under the influence of the French illuminators. Some manuscripts were remarkably illustrated for Bologna University. They are ascribed to French artists, but they were soon replaced by Italians. The National Library, Paris, preserves a beautiful *Latin Bible* of this period. Franco Bolognese* (Dante records his merits) was the greatest illuminator.

Tomaso da Modena, Giovanni da Milano, Paolo Veneziano and Altichiero

Tomaso da Modena belongs among the painters of the school which arose from the Bolognese environment and included Lippo* and Christoforo Dalmasio, Jacopo di Paolo* and Simone dei Crocefissi*. After having studied illumination and produced numerous works in Emilia and Venetia, this original artist settled at Treviso, where in 1352 he painted the frescoes in the Dominican chapter. The fresco of the *Holy Doctors* is an example of the increasingly naturalistic trend in late 14th century Italian art. The scenes from *The Life of St. Ursula* display this tendency by a direct representation, not without occasional traces of humour, which gives this work a cachet of grace and cheerfulness.

About 1365, Giovanni da Milano, a Lombardian settled in Florence, painted the frescoes in the Rinuccini chapel of the Church of Santa Croce, Florence. In a style which was elegant and often precious (but this was the period of full decadence) we see more and more clearly the effects of naturalism which make this painter an artist of high quality, but unfortunately stagnant style, whose facial expressions never passed the conventional stage.

Venice, Padua (where Guariento* and Giusto di Menabuoi* worked) and Verona (the home of Altichiero*) were the three great centres of Italian painting in the second half of the 14th century. For a time they crystallised all the artistic currents in Italy: Byzantine, Tuscan, Emilian and Lombardian.

Paolo Veneziano* worked in Venice during the greater part of his life. He was very influenced by the Byzantine tradition and achieved with reasonable felicity a kind of Gothic-Byzantine synthesis which integrated Giotto's spatiality, contemporary primitive naturalism, and Byzantine gilding and contrasting colours. Saint Mark's, Venice, possesses the beautiful *Episodes in the Life of St. Mark*, painted by Veneziano in 1345 on the back of the Golden Altar-piece.

Altichiero, born in Verona, brilliantly mastered the teachings of the great Sienese painters. He was endowed with a profound inspiration and wide range of expressions, and used luminous colours to translate his gifts, dominated by emotion and delicacy. He painted the Cavalli family's votive fresco in the church of Saint Anastasia, Verona, but is principally known for having decorated the walls of the San Felice del Santo Chapel, Padua, in 1379, and the St. George Oratory, *circa* 1385. Already Altichiero's work was enriched by new forms, more rigorous demands for realism, and more complex dialectic. These are exhibited in, for example, *The Beheading of St. George*, a remarkably orchestrated scene nearer to the Quattrocento than to Giotto. Altichiero displayed a fully developed naturalism and a nascent humanism, and only remained Gothic in inspiration and a certain conventional strictness of composition.

The last Trecento painters

With Giovannino de Grassi (who about 1385 illustrated the *Book of Hours of Gian Galeazzo Visconti*), Michelino da Besozzo*, Pisanello*, Stefano da Zevio* and, one of the greatest, Lorenzo Monaco (discussed in the section on Florentine illuminators) we come to the very end of what can be called authentic Italian Gothic art. All indebted to Giotto and the other Florentine and Sienese masters, they tended towards a subtle mannered style, like that of Michelino da Besozzo. Some, particularly Stefano da Zevio, were already deeply influenced by French Burgundian art. Zevio has left us a very beautiful *Virgin of the Rosary* (Castelvecchio Museum, Verona).

Lorenzo Monaco, Pisanello, and Gentile da Fabriano form the final group of great Italian Gothic painters. We owe to Lorenzo Monaco the scenes of *The Life of St. Nicholas of Bari* (Academy Gallery, Florence), to Pisanello the fresco *St. George and the Princess* (Church of Saint Anastasia, Verona) and to Gentile da Fabriano, the most characteristic of the group, *The Adoration of the Magi*, painted about 1423 (Uffizi, Florence). Gentile da Fabriano has also left us several figures of St. Francis of Assisi which deserve to be ranked among the most beautiful, particularly the picture showing *St. Francis Receiving the Stigmata* (Fornari Museum, Fabriano).

Rhythm; naturalism in the smallest details; sumptuous colour incorporating most complex shades; subtle and delicate movements; refined poetry aimed at a cultured nobility; these attributes were common to all three artists who, at the beginning of the 15th century, created several of the last masterpieces of Trecento painting.

Evidence and Documents

The Successive Aspects of Christian Art

Christianity, which early became the religion of the most civilised Mediterranean races, cultivated art as a friend. It might be supposed that the Church could easily have done without the help of line and colour: the beauty that it brought into the world was of another order. But it judged otherwise: it saw art as an ally. Man not being a pure spirit, it considered he could attain purity through the senses as well as through the soul. Besides, its great teachers pointed to the divine hand in beauty, the presentiment of higher things. To condemn art would have been to mutilate human nature, stifle one of its nobler instincts. The Church has always combated iconoclasts and upheld the struggle of civilisation against ever-recurring barbarism.

It is to the Church that we owe our art, an art that we can term, for nearly fifteen hundred years, Christian art. Through all these centuries, Christian art has been as fluid as life itself. One might have thought that, having to proclaim an immutable dogma, to recount unceasingly the same supernatural story, it would have been stricken with exceptional immobility: the truth has proved to be otherwise. Humanity, meditating on its faith, discovered new aspects of it from age to age. Art expressed these nuances and often rendered them with surprising fidelity. One of the many beauties of Christian art is that it retails the history of Christian thought. It is certainly not all there, since art is not a theology; nevertheless, the different ways of understanding, or rather of sensing Christianity, which are those of the successive generations, are revealed in Christian art. Perhaps it is not impossible to demonstrate this in a few pages.

Emile Mâle

Art and Artists of the Middle Ages
Armand Colin, Paris, 1947

The Illuminators and Their Methods

In the 13th century, this art (illumination) suddenly underwent considerable expansion, and its exercise became divided between the clergy and the laity; at the same time, the miniaturist separated from the calligrapher; not generally and without exception, for they were for a long time included in the same guilds and subject to common taxes, but in certain particular cases, which became increasingly numerous. Already they began to be distinguished by different names: the first was called the illuminator, the *paginator* or page decorator; the second kept the ancient name of *librarius* or *scriptor*, but with a more limited significance. In 1292, the Paris population census counted twelve illuminators established there; in 1300 it counted fifteen. Like most other Parisian artisans, they were nearly all grouped in one street, the *rue Boutebrie*, which took from them the name of the *rue des Enlumineurs*; they were situated in the vicinity of the parchment-makers and the libraries, so that the different industries all concerned in book production were concentrated in the same district, to the great advantage of the public.

The illuminator (of the 14th century) is an independent worker. He exercises his occupation at home, on a table with a drawer, placed in front of a large window which affords him a good light. On this table, a desk or small easel supports the vellum over which his paint-brush moves. He sits on a three-legged stool. Round him are a few phials, vases and pictures hung on the walls. His surroundings, his furniture, and his clothes appear fairly comfortable; he gives the impression of an artist who has "arrived".

Independently of the paint-brush, he continues to use the pen; he also needs a burnisher, a sharp knife, a pair of compasses, a hare's foot and a wolf's tooth, or crystal or agate polisher to polish the surfaces, a pumice stone, pots, shells, porphyry mortars, alambics, and stoves—for most of the time he prepares his own colours. He tries them out first on a scrap of parchment; he is not familiar with the use of the palette. Then he takes the book or the leaflet he is required to illustrate and designs his work directly on it; for it is very rare for him to jot down his preliminary idea in a few rough sketches, as are found in the margins of the *Morality* of St. Gregory the Great, transcribed in the 13th century at Cuissy Abbey (Laon Library). The book has been passed to him already written. The copyist has been careful to leave blank the spaces for the illuminated capitals and the miniatures, and in certain cases where he has doubted his intelligence he has indicated the initials to be designed by faint signs sketched on the extreme edge of the outer margin.

The first operation consists in tracing the outlines with a pen dipped in black or brown ink, or sometimes red. Before taking his brush, the artist still uses a pen to cover certain backgrounds with hatchwork and to execute certain details such as interlacings. Then he fills in this sketch with flat colours, which he will go back over to add the shadows and modelling in darker shades.

Apart from that, the method of applying and preparing the colours generally formed the great preoccupation of medieval artists. They undertook extensive journeys to procure the best recipes; they made collections of them which they guarded jealously for themselves and their friends, and elaborated or corrected them as their experience improved.

A. Lecoy de la Marche

The Manuscripts and the Miniature
Maison Quentin, Paris, 1884

Lights in the West

Entering the immense and shadowy cathedral was always impressive, and instinctively one bowed the head and walked carefully under the formidable majesty of the vaults; and Durtal stopped after a few steps, blinded by the light from the choir contrasting with this sombre avenue of the nave, which was unlit until it joined the transept. The Christ Figure had its legs and feet in shadow, the body in a dead light, and the head flooded by a torrent of colour, at Chartres; and Durtal contemplated, high up, those still ranks of patriarchs and apostles, bishops and saints, flaming in a fire which was quenched in obscure stained-glass windows, guarding the divine body lying at their feet below them; in enormous lancets surmounted by roses they stood ranged along the upper gallery, showing to Jesus nailed on the ground his still-faithful army, his troops numbered in the Scriptures, in Books of Legend, and in Martyrology; and Durtal recognised, among the crowd of blade-like figures in the windows, St. Lawrence, St. Stephen, St. Giles, St. Nicholas of Myre, St. Martin, St. George, St. Symphorian, St. Philip, St. Foix, St. Laumer and countless others whose names he did not know, and he halted, amazed, near the transept, before Abraham raising, in an eternal gesture of menace, over an Isaac for ever bowed, the bright blade of a knife against a sky of infinite azure.

And he admired the conception and workmanship of these 13th century windows, their exaggeration necessitated by the heights, the way the pictures had been made easy to discern from a distance by the introduction, as far as possible, of only a single figure, depicted with massive features in clear colours, so that he could be appreciated from below at a glance.

That day, which was sunny, the three 12th century windows were resplendent with their unsheathed short-sword blades and broad-sword blades on a wide flat ground under the rose that dominates the main portal.

There was a glittering of sparks and flashes, a web of blue fire, a brighter blue than that in which Abraham brandished his knife; this pale, limpid azure recalled the flames on punch, ignited sulphur powder, and the lightning darting from sapphires, but sapphires still young, still ingenuous and trembling, so to speak; and in the glass ogive on the right could be seen delineated by embers the stem of Jesse with its characters mounting one above the other in the blue blaze of the clouds; the middle arch and the left-hand one showed scenes from the life of Jesus, the Annunciation, the entry into Jerusalem, the Transfiguration, the Last Supper, the meal with the disciples at Emmaus, while above these three vaults the Christ Figure flashed in the heart of the great rose and the dead left their tombs at the sound of the trumpet, and St. Michael weighed the souls.

This 12th century blue, Durtal wondered, how had the glass-makers of the time acquired it and, after so long, how had glaziers lost both it and the red? In the 12th century, glass-painters used three main colours: firstly, blue, that ineffable blue of the infinite sky which glorifies the panes of Chartres; then red, a rich, sombre, purplish red; lastly green, inferior in quality to the two other tones. Instead of white they used a greenish shade. In the following century the palette enlarges, but darkens; the glass is thicker; however, what shining azure of pure and virile sapphire those artists of fire attained, and what an amazing red of fresh blood they used! Yellow, less liberally used, was, judging by the robe of a neighbour of Abraham in a crossing near the transept, a brazen tint of lively citron; but, apart from these three colours which vibrate, explode like songs of joy in these transparent pictures, the others darken, the violets are those of plums and aubergines, the browns turn to caramel, the onion greens blacken.

What masterpieces of colour they obtained with the blending and the clash of these tones, and what understanding and skill in manipulating these threads of lead, accentuating certain details, punctuating, separating by these inky marks their paragraphs of flame!

J.-K. Huysmans.

The Cathedral
Librairie Plon, Paris, 1906

Giotto: Balance between St. Thomas Aquinas and St. Francis of Assisi

Psychology was replacing symbolism. Painting in its turn was discovering that to depict the expression of a feeling was a powerful way of conveying it. Giotto's style was to the Neo-Hellenes what the face of his Christ was to a Byzantine Christ. In abandoning the symbolic gesture and substituting a dramatic one, he would himself have invented Gothic if it had not already existed.

The Franciscan in him pursues this tendency. Let us, however, be wary of his legend. Everything advocated by Franciscanism tended to a dissolution of man, but Giotto is as near to Thomas Aquinas as to Francis of Assisi, and the Church's continual effort to strengthen the Christian order by absorbing what most menaces it has largely contributed to the massive character (like the solidity of the Coliseum) of civilisation from Sparta to the United States, massiveness which seems to Asiatics inseparable from Western genius. It took the Roman order to prevent Franciscanism from dissolving into Buddhishm; Giotto is on the side of Rome and perhaps he hides more than he shows of the Franciscan theme's true image.

The irresistible strength of Franciscanism was that it humanised suffering and made it not only a link through Christ between man and God, but also a common bond of sympathy. It is better to regard the Franciscan world as the world of God rather than of St. Francis; that which is most nobly Franciscan in Giotto is no face of the Saint, but the greeting at the Golden Gate. He is never greater than when he embodies the broad sweep of Christian drama, and when his frescoes combine the new teaching with the solitary echo of St. Augustine. His powers of incarnation have certainly never been surpassed, but his greatness lies there no more than in the mark he stamps on the divine figures marching to their destinies, Christs waylaid by Judas, Virgins already touched by the sombre premonition of the Pietà. His command of tenderness brings the pathos of children's suffering into the life of the Virgin: every one of her gestures seems to indicate the most profound sorrow. In his compassion, which embraces all this most meaningful course of fate, he is Christianity personified.

André Malraux

The Voices of Silence
La Galerie de la Pléiade, Paris, 1951

Giotto, or the Divine Made Human

When painting detached itself completely from those Greek prototypes, the way was clear for the easy conception and expression of human individuality, and a more radical adaptation of human faces and bodies to the religious content they were intended to express.

On this point, it is important to remember the profound influence of Giotto and his disciples. Giotto modified the method hitherto used of preparing the pigments as well as the procedure for conceiving and carrying out the actual painting. Just as that sprang from chemical research, so the Neo-Hellenes probably used wax, either for binding the colours, or as a protective surface, which doubtless gave the colours that "greenish yellow, darkening tone", which cannot be altogether explained by the action of lamplight. Now, Giotto rejected this Greek method of viscous fixation and introduced a process of rubbing the colours with the clarified juice of young buds, unripe figs, and other less oily substances, which the early medieval painters perhaps already used before devoting themselves to the strict imitation of the Byzantines... These fixing agents, far from darkening the colours, rendered them on the contrary more clear and brilliant. Far more important, however, was Giotto's innovation in the choice of subjects and their treatment. Already Ghiberti was praising Giotto for having abandoned the crude Greek method and for having introduced spontaneity and charm without going too far; and Boccaccio, speaking of Giotto, says there is nothing in all nature that he could not depict so as to give a totally natural impression. In Byzantine pictures there is no trace of spontaneity: it was Giotto who directed painting towards the real and the actual, and who only painted figures and expressed feelings after attentively studying the life that went on all round him. This tendency was partly due to the fact that in his time manners became generally freer, life became gayer, and, moreover, that people began to cultivate a great number of new saints who were nearer to the painter. These were the subjects which Giotto adopted in his efforts to direct art towards current reality, so that the content itself involved the necessity to make the pictorial representations emerge in all their natural spontaneity and to render characters, actions, feelings, situations, poses and movements with precision and firmness. But as a result of this new emphasis the holy and majestic gravity which characterised the preceding phase of art relatively disappeared. The profane element had come into painting and won there a progressively larger place and, conforming to contemporary taste, Giotto used burlesque side by side with pathos.... (This is why) in his attempt to be human and natural, Giotto himself only occupies a fairly low position in the whole. But it was in following the impulse of Giotto that painting pursued its development. The typical representation of Christ, the apostles and the most important events related in the Gospels passes more and more into the background; by contrast, other subjects multiply: "All hands were occupied in painting phases in the lives of modern saints: their daily life, their sudden awakening to the awareness of holiness, their entry to a life of piety and self-denial, the miracles they accomplished during life and, above all, after death, so many subjects in the representation of which the expression of living feelings takes precedence (which entirely conforms to the social background of the art) over the indication of invisible miracle-working." Nor were the events of the life and Passion of Christ neglected. This is particularly true of the birth and upbringing of Christ: the Virgin and Child has become a favourite subject, depicted in an atmosphere of family intimacy, tenderness, humanity and profound affection, and "as for the subjects borrowed from the story of the Passion, less emphasis was placed on their sublime and triumphant side than on their touching side, a direct consequence of the sentimental compassion for Christ's earthly sufferings, to which St. Francis of Assisi had given an unprecedented impulse by his example and his teachings."

Hegel

Aesthetic of Figurative Painting
Introduction by Bernard Teyssèdre
Hermann, Paris, 1964

Method and Procedure for Working in Fresco

In the name of the most Holy Trinity, I will set you to paint.

It is usual to begin working on a wall; for this, I will show you step by step the path you must follow. When you wish to work on a wall—and it is the most sweet, the most delightful work there is—first take some lime and some sand, both of them well cleaned and sifted. If the lime is very rich and fresh, the mixture should contain two parts of sand to one of lime. Blend them well together with water in sufficient quantity to last you fifteen or twenty days. Let the mixture stand for several days until the lime is well slaked; if it is still hot the plaster may crack. When you come to apply the plaster, brush the wall clean of dust, and wet it thoroughly—it cannot be too wet; take your limewash by the trowelful and plaster it on the wall in one or two coats until you have made a very flat surface. Then when you wish to begin work, do not forget that this well-prepared plaster should be a little roughened. Then, bearing in mind the scene or figure you plan to make, if your plaster is dry, take a stick of carbon and begin to design, compose and set out your measurements, snapping a line to divide your areas and find your vertical, then snapping another to mark the horizon . . . . Then compose your scenes or figures with carbon, as I have told you; and be guided by the spaces which you have evenly marked out. Then take a very small, pointed, hogshair brush, and with a little untempered red ochre (sinopia), as fluid as water, mark and design your figures, shading them in with water-colour as you have done before when I taught you to draw. Lastly, take a bunch of feathers and dust the carbon off your drawing.

That done, take a little sinopia without tempera, and with your soft, pointed brush mark in the nose, eyes, hair, all the extremities and contours of your figures; make sure all these figures are planned in right proportion because they will help you to know and visualise what you have to colour. Next do your borders or whatever you want to surround your picture. Take the lime we have discussed and stir it well with a mattock or the trowel; it should have the consistency of an ointment. Then work out what you can do in one day, for you must finish all the plaster you prepare. It is true that sometimes in winter when it is very damp, on stone walls, the plaster keeps fresh another day, but avoid delay if you can because fresco work done in one day achieves a better and stronger quality, and the work is more enjoyable to do.

Now apply a thin layer (not too much) of well-mixed plaster on the old plaster which you have wetted with your thick hogshair brush dipped in water; moisten this plaster, then with a slip of wood the size of your palm rub the wetted plaster with a circular movement so that the wood removes excess and fills up hollows and makes your plaster very smooth....

When you have drawn a face, if it seems out of proportion or not quite as you would wish, go over the plaster with your thick brush dipped in water and you will be able to eradicate and correct it. Then take a little very liquid green earth (terra-verde) in another jar, and with a soft blunt hogshair brush held between finger and thumb of the right hand, begin to shade under the chin and all the parts which should be darkest, touching and retouching under the lip, in the corners of the mouth, under the nose, under the side of the brows, perhaps on the side of the nose, a little at the edge of the eyes and towards the ears, and so on, as you judge, over the face and hands wherever the flesh colour is to be. Then, with a pointed squirrel brush clearly mark all the outlines of nose, eyes, lips and ears....

Now take a jar; put in it a fraction, next to nothing, of white (bianco sangiovanni) and an equal quantity of light vermilion (cinabrese); make the mixture liquid with clear water; holding your soft hogshair brush firmly in your fingers, as before, go over the face which you have outlined with the green, picking out the lips and cheeks with this reddish colour. My master used to place the red on the cheekbones nearer the ears than the nose, because this helps to model the face. Blend the cheek colour into the rest of the face. Then take three jars and divide them with three different flesh tints, that is the darkest, lighter by half than your reddish colour, and the two others degrees lighter still. Now take the jar with the lightest tint, and with a very soft blunt hogshair brush take some of the flesh colour, squeeze the brush with your fingers, and then pick out all the highlights of your face. Next take the jar of middle colour and with that pick out all the shapes of face, hands, feet, and torso when you are doing a naked figure. Then use the jar of the darkest flesh tint and take it to the edge of the shadows only stopping where it robs the green of its colour value; repeat this procedure several times, blending each tint with the next so that the whole is well covered as far as the nature of the subject demands. Be careful, if you wish your work to shine freshly, not to let your brush stray from one shade of flesh-tint to another, except to soften them gently and skilfully into each other. Work and practice will make you more able than any book can do. When you have used these flesh tints, make another still lighter, almost white, and apply it above the eyebrows, on the highlight of the nose, the tip of the chin, and the eyelids. With a dry squirrel brush and pure white do the whites of the eyes, the tip of the nose and a little on the bow of the lips; do these shapes delicately. Take a little black in another jar, and with the same brush outline the shape of the eyes above the luminous part, mark the nostrils and the earholes. Take a little dark sinopia from another jar and shade under the eyes, the nose contours, the brows, the mouth and under the upper lip, which must be a little darker than the lower. But before outlining these contours take the same paintbrush and the green for retouching the hair. With the same brush and white, do the highlights of the hair, then with a watercolour of light ochre and the soft paintbrush wash over all the hair, as you did for the flesh; then use the same brush dipped in dark ochre to pick out the extremities; then use a very fine pointed squirrel brush with light ochre and white (bianco sangiovanni) to accent the highlights in the hair; lastly outline with the dark sinopia the contours and ends of the hair, as you did with the face.

That will be enough for a young face.

Cennino Cennini

31st July 1437
Extract from the *Book of the Art or Treatise on Painting*

Chronology

Date	Political Events	Arts	Intellectual Life, Journeys and Sciences	Religion
1140		Building of the Abbey of Saint-Denis		
1151	Death of Suger			
1155		1155-75 Manuscript *Hortus Deliciarum*		
1159				1159-77 Schism in the Roman Church
1160			Benoist de Sainte-More: *Romance of Troy* 1160-90 Christian of Troyes: *Breton Romances*	
1163		Notre-Dame-de-Paris started by Bishop Maurice de Sully		
1170				Murder of Thomas à Becket
1180			First canal with locks (Bruges)	
1182				Birth of St. Francis of Assisi
1183	Peace of Constance			
1189	Third Crusade: Frederick Barbarossa, Philip-August, Richard the Lionheart	Building of Bourges Cathedral		
1192				Canonisation of Ladislas, King of Hungary
1194		1194-1260 Building of Chartres Cathedral		
1197		Building of Lincoln Cathedral	Coalmining	
1198				Death of Averroès 1198-1216 Theocracy of Innocent III
1200		c. 1200 Louvre Palace (party of Philip-August) Stained glass at Chartres Rouen Cathedral started	c. 1200 Birth of Rutebeuf Invention of gunpowder (China) W. von Eschenbach: *Parsifal*	
1204	Capture of Constantinople. Founding of Latin Empire in the East			

ate	Political Events	Arts	Intellectual Life, Journeys and Sciences	Religion
206				St. Dominic preaching in Albi
207			Villehardouin: *Conquest of Constantinople*	
208	Albigensian Crusade			Founding of Dominican Order
209		Nicosia Cathedral (Cyprus)		First Franciscan community formed
211		Reims Cathedral		
		1211-28 The "Miracle" of Mont-Saint-Michel		
214	Battle of Bouvines		Oxford University licensed	
215	Magna Carta			Council of Lateran
	Gengis Khan at Peking			
	Mongols in Russia, battle of the Kalka			
218		1218-68 Amiens Cathedral		
221				Death of St. Dominic
222		St. Gudule's Cathedral, Brussels, started	Padua University founded	
		Burgos Cathedral built		
225			*Lancelot of the Lake*	St. Thomas Aquinas born
226				Death of St. Francis of Assisi
228	Formation of Guelph party in Italy			
230	Foundation of the Hanseatic League		Aristotle's *Metaphysics* translated	
231				Tribunals of the Inquisition
236		Lausanne Cathedral built	G. de Lorris: *Le Roman de la Rose* (first part)	
1239	Loss of Jerusalem			
1241	The Mongols in Vienna			
1245		1245-8 The Sainte-Chapelle		Council of Lyons
		1245-75 Building of Westminster Abbey		
1250	Paris Parliament	Building of Cologne Cathedral	Founding of Salamanca University	

Date	Political Events	Arts	Intellectual Life, Journeys and Sciences	Religion
1254			Birth of Marco Polo	
			Founding of the Sorbonne	
1255	Succession of the Paleologi in Byzantium		Jacques de Voragine: *The Golden Legend*	
1265	Charles of Anjou aids the Pope; he relieves the Papal States besieged by Manfred			St. Thomas Aquinas: *Summa Theologica*
1266			Roger Bacon finishes the *Opus Majus*	
1270	Death of St. Louis; eighth and last Crusade			
1274				Death of St. Thomas Aquinas
				Death of St. Bonaventura *(Itinerarium Mentis in De*
1275			Adam de la Halle: *Play of Foliage*	
			Great Chronicles of Saint-Denis	
1276			Jean de Meung: *Le Roman de la Rose* (second part)	
1277		The Campo Santo at Pisa begun.		
1278				The Dominican Order adopts Thomism as doctri
1279			Founding of Coimbra University	
1280				Death of St. Albert the Gr master of St. Thomas
1282	The Sicilian Vespers	Building of Santa Maria Novella, Florence		
1285			Invention of spectacles (Florence)	
1289				The Cardinals vote to contribute half the revenues to the Churc
1290		Cimabue's frescoes in the Church of St. Francis at Assisi		
1291	Fall of Ptolomais and end of the Crusades			
1294	Philip the Fair annexes Guyenne		Death of Roger Bacon	

Date	Political Events	Arts	Intellectual Life, Journeys and Sciences	Religion
295		*Breviary of Philip the Fair* by Master Honoré	Use of alcohol as a drink in Europe	
297				Canonisation of St. Louis
298		Giotto's *Crucifixion* in Santa Maria Novella, Florence	Invention of the spinning wheel	
			Book of *Marco Polo*	
300		c. 1300 Giotto (?): *Scenes from the Life of St. Francis of Assisi*	Invention of the rudder for ships	
301				The Inquisition is placed under the control of the bishops
302	Flemish victory over the French at Courtrai			
303			Dante finishes *The Divine Comedy*	Boniface VIII excommunicates Philip the Fair
304		1304-5 Giotto: *Life and Passion of Christ; Life of the Virgin*, Padua		
307	Revolt of the Swiss cantons			
308				Death of Duns Scotus
309		Duccio's *Maestà* at Sienna	Joinville: *Memoirs of the Reign of St. Louis*	1309-77 Avignon as the seat of the Popes
312	Affair of the Templars			
314	Punishment of Jacques de Molay			
315		Simone Martini's *Maestà*		
317			Death of Joinville	
318		*Psalter of Saint-Omer*		Valdist heresy in Bohemia and Poland
320		1320-30 Frescoes by Pietro Lorenzetti and Simone Martini in the Church of St. Francis at Assisi		
321			Death of Dante	
327	1327-77 Edward III King of England			Death of Master Eckart
330		*Belleville Breviary* by Jean Pucelle	Birth of Nicholas Flamel, writer and scholar	

Date	Political Events	Arts	Intellectual Life, Journeys and Sciences	Religion
1334				Death of Pope John XXI
1336		Death of Giotto		
1337	Outbreak of the Hundred Years War	1337-40 Ambrogio Lorenzetti: *Good and Bad Government*	Birth of Froissart *Chronicles of the Hundred Years War*	
1340			Birth of the poet Eustache Deschamps	
			Birth of Geoffrey Chaucer	
1342				Christian missions to Turkestan
1344		Death of Simone Martini		
1345	First bank crash			
1346	Battle of Crécy			
1347			Death of Guillaume d'Occam	
1348		Death of Bassa Ferrer	Founding of Prague University	
			Boccaccio: *The Decameron*	
1364			Birth of Christine de Pisan, first 'woman of letters'	
1369		Death of Orcagna		
1374			Death of Petrarch	
1377			Death of Guillaume de Machaut, poet and musician at the court of Charles V. One of the creators of the polyphonic school	
1378		Building of Ulm Cathedral		1378-1429 Great schism of the West
1380	Death of Du Guesclin		Invention of the hour-glass	
1384				Death of Wycliffe
1387		Birth of Fra Angelico		
1390		Birth of Jan Van Eyck	Birth of the poet Alain Chartier	
		c. 1390 *Psalter of the Duke of Berry* by A. Beauneveu	First wood-engravings	
1398			First permanent theatrical company: *The Companions of the Passion*	

Date	Political Events	Arts	Intellectual Life, Journeys and Sciences	Religion
400			Death of Geoffrey Chaucer Invention of the capstan	
405				Revolt of Paris University against Benedict XIII
406		Birth of Piero della Francesca		
409				Council of Pisa
1410			First troupes of actors: *The Joyful Societies, The Lawyers, The Carefree Children*	
1411		c. 1411 Roublev: *Image of the Trinity*		
1412	Birth of Joan of Arc			
1415	Battle of Agincourt			
1417				End of schism of the West
1420		Birth of Arnoul Gréban, author of a *Mystery of the Passion*		
1423		Gentile da Fabriano: *Adoration of the Magi*		Opening of the Council of Padua
1429	Joan of Arc escorts Charles VII to Reims		Death of John Gerson, Chancellor of Paris University	
1430		Death of André Roublev c. 1430 Fra Angelico paints *The Annunciation*		
1431	Death of Joan of Arc		Birth of François Villon	Council of Basle
1434		1434-1521 Rouen, Saint-Maclou		
1436			Gutenberg invents printing	
1439				Council of Florence
1447			Birth of Commynes: *(Memoirs of the Reign of Louis XI)*	
1450	French victory over the English at Formigny	1450-60 *Book of Hours of Etienne Chevalier*		
1451				Birth of Isabelle the Catholic
1453	Sack of Constantinople			

Date	Political Events	Arts	Intellectual Life, Journeys and Sciences	Religion
1455	Outbreak of Wars of the Roses	Death of Fra Angelico		
1460		1460-77 Ms. of *The Heart of Smitten Love*		
1464				Attempt at internal Chur reform. Death of Pius II
1465			Birth of Erasmus	
			c. 1465 Death of François Villon	
1469			Birth of Vasco da Gama	
1470			Manufacture of crystal (Venice)	
1471		Birth of Dürer		Death of German mystic Thomas à Kempis
1475		Birth of Michelangelo		
1477	Death of Charles the Rash			
1478			Birth of Thomas More	
1480		Death of Jean Fouquet		
1483	Death of Louis XI			Birth of Luther
1490			Invention of the spring	
1492			Discovery of America by Christopher Columbus	
1494	1494-1515 Franco-Italian Wars			
1498			Discovery of the sea route to India by Vasco da Gama	Execution of Savonarola
1524			Birth of Ronsard	
1525		Death of Carpaccio		

▪rincipal Locations of Gothic Painting

▪untry	Town	Region	Descriptions
▪gium	Bruges		Church of Our Lady. Fresco showing St. Louis, King of France. c. 1340.
	Gand		The ancient abbey of Byloke contains several frescoes (c. 1375): *St. John the Baptist*, *St. Christopher*, *Christ Blessing His Mother*, and a vast composition of *The Last Supper* dating from 1325.
	Hal	Brabant	In the choir of the Basilica of Our Lady can be seen windows reminiscent in style of those in St. Owen's, Rouen. 14th century.
	Huy	Liège	The Collegiate Church of Our Lady has a rosace unique in Belgium. Late 14th century.
	Lierre	Antwerp	The Church of St. Gomer. Stained glass. 15th century.
	Louvain		The Great Beguine Convent has a window showing the Virgin in an almond lozenge (1305).
	Sichem		St. Eustace's Church has a window depicting Calvary (1387).
	Tournai		Cathedral. Fragments of frescoes depicting the legend of St. Margaret and the Holy City of Jerusalem. Early 13th century.
▪cho-▪akia	Karlstein	Bohemia	The castle has frescoes by Tomaso da Modena. c. 1340.
▪land	Canterbury	Kent	The cathedral holds England's richest assembly of stained-glass windows, some of which (e.g. *The New Alliance* and *The Miracles of St. Thomas à Becket*) date from the early 13th century.
	Carlisle	Cumberland	The cathedral window still contains fragments of ancient stained glass representing the Last Judgement. 14th century.
	Eton	Bucks.	The college chapel houses some early murals. 1479-88.
	Exeter	Devon	Several of the cathedral windows were done by the painter-glazier Walter. Early 14th century.
	Gloucester	Glos.	Cathedral. Stained glass. 14th century.
	Lincoln	Lincs.	Cathedral. Stained glass including *The Dean's Eye* (13th century): the rose is remarkable. Some traces of early paintings can be seen. 13th & 14th centuries.
	London		Frescoes in Westminster Abbey. c. 1260-1310.
	Oxford	Oxon.	The chapels of Merton College and New College still have their original windows. 14th century.
	St. Albans	Herts.	The cathedral is the second longest English sanctuary, after Winchester. The painted ceiling of the choir (14th century) is celebrated. The cathedral also houses mural paintings, including a *Crucifixion*, *The Annunciation*, and *The Legend of Saint Christopher*. 13th century.
	Wells	Somerset	Cathedral. The glass of the Golden Window is mid-14th century.
	Winchester	Hants.	Cathedral. Fragments of ancient stained glass. 1380.
	York	Yorks.	Minster. Rich stained glass of all periods (12th-16th centuries) of which the most famous are the *Five Sisters* windows (in grisaille) in the ogival style. 13th century.

Country	Town	Region	Descriptions
France	Albi		Cathedral. Frescoes depicting scenes of hell and purgatory. c. 1490.
	Alet	Aude	Fresco of a *Crucifixion* in the Church of St. Andrew. About the middle of the 14th century.
	Amiens		The cathedral has several four-lobed medallions (13th century) in the ambulatory chapels. Stained glass of 1269, gift of Bishop Bernard of Abbeville.
	Angers		Cathedral. *Scenes from the Life and Passion of Christ* (last quarter of the 13th century). Other assemblies of 12th, 14th and 15th century stained gl
	Asnierès-sur-Vègre	Sarthe	Church. Frescoes of scenes of Hell. 13th century.
	Auzon	Haute-Loire	St. Lawrence's Church has several sets of frescoes: *The Childhood of Christ* and His *Passion*, *Scenes from the Life of St. Michael.* 14th century.
	Avignon		The Papal Palace has the first suite of secular mural paintings. c. 1345.
	Beauvais		The cathedral preserves a few Gothic windows (14th century), unfortunately excessively restored in the 19th century.
	Bonnes	Vienne	The Chateau of Touffou has a mural decoration of heraldic inspiration. 1267-80.
	Bourges		Cathedral. Stained glass in the high windows of the choir, chapels fanning out from the ambulatory (first half of the 13th century); *Virgin and Child* (back of the choir), *St. Stephen*, *Prophets Isaiah and Ezekie* *Annunciation and Last Judgement*. 14th century windows and remarkable collection of stained glass, including those from the Duke of Berry Chapel (14
	Brancion	Saône-et-Loire	St. Peter's Church preserves several frescoes; funeral scenes, pilgrimage sc (c. 1330), and a 14th century *Seraph*.
	Brouet-Vernet	Allier	The ancient chapel of the priory of St. Petronella of Aubeterre has a collec of frescoes (early 13th century): *Baptism of Christ*, *The Scourging* and the *Deposition from the Cross*.
	Cahors		The cathedral preserves France's most beautiful collection of frescoes (early 14th century). On the west cupola: *St. Stephen Stoned* and eight figures of prophets.
	Carcassonne		Cathedral. Windows representing the Passion of Christ and the lives of St. Peter, St. Paul and St. Nazarius. 14th century.
	Chamalieres-sur-Loire	Haute-Loire	The church possesses a fresco representing a Virgin seated with the Infant Je 13th century.
	Chartres		The cathedral preserves a perfect assembly of 12th century stained glass; it is some of the most beautiful known: *Our-Lady-of-the-Beautiful-Window*, scenes from the Old and New Testaments, *The Monthly Occupations*, the *Glorification of Christ;* side transept: *Legend of St. Charlemagne.* 14th century grisaille and silver-yellow stained glass at the south crossing. A few 15th century windows.
	Clermont-Ferrand		The cathedral windows (13th and 14th centuries) are influenced by those of Chartres, and the Sainte-Chapelle in Paris. The cathedral preserves some frescoes depicting scenes from the life of St. George (early 14th cent and, in the crypt, a few small early 13th century scenes.

ntry	Town	Region	Descriptions
	Coutances	Manche	Cathedral. Some 13th and 14th century stained glass deriving from that of Tours and Mans.
	Cunault	Maine-et-Loire	The Priory of Our Lady preserves a 13th century fresco depicting St. Philibert.
	Dijon		Cathedral. Several panels of 15th century stained glass in the Lady Chapel.
	Dol	Ille-et-Vilaine	Beautiful glass in the cathedral's chevet depicting the life of Christ and the history of the first six Bishops of Dol (late 13th or early 14th century).
	Etigny	Yonne	The church preserves some 13th century frescoes showing the miracles of St. Martin.
	Evreux		Cathedral. Assembly of windows which is depleted but typical of medieval Norman stained glass (13th and 14th centuries) with that of St. Owen's, Rouen, and Fécamp. Beautiful examples of glass: high windows of the choir, the Lady Chapel and the south transept (15th century).
	Fécamp	Seine-Maritime	In the Lady Chapel of Trinity Church there are several windows with little figures in them. 13th and 14th centuries.
	Ferrières-en-Gâtinais	Loiret	The church preserves a fresco depicting Christ giving the keys to St. Peter. Late 13th or early 14th century.
	Frétigny	Eure-et-Loir	Church. Frescoes with scenes from the life of St. Andrew. Mid-13th century.
	Friardel	Calvados	The Priory has a fresco depicting the Virgin and Child. Late 14th century.
	Gassicourt	near Mantes	In the church are five beautiful windows strongly influenced by the Masters of Paris and Chartres. Mid-13th century.
	La Chaise-Dieu	Haute-Loire	Church. Fresco of *The Dance of Death.* c. 1450.
	La Clayette	Saône-et-Loire	The château chapel has a fresco of Christ surrounded by angels. c. 1400.
	Landes	Charente-Maritime	In the church are fragments of a fresco showing a hunting scene (Legend of St. Giles ?). Mid-14th century.
	Laon		Cathedral. Three great chevet windows, and the rose; this assembly (13th century) derives some of its colouring from the windows of Chartres. It includes scenes of Christ's nativity, public life and Passion. Other 14th and 15th century windows.
	Lavadieu	Haute-Loire	In the chapter hall of the abbey are frescoes depicting the coming of the Son of Man at the end of time, and the Virgin crowned. Early 13th century.
	Lavardin	Loir-et-Cher	An assembly of 12th to 16th century glass can be seen at the Church of St. Genest.
	Le Loroux-Bottereau	Loire-Atlantique	Ancient chapel of St. Lawrence. Set of frescoes showing scenes from the legend of St. Giles. Late 12th or early 13th century.
	Le Mans		Cathedral. Choir windows: *St. Gervase* and *St. Protais*, patrons of the cathedral. In the chevet: *Christ on the Cross* and *The Virgin Holding the Child.* Late 13th century. 14th and 15th century windows in the side chapels.

Country	Town	Region	Descriptions
	Le Puy		Cathedral. Several original windows: Chapter hall: *Crucifixion* (early 13th century); West porch: *Transfiguration, Virgin and Child* (late 12th or early 13th century). Small apse to the north of the transept: *Martyrdom of St. Catherine, Solomon* (mid-13th century). Second small aps *The Holy Women at the Sepulchre* (mid-13th century).
	Les-Roches-sur-Loir	Loir-et-Cher	Several frescoes in the rupestral chapel depicting scenes of pilgrimage and the legend of St. Giles. Late 12th or early 13th century.
	Limoges		Cathedral. Fine examples of Limousine windows in the apsidal chapels.
	Lutz-en-Dunois	Eure-et-Loir	Church. Several frescoes showing some apostles and Christ's entry to Jerusalem. Mid-13th century.
	Lyons		Cathedral. Glass of seven windows betraying the influence of the master glaziers of Chartres (early 13th century): episodes of the raising of Lazarus, scenes from the childhood of Christ, stories of the Lyonnais Saints Pothin, Irene and Polycarp. 14th and 15th century stained glass.
	Metz		Cathedral. Great façade rose begun by the master glazier Hermann von Münster; it shows Christ on the cross surrounded by angels holding books and musical instruments (late 14th century). Beautiful 15th century windows in the apsidal chapels.
	Montbellet	Saône-et-Loire	Frescoes of apostles and saints can be seen in the chapel of the Knights Templar of St. Catherine. Late 13th or early 14th century.
	Narbonne	Aude	The Archbishop's Palace has a fresco of St. Justus. 14th century.
	Neuvillet-en-Charnie	Sarthe	Church. Frescoes depicting the seated Virgin, holding the Infant. Late 13th or early 14th century.
	Nonac	Charente	A fresco of the Crucifixion can be seen in the crypt of St. Hilary's Church. 14th century.
	Paris		The Sainte-Chapelle. The most consistent collection of 13th century stained glass. The windows were completed for the consecration of 25th April 1248. Some were restored in the 14th century, and again in the 19th century. These windows of Sainte-Chapelle had as great an influence in Europe as those of Chartres.
			Notre-Dame. The west rose depicts the Virgin in Majesty holding the Child (first quarter of the 13th century). It was completed in the 16th century. The south rose (late 13th century), partly remade by Viollet-le-Duc, depicts Christ triumphant. Other 15th century stained glass.
			Saint-Séverin. Fine windows from the abbey of Saint-Germain-des-Prés. 15th century.
	Pernes	Vaucluse	Ferrande Tower. Frescoes of historical scenes. Late 13th century.
	Petit-Quevilly	Seine-Maritime	The Carthusian chapel of Saint Julien preserves several frescoes: *Annunciation, Visitation, Nativity*, several scenes of the Wise Men, *The Flight into Egypt, The Baptism of Christ*. Late 12th century.
	Poitiers	Vienne	St. John's Baptistry. Several frescoes. *Christ Surrounded by the Symbols of the Evangelists, The Life of St. John the Baptist*. Mid-13th century.
			St. Radegunda's Church. Late 13th century stained glass depicting the life of St. Radegunda. Four-lobed and circular medallions of the same period.

ntry	Town	Region	Descriptions
	Quimper	Finistère	Cathedral. Stained glass: choir and transept windows. Late 15th century.
	Ravel	Puy-de-Dôme	The State Room of the castle has a mural painting of heraldic inspiration. Late 13th or early 14th century.
	Reims		Cathedral. Stained glass: choir, chevet, transept and side chapels (13th and 14th centuries). Restored and reset in 1929-31 by Jacques Simon, master glazier.
	Rouen		Abbey church of Saint-Ouen. Fine set of 14th century windows deriving from those of Evreux. Those in the choir are late 14th century; those in the transept, the second half of the 15th century.
			Cathedral. Late 13th and early 14th century windows: scenes from the lives of saints, particularly St. Severus, Bishop of Avranches, and St. Julian the Knight Hospitaller, a window which inspired Flaubert to write *The Legend of St. Julian the Hospitaller*. In the chapel of the south transept, 14th century stained glass. Other 15th century glass.
	Saint-Aignan	Loir-et-Cher	In the church crypt, four groups of frescoes, including *The Legend of St. Giles* and, in the choir, *Christ in Majesty*. Late 12th or early 13th century.
	Saint-Amant-de-Boixe	Charente	Frescoes showing scenes from the life of the Virgin and the childhood of Christ can be seen in the church. Late 13th century.
	Saint-Denis	Seine	Basilica. Fragments of the original stained glass can be seen in the apse and apsidal chapels. 12th and 13th centuries.
	Saint-Dié	Vosges	Cathedral. Rich collection of frescoes: scenes depicting the granting of privileges to Saint-Dié, and in the cathedral chapter *Christ Appearing to Mary Magdalene*, scenes from the life of St. Stephen, the *Trinity*. Mid-14th century.
	Sainte-Croix-en-Jarez	Loire	Carthusian convent. Several frescoes: *Funeral Procession of Theobald of Vassalieu* (the archdeacon of Lyons) *Coronation of the Virgin*, *Crucifixion*. First half of the 14th century.
	Sainte-Radegonde	Aveyron	The church has a series of frescoes about Adam and Eve; pilgrimage scenes. Mid-13th century.
	Saint-Floret	Puy-de-Dôme	A mural decoration depicting episodes from a tale of chivalry can be seen in the château. Second half of the 14th century.
			The church has frescoes of the Virgin and Child with St. John the Baptist. Late 14th century.
	Saint-Geniès	Dordogne	Chalard Chapel. Set of frescoes, including a *St. George on Horseback* and the *Supplication of St. Catherine*. First half of the 13th century.
	Saint-Jacques-des-Guérets	Loir-et-Cher	In the church are frescoes of scenes about the Crusades. Mid-13th century.
	Saint-Jean-au-Bois	Forêt de Compiègne	Church. Fine stained glass, including four windows in grisaille, and several medallions. Mid-13th century.
	Saint-Junien	Haute-Vienne	The St. Martial Chapel in the church contains frescoes showing scenes of the legend of St. Martial. Late 13th century.

Country	Town	Region	Descriptions
	Saint-Romain-Le-Puy	Loire	In the church, 13th century frescoes about St. Romanus of Antioch.
	Saulcet	Allier	Church of St. Julian. Fresco of *St. John the Evangelist*. Second half of the 14th century.
	Sées	Orne	Cathedral. Assembly of stained glass. High windows: *Story of St. Nicholas* and of *St. Peter and St. Paul*; low windows: life of St. Augustin. 13th and 14th centuries.
	Sens		Cathedral. Windows in the ambulatory and the choir (13th century): scenes from the Gospels; *Life of St. Eustace* and *St. Thomas of Canterbury*. Other 14th and 15th century windows.
	Soissons		Cathedral. Assembly of 13th century windows of which some have been restored. In the high windows: *Christ and the Virgin Among the Prophets*, *The Signs of the Zodiac*, *The Liberal Arts*, *Adam and Eve*, etc. 14th and 15th century stained glass.
	Strasbourg		Cathedral. Several 13th century windows and a fine 14th century set. The stained glass of the south crossing was restored in the 19th century afte the miniatures of the *Hortus Deliciarum*.
	Toul	Meurthe-et-Moselle	Cathedral. Several windows donated by Bishop Roger of Ostend in 1253 (apsidal chapels).
	Toulouse		Cathedral. Stained glass. 14th and 15th centuries. St. Antoninus Chapel: fresco c. 1341.
	Tours		Cloister of La Spalette. Set of frescoes illustrating the legend of St. Silvanus from the church of Beaumont-Village (Indre-et-Loire). Late 13th century.
	Vernais	Cher	A fresco depicting the coronation of the Virgin can be seen in the church. Last quarter of the 13th century.
	Vic-le-Comte	Puy-de-Dôme	The Castle Church has frescoes depicting the Virgin and Child, and St. John the Baptist. Late 14th century.
	Vieux-Pouzauges	Vendée	Church. Frescoes illustrating the story of Joachim and Anna, and the childhood of the Virgin. Late 12th or early 13th century.
	Villeneuve-lès-Avignon	Gard	The pontifical chapel of the Carthusian convent has frescoes of the *Crucifixion* and scenes from the life of St. John the Baptist (1352-56 probab
Germany	Augsburg		Cathedral. Stained glass. 14th century.
	Brauweiler		Abbey church. Several frescoes. 1275-1400.
	Cologne		Cathedral. The stained-glass windows include: *The Adoration of the Magi*, *The King of Judah*, *The Forefathers of the Virgin*, c. 1320.
	Freiburg		Cathedral. Several stained-glass windows. 14th century.
	Goslar	Lower Saxony	The Town Hall preserves several frescoes relating to the life of Christ. c. 1500.
	Hildesheim	Lower Saxony	St. Michael's Church has the only example in Germany of a painted ceiling, representing Old Testament scenes. 1200-25.

ntry	Town	Region	Descriptions
	Limburg-am-Lahn		Cathedral. Stained glass. 14th century.
	Marburg		St. Elizabeth's Church has several frescoes. 14th century. A fine *Madonna*, c. 1300, can be seen among the stained glass, which mostly dates from the 14th century.
	Nuremberg		St. Sebald's Church has several original 14th-century windows.
	Ratisbon		Cathedral. 14th century stained glass.
	Soest		The St. Nicholas Chapel preserves some 13th century frescoes. St. Mary-of-the-Hill has frescoes of the mid-13th century.
			The Church of St. Mary-of-the-Meadow preserves some Gothic stained-glass windows. Late 14th century.
	Ulm		The triumphal arch of the cathedral bears a fresco representing the Last Judgement (1471). The stained-glass windows are 15th century.
y	Assisi		Church of St. Francis. Lower Church (13th and 14th centuries): rich series of mural paintings, including a *Virgin* by Cimabue (1290-1295), several frescoes, including a Crucifixion by Pietro Lorenzetti (1320-1330); Stained-glass windows showing scenes from the life of Christ and the life of the Virgin, *The Story of the Creation* and *The Apotheosis of St. Francis* (13th century). Upper Church: Giotto (?) frescoes depicting the legend of St. Francis. c. 1300.
	Bologna		The Church of San Petronio has a stained-glass window of 1466, also some frescoes by Giovanni da Modena: *The Last Judgement* and the *Visit of the Wise Men to Bethlehem*. c. 1420.
	Florence		Santa Croce: Castellani Chapel: Frescoes depicting the legend of the Holy Cross by Agnolo Gaddi, c. 1380. Baroncelli Chapel: frescoes depicting the life of the Virgin by Taddeo Gaddi, c. 1328. Rinuccini Chapel: frescoes showing scenes from the life of the Virgin by Giovanni da Milano (1365). St. Sylvester Chapel: frescoes depicting miracles of St. Sylvester, by Maso. First half of the 14th century. The Bardi and Peruzzi chapels are decorated by Giotto and his pupils: *The Stories of St. John the Baptist, St. John the Evangelist and St. Francis of Assisi.* Early 14th century.
			Santa Maria Novella. Rich series of mural paintings, including: In the nave: *The Trinity*, by Masaccio. Early 15th century. Rucellai Chapel: *Virgin Enthroned*, by Duccio, c. 1285. Spanish Chapel: frescoes by Andrea da Firenze (1365).
			Strozzi Chapel: frescoes by Orcagna and Nardo di Cione *(Last Judgement*, *Heaven* and *Hell)*, 1345-57.
			Santa Maria del Carmine. Brancacci Chapel: frescoes showing scenes from the lives of the Apostles by Masaccio (1426-1428), and his *Adam and Eve Cast Out of the Garden of Eden.*
	Orvieto		Cathedral. Several 14th and 15th century frescoes.
	Padua		Arena Chapel (or Scrovegni Chapel). Frescoes showing scenes from the lives of Christ and the Virgin, and *Christ's Passion* by Giotto (1304-6).

Country	Town	Region	Descriptions
			St. Anthony's Church. St. Felix Chapel: frescoes by Altichiero and Avanzo (1376).
			St. George's Oratory. Frescoes by Altichiero and Avanzo (1385).
	Pisa		Campo Santo. Frescoes (south wall): *The Triumph of Death*, *The Last Judgement*, *Hell*, c. 1350; North wall: *Creation of the World*, *Creation of Man*, *Original Sin*, c. 1390.
			Cathedral. Mosaic by Cimabue depicting St. John the Evangelist (1302).
	Rimini		St. Augustin's Church. Frescoes of the Rimini school (1330-1340).
	Siena		Town Hall. Numerous frescoes of the Siena school (14th and 15th centuries) including: *La Maestà* by Simone Martini (1315) and the *Allegory of Good and Bad Government* by Ambrogio Lorenzetti (1337-4
	Treviso	Venetia	Monastery of San Niccolo, frescoes by Tomaso da Modena (1352).
	Venice		St. Mark's Church. Panels depicting episodes in the life of St. Mark by Paolo Veneziano (1345).
	Verona		St. Anastasia's Church. Frescoes illustrating the legend of St. George. c. 14
Netherlands	Deventer	Overijssel	St. Nicholas' Church. Fresco of a bishop with Christ and angels. Early 13th century.
	Utrecht		St. Peter's Church. Fragment of a fresco of the crucifixion. Early 13th century.
	Zutphen	Guelders	Great Church. Several 14th and 15th century frescoes.
Spain	Burgos	Castille	Cathedral. Rosace and other stained-glass windows. 15th century.
	León		Cathedral. Magnificent assembly of windows (13th century onwards); the façade rosace is 13th century, and that in the main chapel 14th century. In the St. James' Chapel, windows depicting the Virgin and St. John the Bapt 15th century. The cathedral cloister has a few fragments of frescoes. 15th century.
	Manresa	Barcelona	The cathedral houses a reredos of *The Holy Spirit* painted by Father Serra (13
	Palma-Majorca		Cathedral. Roses and other windows. 14th century.
	Pedralbes	Catalonia	Monastery of St. Mary. Stained glass (14th century). The St. Michael Chapel in the same monastery was painted by Bassa Ferrer (1345); including a mural painting in oil of *St. Bonaventura*.
	Salamanca	Léon	Ancient cathedral. A fresco of the *Last Judgement* (1466). The St. Martin cha in the same cathedral contains some 13th century frescoes.
	Toledo	Castille	The cathedral has a rich assembly of stained glass (1418-1560) depicting scenes from the New Testament, and the *Lives of Saints*. In the vestry, *The St. Louis Bible*. 13th century. In the cloister, frescoes by Amaldo di Cremona, pupil of Giotto. 14th century.
	Valencia		The cathedral has Gothic windows with alabaster panes. Late 14th century.

ountry	Town	Region	Descriptions
itzerland	Königsfelden		The Abbey has windows showing the Passion of Christ and the lives of the Virgin and certain saints (1311-1337).
	Lausanne		The Cathedral has a fine 13th century rose window.
	Wettingen	Argovia	The Cistercian convent has several 13th century windows.

Manuscripts

Country	Town	Museum	Title	Artist	Date
Austria	Vienna	National Library	Missal for the Abbot of Admont	Workshop of Admont convent	1288
	Vienna	National Library	*Biblia Pauperum*		1325
	Vienna	National Library	*Life of Mary*	Workshop of Waldhausen convent	1325
	Vienna	National Library	Klosterneuburg Bible		Early 14th C.
	Vienna	National Library	*Speculum humanae Salvationis*		c. 1350
	Vienna	National Library	Wenceslas Bible		1380-90
	Vienna	National Library	*Rationale divinorum Officiorum*		1384-1406
	Vienna	National Library	The Tyrolean Fishery Book	Jörg Kölderer, follower of	1504
	Vienna	National Library	*Sermons* of St. Augustine	Henry Aurhaym	1406-24
	Vienna	National Library	Book of Prayers	Miniaturist of Albert V	c. 1437
	Vienna	National Library	*The Trojan War* by Guido Colonna	Martinus Opifex	c. 1445
	Vienna	National Library	Romance by Girart de Roussillon	Workshop of Jean Wauquelin	Before 1448
	Vienna	National Library	*Roman de la Rose*		Mid-15th C.
	Vienna	National Library	*Theseid*	René of Anjou (?)	Mid-15th C.
	Vienna	National Library	*Heart of Smitten Love*	René of Anjou (?)	Mid-15th C.
	Vienna	National Library	*Privileges of Ghent*		After 1453
	Vienna	National Library	*Jerusalem Chronicle*	Workshop of Jean Dreux	1462-67
	Vienna	National Library	*Hortus animae*	Workshop of Sander Bening	Second half of the 15th C.
	Vienna	National Library	Black Prayer Book (black parchment)	Master of Anthony of Burgundy	1466-67
	Vienna	National Library	Book of Hours	Philip of Mazerolles	c. 1470
	Vienna	Schottenstift Library	*The Flower of Stories*		Mid-15th C.
Belgium	Antwerp	Mayer Van den Bergh Museum	Breviary	Workshop of Sander Bening	Early 16th C.
	Bruges	Grand Seminary Library	Missal of Jacquemine of Ossenbrugge		1454
	Brussels	Royal Library	Peterborough Psalter		c. 1290
	Brussels	Royal Library	Very Beautiful Hours of Our Lady	Jacquemart de Hesdin	Early 15th C.

Country	Town	Museum	Title	Artist	Date
	Brussels	Royal Library	Missal	Louis de Male	Early 15th C.
	Brussels	Royal Library	Breviary of Philip the Good		Early 15th C.
	Brussels	Royal Library	Historiated Bible	Utrecht school	1431
	Brussels	Royal Library	*The City of God*	Workshop of Gilbert of Metz	c. 1440
	Brussels	Royal Library	*Chronicles of Hainault I and III*	Workshop of Jean Wauquelin	1448-50
	Brussels	Royal Library	*Maritien Chronicles*	Workshop of Pilavaine	Mid-15th C.
	Brussels	Royal Library	*Life and Miracles of Saint Josse*	Lille school	Mid-15th C.
	Brussels	Royal Library	*Flower of Stories*		c. 1460
	Brussels	Royal Library	*Treatise on the Lord's Prayer*	Workshop of Jean Miélot	c. 1460
	Brussels	Royal Library	*Life of St. Hubert*	Loyset Liedet	Second half of the 15th C.
	Ghent	University Library	*History of Oliver of Castille*	Workshop of the Master of Wavrin	Mid-15th C.
	Liège	University Library	Book of Hours	Guelders school	c. 1410
	Liège	University Library	Book of Hours	Utrecht school	c. 1460
	Mons	Municipal Library	*Chronicles of Hainault II*	Workshop of Jean Wauquelin	1448
Czecho-lovakia	Prague	National Library	Codex Vysehradensis	Bohemian school	14th C.
	Prague	University Library	Passionale of the Abbess Cunegunda	Bohemian school	c. 1320
	Prague	University Library	Velislav Bible	Bohemian school	c. 1340
	Prague	National Museum	Liber viaticus of Bishop John of Streda	Bohemian school	Mid-14th C.
	Prague	National Museum	*Laus Mariae* of Konrad von Haimburg	Bohemian school	c. 1364
England nd Scotland	Cambridge	Corpus Christi College	Chaucer's *Troilus*		Second half of 14th C.
	Cambridge	St. John's College	Prayerbook of Margaret of York	Ghent workshop	Second half of 15th C.
	Cambridge	Trinity College	Apocalypse	Workshop of St. Albans Abbey	First half of 13th C.
	Glasgow	Hunterian Museum	Vincent de Beauvais *Mirror of Human Salvation*	Workshop of Willem Vrelandt	1455

Country	Town	Museum	Title	Artist	Date
	Glasgow	University Library	Book of Hours	Flemish workshop	c. 1450
	Leeds	University Library	Book of Hours of Hugues de Mazinghem		Mid-15th C.
	London	British Museum	*Historia Anglorum*	Matthew Paris	c. 1260
	London	British Museum	Robert of Bello's Bible	Canterbury school	c. 1250
	London	British Museum	Westminster Psalter		13th C.
	London	British Museum	French Apocalypse		Late 13th C.
	London	British Museum	Tenison Psalter		1284
	London	British Museum	Queen Mary's Psalter	Peterborough workshop (?)	First half of 14th C.
	London	British Museum	Saint-Omer Psalter		1320-30
	London	British Museum	Robert of Lisle's Psalter		Between 1280 and 1340, probably c. 1300
	London	British Museum	Lutrell Psalter		c. 1345
	London	British Museum	Carmelite Missal		Late 14th C.
	London	British Museum	Lectionary ordered by John Lovell	Hermannus Scheere	Late 14th C.
	London	British Museum	Bible said to be Richard II's	School of Hermannus Scheere	Early 15th C.
	London	British Museum	Breviary of John the Fearless	Pol of Limbourg	Early 15th C.
	London	British Museum	Bedford Breviary		1424-35
	Manchester	John Rylands Library	Henry of Chichester's Missal	Salisbury workshop	Mid-13th C.
	Oxford	Bodleian Library	*Pronostica Socratis*	Matthew Paris	Mid-13th C.
	Oxford	Bodleian Library	Bible		1265
	Oxford	Bodleian Library	Book of Hours	Hermannus Scheere	Late 14th C.
	Oxford	Bodleian Library	Book of Hours of Yolande de Lalaing	Convent of St. Agnes-of-Delft	1459-60
	Oxford	Bodleian Library	Moral and religious tracts		1475
	Oxford	New College	Oxford Psalter	William of Brailes	1230-50
	Sheffield	Ruskin Museum	Book of Hours of Diana of Croy	School of Jean Fouquet	Second half of the 15th C.
	Westminster	Abbey Library	*Liber Regalis*		Late 14th C.
	Winchester	Cathedral Library	Winchester Bible		1150-60

ountry	Town	Museum	Title	Artist	Date
France	Chantilly	Library	Ingeburge Psalter		c. 1210
	Chantilly	Condé Museum	*The Very Rich Hours of the Duke of Berry*	Limbourg Brothers (finished by Jean Colombe of Bourges)	Early 15th C.
	Chantilly	Condé Museum	Book of Hours of Etienne Chevalier	Jean Fouquet	1445-61
	Chateauroux	Municipal Library	Paris Breviary	Master of Boucicaut	Early 15th C.
	Dijon	Municipal Library	*Romance of the Holy Grail*		Mid-15th C.
	Grenoble	Library	*The Ladies' Champion*		Mid-15th C.
	Lille	Municipal Library	*The Moral Sayings of Philosophers*	Master of Gilbert of Metz	Mid-15th C.
	Metz	Library	*Mortification of Vain Pleasure*		1453
	Montpelier	Library of the Medical Faculty	*Song Book*		Late 13th C.
	Paris	Arsenal Library	Psalter of Blanche of Castille (Paris Psalter)		c. 1230
	Paris	Arsenal Library	*La Somme le Roi*		1311
	Paris	Arsenal Library	*Térence des Ducs*		c. 1405-10
	Paris	Arsenal Library	Boccaccio: *Decameron*	Master of Gilbert of Metz	c. 1440
	Paris	Arsenal Library	*Roman History*	Loyset Lyédet	c. 1460
	Paris	Arsenal Library	*Chronicle of the Emperors*	Workshop of David Aubert	1462-65
	Paris	Arsenal Library	*Judaic Antiquities* by Flavius Josèphe	Workshop of Sander Bening	Second half of the 15th C.
	Paris	Arsenal Library	*Instruction for a Young Prince*	Workshop of Jean Hennecart	1470
	Paris	Mazarine Library	*The Golden Legend* by Jacques de Voragine	Master of the Copses	Second half of the 14th C.
	Paris	National Library	St. Louis Psalter		1250-70
	Paris	National Library	*Great Chronicles of France*	Saint-Denis Scriptorium	13th C.
	Paris	National Library	Martyrology		c. 1270
	Paris	National Library	Breviary of Philip the Fair	Master Honoré	Late 13th C.
	Paris	National Library	Clement VII's Bible	Bologne school	Late 13th-early 14th C.
	Paris	National Library	Belleville Breviary	Jean Pucelle	1323-26

Country	Town	Museum	Title	Artist	Date
	Paris	National Library	Robert de Billyng's Bible	Jean Pucelle Anciau de Cens Jacquet Maci	1327
	Paris	National Library	Little Hours	Jean Pucelle	First half of 14th C.
	Paris	National Library	*Tristan*	Lombardy school	14th C.
	Paris	National Library	*Pantheon*	Goffredo di Viterbo	14th C.
	Paris	National Library	*Funeral Oration for Gian Galeazzo Visconti*	Michelino da Besozzo	14th C.
	Paris	National Library	Roman Pontifical	Siena school	Mid-14th C.
	Paris	National Library	*The City of God*	Master of the Copses	Mid-14th C.
	Paris	National Library	*Great Chronicles of France*	Master of the Copses	Mid-14th C.
	Paris	National Library	Bible of Jean de Sy	Master of the Copses	1356
	Paris	National Library	*Poems* by Guillaume de Machaut	Master of the Copses	c. 1370
	Paris	National Library	Book of Hours of Blanche of Savoy	Giovanni di Benedetto	Late 14th C.
	Paris	National Library	Psalter for the Duke of Berry	André Beauneveau	c. 1400
	Paris	National Library	Duke of Burgundy's Bible	Limbourg Brothers	1402
	Paris	National Library	The Great Hours of the Duke of Berry	Jacquemart de Hesdin	1409
	Paris	National Library	The Little Hours of the Duke of Berry	Jacquemart de Hesdin	Early 15th C.
	Paris	National Library	Historiated Bible	Limbourg Brothers	Early 15th C.
	Paris	National Library	Very Beautiful Hours of Our Lady		Early 15th C.
	Paris	National Library	*Book of Marvels*	Master of Bedford Master of Boucicaut	Early 15th C.
	Paris	National Library	Philip the Good's Book of Hours	Workshop of the Master of Boucicaut	Early 15th C.
	Paris	National Library	Rohan Hours	Master of Rohan	Early 15th C.
	Paris	National Library	Breviary	Master of Bedford	1424-35
	Paris	National Library	Hunting book of Gaston de Foix	Master of Bedford	First half of the 15th C.
	Paris	National Library	Margaret of York's Book of Hours		First half of the 15th C.
	Paris	National Library	*The Tale of Alexander*	Workshop of Jean Wauquelin	1448
	Paris	National Library	*Judaic Antiquities* by Flavius Josephus	Several pages are by Jean Fouquet	Mid-15th C.

ntry	Town	Museum	Title	Artist	Date
	Paris	National Library	*Great Chronicles of France*	Jean Fouquet	1450-70
	Paris	National Library	*Miracles of Our Lady*	Jean le Tavernier	1450-70
	Paris	National Library	Laval Hours	School of Jean Fouquet	Second half of 15th C.
	Paris	National Library	*The Winning of the Golden Fleece*	Workshop of Lieven of Lathem	c. 1470
	Paris	National Library	Book of Hours of Charles of Angoulême	Jean Bourdichon	1485
	Paris	National Library	Hours of Anne of Brittany	Jean Bourdichon	1500-08
	Paris	National Library	Hours of Ferdinand, King of Naples	Jean Bourdichon	Early 16th C.
	Paris	National Library	Hours of King Charles VIII	Jean Bourdichon	Early 16th C.
	Paris	Jacquemart-André Museum	Marshall Boucicaut's Book of Hours	Master of Boucicaut	Early 15th C.
	Rouen	Municipal Library	Aristotle: *Political and Economic Ethics*	Workshop of Loyset Liédet	Before 1454
	Tours	Library	Decree of Gratien	Master Honoré (Finished by Thomas of Wymonduswold)	Late 13th C. 1323
rmany	Aschaffenburg	Library	Evangeliary of Fritz von Erthal		c. 1260
	Berlin	Library	*Mortification of Vain Pleasure*		1453
	Bonn	National Rhenish Museum	*Speculum Virginum*	Conrad von Hirsau	Late 12th C.
	Hamburg	State Library	Cistercian Breviary		c. 1260
	Heidelberg	University Library	Troubadour Manuscript		1315-40
	Munich	Library	*Lives and Martyrdoms of the Apostles*	School of Regensburg-Prüfening	1170-1200
	Munich	Library	*Liber Matutinalis*	Conrad von Scheyern	1230
	Munich	Library	*Carmina Burana*	Bavarian workshop	c. 1430
	Munich	Library	*Cases of Unfortunate Noblemen and Noblewomen*	Jean Fouquet	Mid-15th C.
	Munich	Castle Library	Evangeliary	Abbess of Niedermünster	Early 13th C.
	Münster	University Library	Missal of Johannes Van Hoya	Workshop of the Master of Zweder Van Culemborg	c. 1430
	Stuttgart	Library	Psalter of the Landgrave Hermann von Thüringen		c. 1230

Country	Town	Museum	Title	Artist	Date
	Stuttgart	Würtember-gerische Landesbibliothek	*Book of the Chase*		15th C.
	Tübingen	University Library	Manuscript for Otto Van Moerdrecht		Early 15th C.
	Tübingen	University Library	Book of Hours for Maria of Guelders	Master of Otto Van Moerdrecht	c. 1415
Hungary	Budapest	National Library	Missal of the Poszoni chapter	Nagyszombati Mahali	1403
	Budapest	Széchényo	Missal	Vaci Janoš	1423
Italy	Bologna	University Library	Book of Hours	Master of William of Metz	Second half of the 15th C.
	Bologna Museum	Municipal	Corale 5	Niccolo di Giacomo	Late 12th C.
	Bologna	Municipal Museum	Corale	School of Cimabue	Late 13th C.
	Bologna	Municipal Museum	Antiphonary	Neri da Rimini	Early 14th C.
	Cividale del Friuli	Museum	St. Elizabeth's Psalter	Thuringo-Saxon school	Second half of the 13th C.
	Florence	Laurentiana Library	Biadaiolo Manuscript	School of Giotto	Late 14th C.
	Florence	Laurentiana Library	Gradual	School of the Angels	Late 14th C.
	Florence	Laurentiana Library	Corale 3	School of Lorenzo Monaco	Early 15th C.
	Florence	Laurentiana Library	Pliny's *Natural History*	Petrus of Slagosia	Early 15th C.
	Florence	Laurentiana Library	Roberto della Porta: *Romuleon*	Workshop of David Aubert	1465
	Florence	National Library	Book of Hours of Filippo Maria Visconti	Giovannino de' Grassi	Late 14th C.
	Florence	Santa Croce	Antiphonary	Don Simone Camaldolese	Late 14th C.
	Milan	Ambrosiana Library	Decretals	Niccolò di Giacomo	1354
	Milan	Ambrosiana Library	Coronation Missal	Anovelo da Imbonate	14th C.
	Milan	Ambrosiana Library	Frontispiece to Virgil	Simone Martini	Late 14th C.
	Milan	Ambrosiana Library	*De Balneis puteolanis*	Neapolitan school	Late 14th C.
	Milan	Braidence Library	*Register of Notaries*	Matteo di Ser Cambio	Late 14th C.

ıntry	Town	Museum	Title	Artist	Date
	Milan	Trivulziana Library	*Pharsalia*	Niccolò di Giacomo	Mid-14th C.
	Milan	Trivulziana Library	Beroldo	Giovannino de' Grassi	Late 14th C.
	Milan	Trivulziana Library	*The Divine Comedy* by Dante		1405
	Milan	Visconti di Modrone Collection	Book of Hours of Gian Galeazzo Visconti	Giovannino de' Grassi	c. 1385
	Modena	Este Library	Book of Hours of Isabelle of Castille	Verona school	14th C.
	Naples	National Library	Boethius: *De Musica, De Arithmetica*	School of the Anjou Court	Late 14th C.
	Padua	Cathedral	Collection of letters	Engelbert of Admont	1280
	Rome	Angelica Library	*De Balneis puteolanis*	Neapolitan school	Late 14th C.
	Siena	Public Library	Book of Hours	Bruges workshop	c. 1455
	Siena	Public Library	Missal of Ferry of Clugny	Workshop of Willem Vrelandt	1473
	Turin	Public Museum	Very Beautiful Hours of Our Lady		Early 15th C.
	Vatican	Library	Several Manuscripts executed for Pope Boniface VIII		Early 14th C.
	Vatican	Library	Villani Chronicle		Late 14th C.
	Venice	St. Mark's Library	Mariegola dei Calderari		Late 14th C.
	Venice	St. Mark's Library	*The Entry of Spain*		Late 14th C.
	Venice	St. Mark's Library	Roman Missal	School of Niccolò di Giacomo	Early 15th C.
	Venice	Civic Museum Correr	*Mariegole*	School of S. Caterina-dei-Sacchi	Late 14th C.
	Venice	Civic Museum Correr	*Mariegole*	School of S. Marco	Late 14th C.
ıerlands	Amsterdam	Koninklijk Oudheidkundig Genootschap	Bible	Utrecht school	c. 1445
	Groningen	University Library	Rhymed Bible of Jakob Van Maerlant	Michel Van der Borch	1332
	Haarlem	Municipal Library	Missal of the Haarlem Weavers' Guild	Utrecht school	c. 1400
	The Hague	Royal Library	Book of Hours of Catherine of Aragon	Workshop of Willem Vrelandt	Mid-15th C.

Country	Town	Museum	Title	Artist	Date
	The Hague	Royal Library	*The Mirror of the Sinful Soul*	Workshop of Jean Miélot	1451
	The Hague	Royal Library	Book of Hours of Philip the Good	Workshop of Jean le Tavernier	1454
	The Hague	Royal Library	*Legend and Miracles St. Hubert*	Workshop of Loyset Liédet	1463
	The Hague	Meermann-Westreenen Museum	Bible of Jean de Vantar	Jean de Bandol	Late 14th C.
	The Hague	Meermann-Westreenen Museum	Aristotle's *Ethics*		1376
	The Hague	Meermann-Westreenen Museum	Book of Prayers	Master of Catherine of Cleves	c. 1438
	The Hague	Meermann-Westreenen Museum	Chronicle of Aegidius of Roya	Master of Anthony of Burgundy	Second half of the 15th C.
	Leyden	University Library	Psalter		Late 12th C.
	Leyden	University Library	*On the Flowers of Nature* by Van Maerlant	Nicholas Van Delft	1350-70
	Leyden	University Library	Book of Hours	Master of Catherine of Cleves	1440-45
Poland	Breslau	Library	Valerius Maximus	Master of Anthony of Burgundy	Second half of the 15th C.
Spain	Madrid	National Library	Book of Hours	Workshop of Willem Vrelandt	Mid-15th C.
	Madrid	National Library	Moral Treatises by St. Augustin	Workshop of Jean Dreux	1462
	Toledo	Cathedral Vestry	St. Louis Bible		13th C.
Sweden	Stockholm	National Museum	Book of Hours	Guelders school	c. 1420
Switzerland	Geneva	University Library	William of Tyr: *History of the Crusades*	Workshop of Loyset Liédet	Mid-15th C.
	Geneva	University Library	*The Flower of Stories*		Mid-15th C.
	Wettingen	Abbey	Gradual	Master of William of Cassel	First half of 14th C.
U.S.A.	Baltimore	Walter's Art Gallery	Biblical scenes	William of Brailes	1230-50
	Baltimore	Walter's Art Gallery	Book of Hours	Master of Zweder Van Culemborg	c. 1435

untry	Town	Museum	Title	Artist	Date
	Baltimore	Walter's Art Gallery	*The Flower of Stories*	Workshop of Loyset Liédet	Mid-15th C.
	Baltimore	Walter's Art Gallery	Book of Hours	Workshop of Willem Vrelandt	Second half of 15th C.
	Baltimore	Walter's Art Gallery	Jehan de Wavrin *Chronicle of England*	Workshop of Ghent	Second half of 15th C.
	Cambridge (Mass.)	Harvard College Library	Guy de Thurno: *The Vision of the Soul*	Workshop of David Aubert	1474
	New York	Guennol Collection	Book of Hours of Catherine of Cleves	Utrecht school	c. 1435
	New York	Metropolitan Museum	Book of Hours of Jeanne d'Evreux	Jean Pucelle	c. 1328
	New York	Metropolitan Museum	Beautiful Hours	Limbourg Brothers	E[illegible]y 15th C.
	New York	Pierpoint Morgan Library	Scenes from the Life of Christ	Pacino de Bonaguida	[illegible]y 14th C.
	New York	Pierpoint Morgan Library	Breviary of Duke Reinoud IV of Guelders	Master of Otto Van Moerdrecht	1417
	New York	Pierpoint Morgan Library	*Table of the Christian Faith*	Dierck Van Delft	Early 15th C.
	New York	Pierpoint Morgan Library	Book of Hours	Mons Wor[illegible]	Before 1450
	New York	Pierpoint Morgan Library	*Mortification of Vain Pleasure*		1453
	New York	Pierpoint Morgan Library	Pietro di Crescenzi: *Book of Rural Profits*	Workshop of the Master of Margaret of York	c. 1470
	New York	Pierpoint Morgan Library	Book of Hours (on black parchment)	Workshop of the Master of Anthony of Burgundy	c. 1475
	New York	Public Library	John Tickill's Psalter	Prior of Worksop	Early 14th C.

Frescoes — Stained Glass — Tapestries — Altar Screens

Country	Town	Museum	Origin	Genre	Date
Belgium	Antwerp	Royal Fine-Arts Museum	*Calvary* by Hendrik Van Rijn (one of the few pre-Eyck paintings) from St. John's Church, Utrecht	Reredos	c. 1363
	Brussels	Quinquagenary	*Presentation in the Temple*	Tapestry	14th C.
	Brussels	Quinquagenary	*Battle of Roncevaux*	Tapestry	Mid-15th C.
	Tournai	Cathedral Treasury	*Lives of St. Piat and St. Eleuthera* by Pierrot Féré	Tapestry	1402
England	London	National Gallery	*Wilton Diptych*	Panels	c. 1395
France	Angers	Tapestry Museum	*Apocalypse* by Nicholas Bataille	Tapestry	1377-81
	Paris	Museum of Decorative Arts	Scene from a romance, from the Arras workroom	Tapestry	c. 1420
	Paris	Museum of Decorative Arts	Monograms and a device	Tapestry	Late 15th C.
	Paris	Museum of Decorative Arts	Important selection of French Gothic frescoes		
	Paris	Cluny Museum	*Scenes from the Life of St. Martin* from an Icelandic workroom	Tapestry	13th C.
	Paris	Cluny Museum	*Life of St. Mark*, German altar facing	Tapestry	14th C.
	Paris	Cluny Museum	*The Resurrection*, from the Arras workroom	Tapestry	Late 14th C.
	Paris	Cluny Museum	*The Oblation of the Heart*, from the Arras workroom	Tapestry	Early 15th C.
	Paris	Louvre	*Narbonne Facing*	Silk painting	c. 1375
	Paris	Louvre	*The Legend of St. Nicasius and St. Eutropius*	Stained glass	Second half of the 13th C.
Germany	Cologne	Museum	Scenes from the life of Christ by a Cologne master, from the ancient Convent of St. Clare at Cologne	Reredos	c. 1330
	Halberstadt	Cathedral	*Charlemagne with Four Philosophers*	Tapestry	c. 1200
	Munich	National Museum	Fresco from the Convent of Rebdorf		c. 1300
	Munich	National Museum	Stained glass from the Minorite church at Ratison		c. 1400
Spain	Burgos	Diocesan Museum	Several Gothic tapestries		
	Valencia	National Museum	Triptych from the Carthusian convent at Porta Coeli		c. 1400

untry	Town	Museum	Origin	Genre	Date
	Vich	Museum	Panels of the Poor Clares' reredos by Luis Borrassa		1415
	Zamora	Cathedral Museum	*Trojan War* woven at Tournai	Tapestry	c. 1465
itzerland	Basle	History Museum	Fragments of *The Dance of Death*, from the Dominican church cemetery	Fresco	Early 15th C.
	Zürich	National Museum	*Virgin and Child*, from Flums (Saint-Gall)	Stained glass	Late 12th C.
	Zürich	National Museum	Ceiling with New Testament scenes after those in Zillis church	Frescoes	13th C.
S.A.	New York	Metropolitan	*The Nine Heroes*, from the workroom of Nicholas Bataille	Tapestry	c. 1385

Painters

Name	Town	Museum	Name of Work	Date
Altichiero (1330-85)	Padua	St. Felix Chapel	Scenes from the life of St. James	1379
	Padua	St. George's Oratory	Scenes from the life of St. George	1385
Barna	Arezzo	Cathedral	*Crucifixion*	1369 (?)
	San Gimignano	Collegiate Church	Scenes from the life of Christ	
Baronzio, Giovanni (d. before 1362)	New York	Metropolitan Museum	Scenes from the Holy Story	
	Paris	Louvre	*Deposition from the Cross*	
	Urbino	National Museum	Polyptych	1345
Bartolo di Fredi (c. 1330-c. 1410)	Amsterdam	Rijksmuseum	*Madonna and Child*	
	New York	Lehman Collection	*Adoration of the Magi*	
	Paris	Louvre	*Presentation in the Temple*	
	Siena	Picture Gallery	*Baptism of a Prisoner*	
	Siena	Picture Gallery	Stories of Saints	
	Siena	Picture Gallery	*Jesus and His Disciples at Table*	
Bellechose, Henri (d. between 1440 and 1444)	Paris	Louvre	*The Last Communion and Martyrdom of St. Denis*	c. 1415
	Paris	Louvre	*Christ on the Cross*	
Broederlam, Melchior (active 1381-1409)	Dijon	Museum	*The Annunciation* and *The Visitation*	
	Dijon	Museum	*The Presentation in the Temple* and *The Flight into Egypt*	
Buonaiuti da Firenze, Andrea (d. 1377)	Florence	Santa Maria Novella	Scenes of the Passion	1365-67
	Florence	Santa Maria Novella	*The Church Triumphant*	1365-67
	Florence	Santa Maria Novella	*The Triumph of St. Thomas Aquinas*	1365-67
Cavallini, Pietro (c. 1250-1330)	Trastavere	St. Cecilia's Church	*Last Judgment*	
Cimabue (1240-c. 1302)	Assisi	St. Francis' Church	Scenes of the life of the Virgin, the Apocalypse, and Sts. Peter and Paul, Evangelists	1277-81
	Paris	Louvre	Virgin with Angels (school)	
	Pisa	Cathedral	*St. John the Evangelist* (Mosaic)	1302
Cione, Bernado (mid-14th C.)	Florence	Santa Maria Novella	*Paradise*, *Inferno*, *Last Judgment* with the portrait of Dante	1345-57
Daddi, Bernado (died c. 1350)	Florence	Uffizi Gallery	*Virgin and Child* and *Saints*	

ıme	Town	Museum	Name of Work	Date
	New York	Lehman Collection	*The Virgin and Child*	
	Paris	Louvre	*Crucifixion*	
	Paris	Louvre	*Annunciation*	
	Pisa	Civic Museum	*Scene from the life of St. Cecilia*	c. 1335
	Turin	Picture Gallery	*Coronation of the Virgin*	
ılmau, Luis ctive 1428-60)	Barcelona	Museum	Reredos of the Virgin of the Councillors of Barcelona	1445
ıccio di ıoninsegni (d. 1318)	Florence	Santa Maria Novella	*Virgin enthroned*	c. 1285
	London	National Gallery	Triptych	
	Perugia	Picture Gallery	*Madonna*	
	Siena	Cathedral Museum	*La Maestà*	
	Siena	Cathedral Museum	*The Virgin Triumphant with Saints*	
	Siena	Picture Gallery	*The Franciscan Madonna*	
rrer, Bassa 290-1348)	Barcelona	Monastery at Pedralbes	*St. Bonaventura*	1345
ıddi, Angelo ddeo (c. 1333-96)	Florence	Santa Croce	*The Legend of the Holy Cross*	c. 1380
	Paris	Louvre	*Annunciation*	
addi, Taddeo . 1366)	Florence	Santa Croce	*Life of the Virgin*	c. 1332-38
	Florence	Uffizi Gallery	*Madonna*	
entile da Fabriano 1370-1450)	Florence	Uffizi Gallery	*Adoration of the Magi*	1423
	Florence	St. Nicholas Church	Reredos of the Virgin's Altar	
	Paris	Louvre	*Presentation in the Temple*	
	Paris	Louvre	*Virgin and Child*	
	Rome	Colonna Gallery	*Madonna surrounded by Angels*	
Giottino"? 4th C.)	Florence	Uffizi Gallery	*Descent from the Cross*	
otto (1266-1336)	Assisi	St. Francis' Church	Scenes from the lives of St. Francis, Christ, and St. Mary Magdalene	c. 1300
	Florence	Santa Croce	Stories of St. John the Baptist, St. John the Evangelist, and St. Francis of Assisi	Early 14th C.
	Florence	Santa Maria Novella	*Crucifixion*	
	Florence	Uffizi Gallery	*Throned Madonna*	
	Munich	Picture Gallery	*Christ on the Cross*	

Name	Town	Museum	Name of Work	Date
	Munich	Picture Gallery	*The Last Supper*	
	Padua	Arena Chapel	Scenes from the lives of Christ and the Virgin	1304-06
	Paris	Louvre	*St. Francis receiving the Stigmata*	
	Rome	St. John Lateran	*Boniface VIII proclaiming the Jubilee of 1300*	
Giovanni da Milano (14th C.)	Florence	Santa Croce	Scenes from the life of the Virgin	1365
	Florence	Fine-Arts Academy	*The Dead Christ*	
	Florence	Fine-Arts Academy	*The Virgin at the Crucifixion*	
	New York	Metropolitan Museum	*Virgin with Donors*	
Giusto di Menabuoi (d. 1393)	London	National Gallery	*Coronation of the Virgin*	
	Padua	Baptistry	*Redeemer in Glory*	c. 1380
Jacopo del Casentino (1297-1356)	Arezzo	San Bartolomeo	*Dead Christ* with Virgin and St. John the Baptist	
Lorenzetti, Ambrogio (d. 1348)	Florence	Uffizi	*Presentation in the Temple*	1342
	Florence	Uffizi	Scenes from the lives of the Saints	
	Siena	Municipal Palace	*Allegory of Good and Bad Government*	1337-40
	Siena	Picture Gallery	*Townscape*	1335-40
	Siena	Picture Gallery	*Madonna and Child*	c. 1340
	Siena	Picture Gallery	*Annunciation*	1344
Lorenzetti, Pietro (first half of the 14th C.)	Arezzo	Pieve	*Virgin with several Saints*	1320
	Assisi	Church of St. Francis	*Crucifixion*	1320-30
	Florence	Uffizi	*Madonna Enthroned*	1340
	Siena	Cathedral Museum	*Birth of the Virgin*	1342
	Siena	Picture Gallery	Predella of the Carmelite reredos	1328-29
	Siena	Picture Gallery	*Madonna between St. Francis and St. John the Evangelist*	
Malouel, Jean (d. 1419)	Paris	Louvre	*Martyrdom of St. Denis*	1398
	Paris	Louvre	*Dead Christ Sustained by the Eternal Father* (from the Carthusian Convent of Champmol)	

Name	Town	Museum	Name of Work	Date
Martini, Simone (1284-1344)	Antwerp	Royal Museum	*The Virgin and the Angel of the Annunciation*	After 1339
	Antwerp	Royal Museum	*The Blow with the Lance* and *The Descent from the Cross*	After 1339
	Assisi	St. Francis' Church	*Legend of St. Martin*	1320-30
	Florence	Uffizi	*Annunciation*	1333
	Pisa	Civic Museum	Polyptych: Madonna, Infant and saints	c. 1340
	Rome	National Museum of Ancient Art	*Virgin and Child*	
	Siena	Municipal Palace	*La Maestà*	1315
	Siena	Municipal Palace	*Equestrian portrait of the Soldier of fortune Guido da Fogliano*	1328
Martorell, Bernardo (d. 1453)	Barcelona	Cathedral	Reredos of *The Transfiguration*	
Maso (14th C.)	Florence	Santa Croce	*Legend of St. Sylvester*	
Master Bertram (c. 1345-1415)	Hamburg	Kunsthalle	Grabow reredos	1379-83
	Hamburg	Kunsthalle	Reredos of St. Peter's, Hamburg	
	Hamburg	Kunsthalle	Buxtehude Altar	c. 1390
Master of the Vyšši Brod Cycle (14th C.)	Prague	National Gallery	Scenes from the Life and Martyrdom of Christ	c. 1350
Master of Heiligenkreuz (early 15th C.)	Vienna	Museum	Reredos of the Church of Heiligerkreuz	
Master of the Trebon Reredos (second half of the 14th C.)	Prague	National Gallery	Cycle of the Passion	c. 1380
Monaco, Lorenzo (before 1372-before 1425)	Florence	Gallery of the Academy	Scenes from the life of St. Nicholas of Bari	
	Florence	Uffizi	*Coronation of the Virgin*	
	Florence	Uffizi	*Adoration of the Magi*	
	New York	Lehman Collection	*Nativity*	1405-10
	Paris	Louvre	*Jesus on the Mount of Olives*	
	Paris	Louvre	*The Holy Women at the Tomb*	
	Paris	Louvre	*Virgin and Child*	
	Rome	Gallery of Painting	Scenes from the life of St. Benedict	
Orcagna, Andrea di Cione (1329-89)	New York	Lehman Collection	*Crucifixion*	

Name	Town	Museum	Name of Work	Date
	Pisa	Campo Santo	*Death and the Last Judgement*	
Sano di Pietro (1406-81)	Chantilly	Condé Museum	*Mystic Marriage of St. Francis with Lady Poverty*	
	London	National Gallery	*Coronation of the Virgin*	
	New York	Lehman Collection	*Virgin and Child*	1436
	Paris	Louvre	Scenes from the life of St. Jerome	
	Siena	Picture Gallery	*The Madonna appears to Calistus III*	
Stefano da Zevio (c. 1375-c. 1451)	Budapest	Museum	*Virgin and the Infant Jesus*	
	Milan	Brera Gallery	*Adoration of the Magi*	
	Rome	Colonna Gallery	*Madonna*	
	Verona	Castelvecchio Museum	*The Virgin of the Rosary*	Early 15th C.
Tomaso da Modena (c. 1325-c. 1379)	Treviso	Museum	Scenes from the life of St. Ursula	1352
	Treviso	Seminary	*St. Albert the Great*	
	Vienna	Museum	*Virgin and the Infant Jesus*	
Veneziano, Paolo (c. 1340-c. 1368)	Paris	Louvre	*Virgin*	
	Venice	St. Mark's Church	Scenes from the life of St. Mark	1345
	Venice	Academy	*Madonna Enthroned with the Child*	
	Vicenza	Municipal Museum	*The Death of the Virgin*	
Vitale da Bologna (first half of the 14th C.)	Bologna	Picture Gallery	Frescoes of Mezzarata	c. 1345
	Vatican	Museum	*La Madonna dei Battuti*	

Maps

NORTH
SEA
ATLANTIC
OCEAN
Glasgow
Melrose
Fountains Abbey
York
Lincoln
Lichfield
Gloucester
St. Albans
Cambridge
Oxford
Glastonbury
Wells
London
Canterbury
Salisbury
Winchester
Chichester
Utrecht
Bois-le-Duc
Bruges
Mechlin
Antwerp
Maastricht
Gand
Brussels
Liège
Amiens
Laon
Bayeux
St-Wandrille
Rouen
Beauvais
Soissons
Reims
Mont St. Michel
Sées
Pierrefonds
Paris
Meaux
Coutances
Chartres
Sens
Toul
Le Mans
Quimper
Auxerre
Tours
Semur
Dijon
Bourges
Poitiers
Nevers
Noirlac
Riom
Lyons
Bassac
Clermont-F.
Montbrison
Bordeaux
St-Junien
Bazas
Agen
Avignon
Albi
Valmagne
Dax
Orthez
Béziers
Aix
León
Carcassonne
Burgos
Las Huelgas
Gerona
Manresa
Coimbra
Avila
Burgo de Osma
Barcelona
Leiria
Cuenca
Palma-Majorca
Toledo
Valencia
Evora
Huerto

Gothic Art
Principal European locations

NORTH SEA
BALTIC SEA
ATLANTIC OCEAN
ENGLISH CHANNEL
ADRIATIC SEA
MEDITERRANEAN SEA
Carlisle
York
Lincoln
Gloucester
Oxford
Wells
Canterbury
Exeter
Winchester
Lierre (Antwerp)
Louvain
Cologne
Marburg
Sichem
Fécamp
Amiens
Hal
Huy (Liège)
Limburg am Lahn
Sées
Rouen
Laon
Coutances
Beauvais
Soissons
Dol
Chartres
Paris
Reims
Metz
Evreux
Quimper
Le Mans
Toul
Sens
Strasbourg
Fribourg
Augsburg
Angers
Bourges
Poitiers
Dijon
Wettingen
Limoges
Königsfelden
Lausanne
Clermont-Ferrand
Lyons
Bologna
Toulouse
Assisi
León
Carcassonne
Burgos
Toledo
Palma-Majorca
Valencia

Frescoes in France

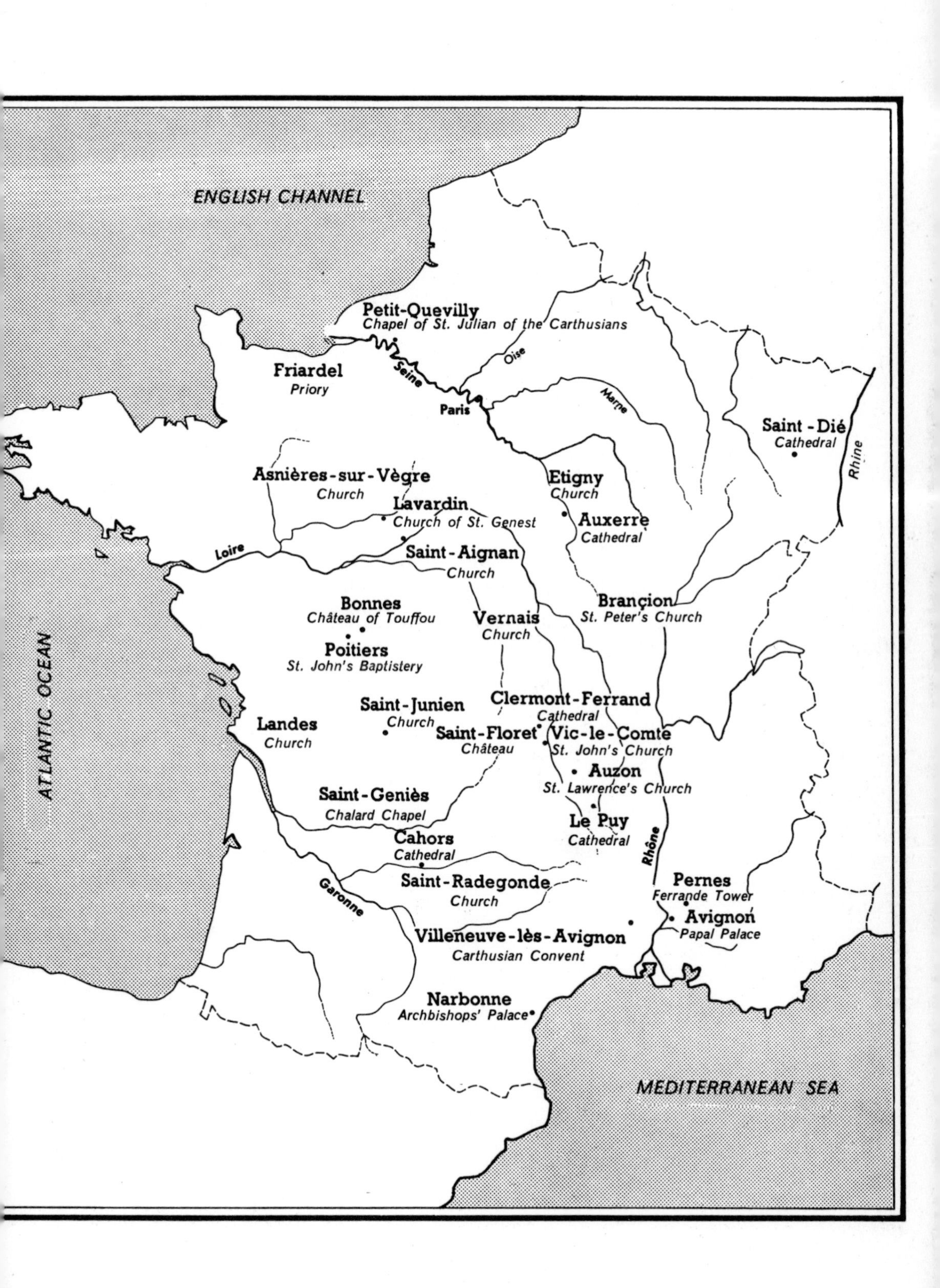
ENGLISH CHANNEL
ATLANTIC OCEAN
MEDITERRANEAN SEA
Petit-Quevilly
Chapel of St. Julian of the Carthusians
Oise
Seine
Paris
Marne
Friardel
Priory
Saint-Dié
Cathedral
Rhine
Asnières-sur-Vègre
Church
Lavardin
Church of St. Genest
Etigny
Church
Auxerre
Cathedral
Loire
Saint-Aignan
Church
Brançion
St. Peter's Church
Bonnes
Château of Touffou
Vernais
Church
Poitiers
St. John's Baptistery
Clermont-Ferrand
Cathedral
Saint-Junien
Church
Landes
Church
Saint-Floret
Château
Vic-le-Comte
St. John's Church
Auzon
St. Lawrence's Church
Saint-Geniès
Chalard Chapel
Le Puy
Cathedral
Cahors
Cathedral
Rhône
Saint-Radegonde
Church
Pernes
Ferrande Tower
Garonne
Avignon
Papal Palace
Villeneuve-lès-Avignon
Carthusian Convent
Narbonne
Archbishops' Palace

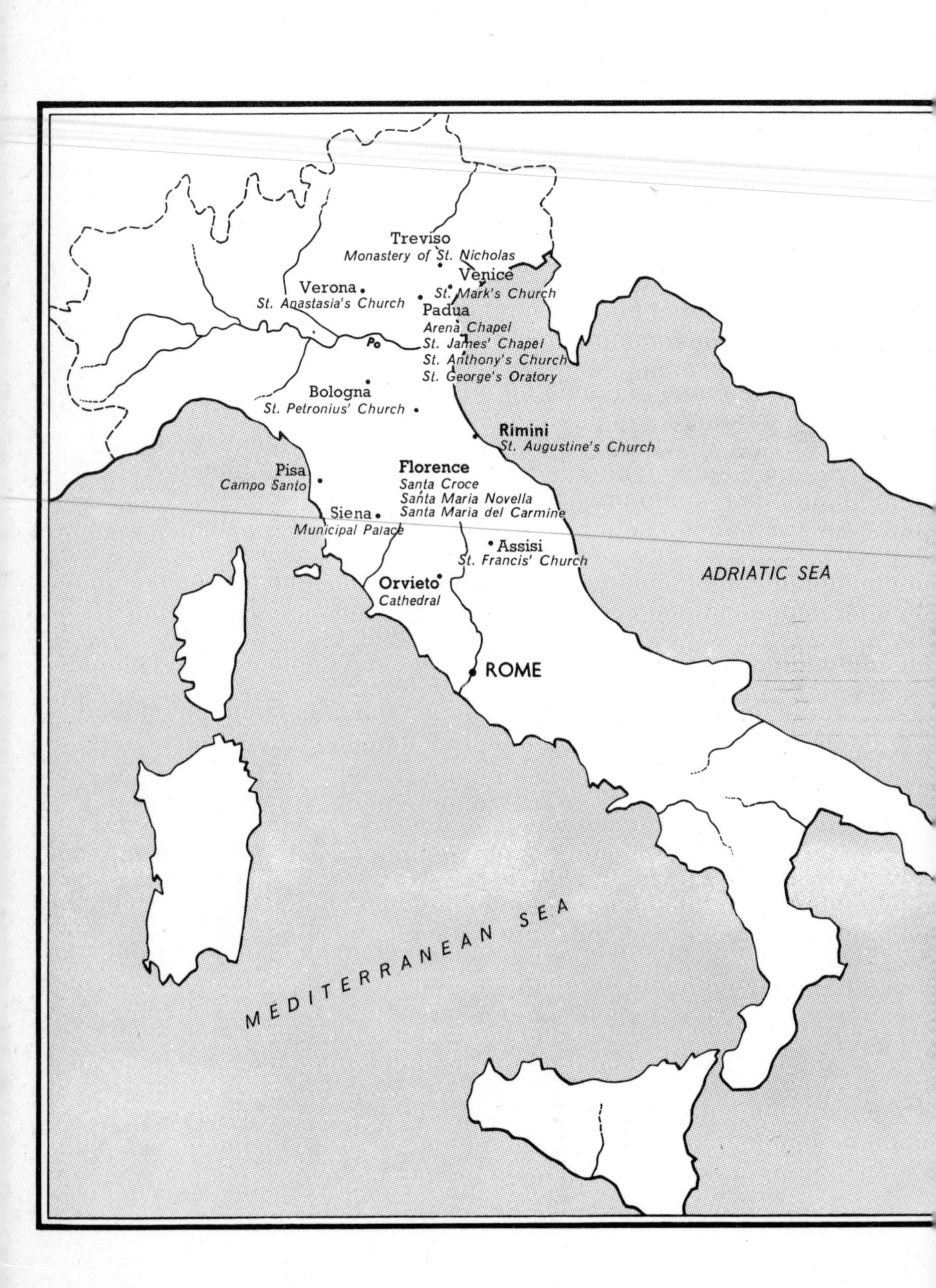
Treviso
Monastery of St. Nicholas
Venice
St. Mark's Church
Verona
St. Anastasia's Church
Padua
Arena Chapel
St. James' Chapel
St. Anthony's Church
St. George's Oratory
Po
Bologna
St. Petronius' Church
Rimini
St. Augustine's Church
Pisa
Campo Santo
Florence
Santa Croce
Santa Maria Novella
Santa Maria del Carmine
Siena
Municipal Palace
Assisi
St. Francis' Church
Orvieto
Cathedral
ADRIATIC SEA
ROME
MEDITERRANEAN SEA

Dictionary

Passionale for the Abbess Cunegunda
c. 1320
University Library, Prague

Abelard, Peter (1079-1142)

Born at Palet near Nantes. He taught in turn at Melun, Corbeil, Paris, Laon, then again at Paris on the Mont-Sainte-Geneviève. At that time he formed his liaison with Heloise; they lived in a house in the City, on the site of the Quai des Fleurs. His philosophy was condemned first at Soissons in 1121 and later in the Chapter of Sens in 1141. He was a theologian, but primarily a philosopher who advocated a degree of rationalism and opposed the uncompromising mysticism of St. Bernard. He was a poet and has left us some religious hymns; he also wrote love songs in honour of his mistress. He celebrated the lives and doctrines of the ancient philosophers who seemed to him not so far from Christianity; he defended the idea among others that Plato had understood the Trinity and all his life he tried to explain this understanding of mystery by Pagans. Numerous works are attributed to him, particularly a treatise on *Logic*, in which he defined the meaning of the doctrine "of names" which subsequently caused a stir under the title of Nominalism.

Altichiero

Altichiero was born at Zevio near Verona. He was one of the greatest Italian primitive painters. In collaboration with Avanza, he painted the frescoes in the chapels of St. Felix and St. George at Padua. These frescoes are valuable for their realistic conception and rich colour. Altichiero's work, with that of Giotto and Orcagna, is the most beautiful of that period. His *Birth of the Virgin* is in the Strasbourg museum.

Anciau de Cens

Early 14th century French miniaturist, pupil and colleague of Jean Pucelle. Two pages of a Bible illuminated by Jean Pucelle, Anciau de Cens and Jacquet Maci are preserved in the National Library, Paris. One of the illuminations is signed and dated.

Anjou (Duke of) (1409-80)

Familiarly called King René, born at Angers and died at Aix-en-Provence. He was Duke of Bar and of Lorraine and Count of Provence. The crown of the kingdom of Sicily descended to him in 1417, but he was never able to take possession of his kingdom. He was a talented

Jean Bourdichon
Anne of Brittany with Two Saints
National Library, Paris

administrator and a protector of the arts. He maintained a brilliant court at Aix-en-Provence. He was the patron of numerous artists and poets, and himself painted and wrote poems and essays.

Anne of Brittany (1477-1514)

Born at Nantes, daughter of Duke Francis II of Brittany. In 1491 she married Charles VIII, King of France, and became his widow a few years later. By her marriage to Louis XII she once more became Queen of France, and annexed Brittany to France as her dowry. Bourdichon, or his pupils, illustrated *The Hours of Anne of Brittany*.

Antiphonary

Song-book, usually placed in the middle of the choir, and containing psalms, hymns and alternate chants.

Apocalypse of Saint-Sever

This Romanesque manuscript was derived from copies of the *Apocalypse of Beatus* about the middle of the 11th century in the monastery of Saint-Sever in Gascony, and is now in the National Library, Paris. The miniatures in this work suggest that they were done under Spanish influence.

Aragon

Ancient kingdom of Spain which was united with Catalonia in the 12th century. When Isabelle married King Ferdinand II in 1649 she brought Castille to Aragon.

Architrave

Lowest division of the entablature resting directly on the capitals of columns.

Arras

The production of tapestries from the Arras workrooms mingles with that of Paris. We do not know of any Arras work before the second half of the 14th century; only the tapestry depicting the *Life of St. Piat and St. Eleuthera*, made in 1402, can be attributed with certainty to these workshops. This tapestry is now in Tournai Cathedral.

Asceticism

Religious doctrine advocating mortification of the flesh, to attain a higher degree of spiritual perfection. It can be considered that the Cistercian reform reserved an important place for asceticism.

Aubert, Marcel (1884-1963)

French archeologist, specialising in the Middle Ages. He is the author of several studies on French medieval monuments. Among his principal publications concerning the Middle Ages are: *Notre Dame de Paris*, Paris 1920; *Vitraux des Cathédrales de France, XIIe-XIIIe siècles*, Paris, 1937; *Le Vitrail en France*, Paris 1946; *La France Glorieuse du Moyen Age*, Paris 1950.

Averroès, Ibn Roschd (1126-98)

One of the greatest Arab thinkers of the Middle Ages. Born at Córdoba. Admirer of Alexander's tutor, Aristotle, he introduced his ideas into Europe. Dante associates him with Avicenna among the greatest names in Greek knowledge: Euclid, Ptolemy, Hippocrates, Galen. Like most of his coreligionaries, Averroès was also influenced by neo-Platonic thinking. Averroès set himself to solve the problems arising from the relationship between philosophy and faith. He wrote the *Commentaries on the Philosophy of Aristotle*.

Avicenna, Ibn Sinâ (980-1037)

Of Persian origin. He wrote about a hundred works on various subjects. It was through him " that the Middle Ages learnt of the doctrine so disconcerting for Christians, of the Universal Intelligence, instrument and source of all intellectual knowledge of the entire human race" (E. Gilson). Avicenna was also a doctor. Among his principal works are: *The Canon of Medicine* and the *Ach Chafa*, or *Philosophical Encyclopaedia*.

Miniature
Averroès Conversing
National Library, Paris

Avignon (Cathedral of)

The Cathedral of Notre-Dame-des-Doms, Avignon, was built during the early centuries of the Church, and was entirely reconstructed about the middle of the 12th century. The porch was decorated with Simone Martini's beautiful frescoes, but only those on the tympanum remain, representing the eternal Father surrounded by angels and Cardinal Ceccano at the feet of the Virgin. Inside, near the door, the remains of a 13th century fresco of a *Virgin and Child* may still be seen.

The Hunt
Detail of a falconer
14th century
Papal Palace, Avignon

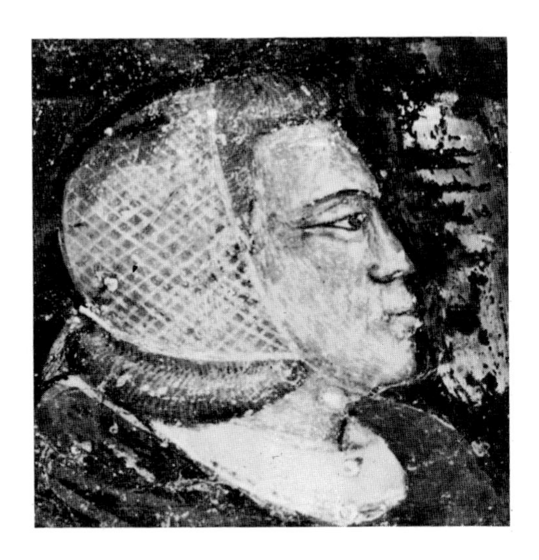

Avignon (Papal Court at)

Ancient capital of the County of Venaissin. Rich in monuments: Papal Palace (1334-92), Notre-Dame-des-Doms, the St. Benezet Bridge over the Rhône. Avignon was the seat of the papacy from 1309 to 1376. The town remained the property of the Roman Catholic Church until 1791.

Bacon, Roger (1214-92)

Franciscan monk and English philosopher, nicknamed " the admirable doctor ", born in Ilchester and died at Oxford. Bacon " saw the history of philosophy rather as an atrophication or an obliteration than a burgeoning " (Edouard Jeauneau). He was also an alchemist and made some interesting discoveries in optics. Among his works are: *Speculum Alchimiae*, and the *Opus Majus*. Bacon is held to be one of the foremost experimental philosophers of the Middle Ages.

Bandol, Jean de

Known as Jean or Hennequin of Bruges. Fourteenth century Flemish illuminator. The Meermann-Westreenen Museum, The Hague, possesses the title-page of a Bible by him, dated 1372. He is equally well known for his drawings and for his designs for tapestries, particularly that for the *Apocalypse* of which a great number were made by the tapestry-maker Nicolas Bataille.

Barna

Italian painter, originally from Siena. The frescoes Barna painted in St. Augustine's, Siena, in the Church of the Holy Spirit, Florence, and other churches in Cortona and Arezzo have disappeared. In 1369(?) he painted a *Crucifixion*, preserved in the episcopal palace at Arezzo, and the *Legend of St. James*, which is in Florence. The *Scenes from the Life of Christ* in the Church

Giovanni Baronzio (da Rimini) (died before 1362)
Scenes from the Life of Christ (detail)
Descent from the Cross
National Museum of Ancient Art,
Barberini Palace, Rome

of San Gimignano, an unfinished work, are among his most celebrated frescoes. According to Vasari, Barna met his death in this church when a scaffolding collapsed.

Baronzio, Giovanni

Italian painter of the Rimini school, died before 1362. Baronzio was the author of a polyptych carried out in 1345; this picture was once thought lost but is now in the Urbino Gallery. Among his known works are: *Scenes from the Holy Story* (New York (School) Museum); and the *Samaritan Woman at the Well* (Pesaro Museum).

Barrel Vault

Name given to an arch whose section forms a semi-circle. The barrel vault was much used in Romanesque architecture, e.g. at the Trinity of Caen and the Abbey of Jumièges, etc.

Bartoli di Fredi (c. 1330-c. 1410)

Italian painter working in Siena; we still have some of his frescoes at San Gimignano. The Siena Museum preserved many works including *The Death of the Virgin* and a *Madonna*; the Louvre has a *Presentation at the Temple* on display.

Bataille, Nicolas (c. 1330-c. 1405)

French tapestry-maker who between 1377 and 1381 made for the Duke of Anjou the tapestries of the *Apocalypse* designed by Jean de Bandol and preserved in the Tapestry Museum at Angers. The *Apocalypse* was ordered by Louis I of Anjou for his castle at Angers. Originally, it comprised seven great pieces each forming fifteen pictures of which seventy scenes have come down to us. The *Apocalypse* is the oldest known tapestry—Queen Mathilda's embroidery at Bayeux has always wrongly been called tapestry. With Pierre Beaumetz and Jacques Dourdin, Nicolas Bataille made several tapestries depicting the life of Du Guesclin.

Bayeux (Cathedral of)

Notre-Dame Cathedral, Bayeux, was consecrated in 1077. The nave was constructed in Romanesque style. Bishop Henri continued the decoration in Gothic style at the beginning of the 13th century. The stained glass of the great window in the façade is 15th century. In the Capitular room are preserved some frescoes representing Notre-Dame of Bayeux. The cathedral treasury possesses a fine collection of

12th and 13th century illuminated manuscripts, and until the Revolution it housed Queen Mathilda's famous embroidery, which is now in the former residence of the archbishop.

Beaumetz, Jean de (d. 1396)

French painter, born in Cambrai, attached to the court of Philip the Bold, Duke of Burgundy. Between 1384 and 1387 he produced many pictures for the Carthusian convent at Champmol. Also between 1388 and 1391 he decorated both the chapel of Argilly Castle (Côte-d'Or) and the Château de Germolle. Both these castles have since been destroyed and none of this artist's work has come down to us. It is only known from contemporary writings.

Beaumetz, Pierre

Late 14th century French tapestry-maker who, with Nicolas Bataille and Jacques Dourdin, many times depicted the life of Du Guesclin.

Beauneveu, André

French painter, illuminator and sculptor, born at Valenciennes in the first half of the 14th century, died at Bourges c. 1413. In 1360 he decorated the castle of Yolande de Bar at Nieppe. Three years after his return to Valenciennes in 1361 he made a certain number of statues for Charles V intended for the Basilica of St. Denis. The King's brother, the Duke of Berry, took Beauneveu into his service; among other works, the painter illustrated a *Psalter for the Duke of Berry* and *The Very Beautiful Hours*. Among his sculptures are: the tombs of Philip VI of Valois, of John the Good, of Jeanne of Burgundy, and of Charles V, which are in the Basilica of St. Denis.

Bellechose, Henri

Flemish painter born in Brabant, attached to the courts of the Dukes of Burgundy between 1415 and 1440, died some time between 1440 and 1444. Henri Bellechose worked mostly in Dijon. In 1415 while he was court painter to John the Fearless, the latter commissioned him to do some paintings for the Carthusian convent of Champmol, which have since disappeared; two of his paintings are in the Louvre: *The Last Communion and Martyrdom of St. Denis* (begun by Malouel) and the *Christ on the Cross.*

Bellini

Family of Venetian painters: Jacopo, who was born in Venice, worked there, and died in 1470; and his two sons, Gentile (1429-1507) who worked in Venice and in Constantinople, and Giovanni, the most illustrious. Gentile's *Portrait of Mahomet*

Gentile Bellini (1429-1507)
Procession in St. Mark's Square (detail)
Academy Museum, Venice

Bonaventura di Berlinghiero
Saint Francis
Church of St. Francis, Pescia

II is in London; Giovanni has left, among other works, *The Miracle of the Holy Cross*, the *Dead Christ* and a *Transfiguration*, in the Venice Museum.

Berlinghiero, Bonaventura di

Italian painter retaining the Byzantine style. He is best known for his picture of St. Francis of Assisi, from about 1235, which is in the church of St. Francis at Pescia.

Berry (Duke of) (1340-1416)

John of France, Duke of Berry, son of John II, born at Vincennes. The court of the Duke of Berry at Bourges was the most brilliant in all France at that time. The Duke was a collector of tapestries, precious metalwork and jewellery, paintings and illuminated manuscripts, and attached a great number of artists to his court from whom he ordered numerous works, among them: *The Great Hours of the Duke of Berry* illuminated by Jacquemart de Hesdin, National Library, Paris; the same library also possesses this artist's *The Little Hours of the Duke of Berry*; André Beauneveu, attached to the court of the Duke of Berry in 1396, made the stained glass for the Sainte-Chapelle, Bourges, and illuminated a psalter for the Duke which is in the French National Library. *The Very Rich Hours of the Duke of Berry*, produced c. 1416 by the Limbourg brothers, is preserved in the Condé Museum, Chantilly.

Besozzo, Michelino da

Italian painter and illuminator who lived during the 15th century. At the beginning of his career he lived in Pavia and belonged to the Lombardian school. Between 1420 and 1425 Besozzo worked in Milan Cathedral. In 1430 he went to Venice, but returned to work in Milan from 1439 to 1442. The pictures in Milan Cathedral depicting a *Madonna Enthroned* and the *Presentation in the Temple* are attributed to him.

Blanche of Navarre

Daughter of Philip III of Evreux, King of Navarre, and of Jeanne II; she became the second wife of Philip VI of Valois, King of France from 1328-50.

Bonaiuti da Firenze, Andrea (d. 1377)

Italian painter who in 1365 carried out the frescoes in the Spanish chapel of Santa Maria Novella, Florence. The wall behind the altar is decorated with scenes of the Passion; on the ceiling, among other subjects, are *The Resurrection* and *The Ascension*: on the right and left walls respectively, *The Church Triumphant* and *The Triumph of St. Thomas Aquinas*.

Luis Borrassa (late 14th and early 15th century)
Pentecost reredos (1394)
Centre panel of the predella (1411)
Manresa Cathedral

Jean Bourdichon (1494)
The Dauphin Charles of Orland
Private Collection, London

Borch, Michel Van der

Dutch miniaturist and illuminator of the first half of the 14th century. The name Michel Van der Borch appears on the title-page of a Flemish Bible by Jacob Van Maelant, a Flemish calligrapher of the second half of the 13th century. This Bible is ornamented with seventy-two miniatures and numerous illuminated capitals. The manuscript is preserved in the Meermann Westreenen Museum at The Hague.

Borrassa, Luis (d. 1424)

Late 14th and early 15th century Spanish painter born in Gerona, of a long line of painters. It is not known how Borrassa started, but he is first encountered at the court of Juan I of Aragon, the rendezvous

for artists at that period. After having carried out a reredos for the Minorites of Tarragona in 1389, he set up his workshop in Barcelona and worked there from 1390 until his death. The polyptych tracing the life of St. John the Baptist now in the Museum of Decorative Arts, Paris, is attributed to the workshop of Luis Borrassa. Borrassa's painting is distinguished by a natural style; he, Bassa Ferrer and Bernado Martorell represent the Valencian group.

Bosch, Hieronymus (c. 1450/1460-1516)

Dutch painter and engraver, born and died at Bois-le-Duc in the Low Countries. His moralistic tendency and his strongly fantastic vision link Bosch to a certain extent with medieval painting. His representation of the details of daily life classes him as the precursor of the realist school of the Low Countries. Bosch possessed a boundless imagination, and depicted man's eternal struggle with himself and with his enemy represented in the form of devils and fantastic beings and animals, half-human, half-beast. In 1504, at the request of Philip the Fair, he painted his *Last Judgement*, now in the Fine Arts Museum, Antwerp. His works are divided among the principal European museums.

Bourdichon, Jean (c. 1457-1521)

French painter and miniaturist, born and died at Tours. It is known that Bourdichon was painter to Louis XI, Charles VIII, Louis XII and Francis I. The miniatures in the *Hours of Anne of Brittany* in the National Library, Paris, are attributed to him. This work shows great delicacy and reliable integrity. The same library has his *Hours of Ferdinand King of Naples*, the *Hours of King Charles VIII* and an early 16th century Roman missal.

Bourges (Cathedral)

Bourges Cathedral was built in the 13th century and consecrated in 1324. Its nave is remarkable for the absence of transepts. The stained glass in the cathedral choir dates from the first third of the 13th century: *Virgin and Infant Jesus*, *St. Stephen*, prophets, evangelists and apostles. In the first ambulatory can be seen *The Virgin and Christ the Judge*, *The Annunciation*, *The Last Judgement*, *St. Stephen*, *St. Lawrence* and eight more medallions of archbishops of Bourges (twenty-eight others were destroyed in the 18th century to improve the lighting). The West Door is remarkable and the statuary there is some of the most perfect in all Gothic art. In the Middle Ages the Cathedral environs sheltered the famous workshops of painters, glaziers and illuminators.

Breughel, Pieter (c. 1525-69)

Flemish painter born at Bruegel in Brabant, died in Brussels. Pieter Breughel served his artistic apprenticeship under the instruction of a disciple of Hieronymus Bosch, who persuaded him to travel to Antwerp with Pierre Coeck d'Alast, painter to Charles V. In 1551, Breughel left for Italy. He had to go through France and stayed there two years. He arrived in Rome in 1553. At this time he produced his *Naval Battle in the Straits of Messina*. He was little influenced by Italy, and returned to Flanders in 1554. He married the daughter of Pierre Coeck d'Alast, settled in Brussels, and lived there until his death. From his return to Brussels, Breughel's art moved to its height. He concentrated first on landscapes, then on religious compositions which show the dramatic realism so characteristic of his work. Of this period are: the *Tower of Babel* in the Vienna Museum; and the *Road to Calvary*. During the last years of his life Breughel abandoned the canvases of enormous scope and treated mainly familiar scenes with a smaller number of people. He was misunderstood by his contemporaries, who nicknamed him Breughel the Peasant, and the Jester.

Broederlam, Melchior

Flemish painter, born at Ypres, where he worked from 1381 to 1409. Broederlam was painter and valet to Philip the Bold, Duke of Burgundy. In 1387, he designed the encaustic tiles in the castle of Hesdin. In 1395 he worked at Ghent and on the request of Philip the Bold soon began the triptychs of the two altars at Dijon. Two panels are in the Dijon museum: *The Annunciation and the Visitation*, *The Presentation in the Temple*, and *The Flight into Egypt*. The Valencia Museum has a *Christ in the Tomb*. A votive tablet now in the chapel of the Civil Hospital, Ypres, is very likely also by him.

Cahors (Cathedral of)

Cathedral with cupolas, built in the 12th century. The west cupola is decorated with 14th century frescoes due to the generosity of Pope John XXII, a native of Cahors. They were carried out by an Avignon workshop and depict the stoning of St. Stephen. At the end of the last century, the Gothic frescoes in the east cupola were criminally distempered; they are now irrecoverable.

Calligrapher

Copyist who was a past master in the art of designing letters. Calligraphy was the highest art of the monk copyists in the Middle Ages. Due to them a large proportion of ancient philosophical works were translated and preserved in the monasteries. Originally, the occupations of calligrapher and miniaturist were one and the same.

Cameo-painting

Term given to a type of painting where the artist uses only different shades of the same colour. It was employed mainly in the later illumination period; manuscripts illustrated with cameo plates include *Philip the Good's Book of Hours* executed at the end of the first half of the 15th century in the workshop of Jean le Tavernier.

Canonisation

Canonisation is the decision of the Pope by which he appoints a churchman or a layman to the number of Saints of the Church. Canonisation is always governed by precise rules. If the person is accepted by the Congregation of rites, he is first of all declared "venerable". It is only when his exercise of Christian virtues has been proved and evidence of at least two miracles has been obtained that the Pope accords him "beatification". Two more miracles are necessary to introduce the procedure which consists of examining the virtues and the writings of the elect; this procedure is followed by pleadings between "God's Advocate" and the "Devil's Advocate". Only then does the Pope agree to or reject the canonisation.

Canterbury (Cathedral of)

Canterbury Cathedral was built on the site of a church dedicated by St. Augustin in 587 when he came to England from Rome with his forty monks. The first choir of the final construction was destroyed by fire in 1174; the present choir was constructed between 1174 and 1180 by Guillaume de Sens (known as William the Frenchman) in a transitional style between Norman and Early English. The nave and transepts were rebuilt in 1421. It was in this cathedral that Thomas à Becket, Archbishop of Canterbury, was assassinated on 29th December 1170. In the choir are several beautiful 13th century windows.

Cathedral

Church containing the liturgical seat of the bishop or archbishop. Cathedrals usually form an immense cross consisting of the nave leading up to the choir and the transepts to left and right. There are many exceptions to this rule, such as

Head of Christ, attributed to Pietro Cavallini
Last Judgement (detail)
Convent of St. Cecilia, Rome

Bourges, which has no transept, Beauvais, which has no nave, and Cahors, where cupolas crown the nave and the transepts. Most cathedrals are orientated: the choir points to Jerusalem. Winchester Cathedral is one of the longest in Europe, Ulm has one of the highest bell-towers—542 feet.

Cavallini, Pietro

Italian painter who lived between 1250 and 1330. He was probably born in Rome. He worked in Naples in 1308 in the service of King Robert II of Anjou. Cavallini also had a workshop at Rimini.

Celtic

Pertaining to the Celts. This was the name given by the Romans to that part of ancient Gaul between the Seine and the Garonne. The Celtic people, of Indo-European origin, settled in central Europe around the 10th century B.C. They were shortly driven back towards the Atlantic and settled in Spain, France, Ireland, Scotland, Wales and parts of England.

Charlemagne (742-814)

Born in Neustria, died in Aix-la-Chapelle. He was the son of Pépin the Short, and in 768 succeeded his father and reigned with his brother Carloman until the latter died in 771. After his glorious campaign against Lombardy (773-4) he took the title of King of Lombardy. Between 781 and 799 he conquered Bavaria and the country of the Avars. Pope Leo III crowned him Emperor of the West in the year 800. The later years of his reign were darkened by the incursions of the Normans. He was a great patron of learning and founded numerous schools and universities. The project of forming a centralised Europe, as it was under Roman domination, crumbled at his death and the empire was divided into three parts. The Treaty of Verdun in 843 ratified this division.

Charles IV the Fair (1294-1328)

Third son of Philip IV the Fair and Jeanne of Navarre. Charles IV was King of France from 1322 until his death in 1328. He is the last king of the Capetian dynasty in direct line. He drove the Lombardian bankers out of France; he neutralised Guyenne and made peace with England.

Charles V (1338-80)

Son of John II the Good and Bona of Luxembourg. Charles V was King of

Froissart Chronicles
Baptism of Charles the Dauphin
National Library, Paris

France from 1364 until his death in 1380. His reign was distinguished by prudent policy, which was happily applied during the War of Burgundian Succession. Aided by great captains, Du Guesclin, Clisson and Boucicaut, he rid France of the pillagers who infested the roads—the Great Companies. After a methodic war of attrition, he threw the English out of France, leaving them with only Calais, Cherbourg, Brest and Bordeaux. Charles V was responsible for financial reforms and the extension of university privileges. He had many palaces built or improved, including the Louvre, Vincennes Castle, and the Hôtel Saint-Pol. He also gathered a large collection of manuscripts which formed the basis of the future National Library of France.

Charles VI (1368-1422)

Son of Charles V and Jeanne of Bourbon. Charles VI was King of France from 1380 until his death in 1422. At the beginning of his reign he was advised by his uncles whose policy led to the Maillotin Revolt. After defeating the Flemish at Roosebeke Charles VI dismissed his uncles and replaced them with his father's former councillors, the Marmousets, who gave him the nickname of the Well-Loved. During an expedition against the Duke of Brittany, Charles VI was struck by insanity. With the Treaty of Troyes, 1420, the kingdom fell almost entirely into the hands of the English after the bloody battle of Agincourt in 1415.

Charles the Bold (1433-77)

Born at Dijon. Son of Philip the Good and Isabella of Portugal. Charles the Bold, last Duke of Burgundy, tried to reconstitute the Kingdom of Lotharingia. After the battle of Montlhéry in 1465, he made Louis XI sign the Treaties of Conflans and St. Maur on behalf of the League of Public Good. Then he formed a new league against the King after the Liège insurrection of 1467-8. At the head of a third league, he miscarried before Beauvais and Rouen. He was killed before Nancy while fighting René II, Duke of Lorraine, whom he had deprived of his dukedom.

Chartres (Cathedral of)

From the architectural point of view, the Cathedral of Notre-Dame of Chartres, with Reims and Amiens, marks one of the most important stages in the development of the Gothic style. It was, as Emile Mâle writes: "the very thought of the Middle Ages made visible". Except for the porches and the gables of the transept, the construction of the cathedral was completed in 1225. The rose window of the façade dates from the beginning of the 13th century and represents the *Last Judge-*

ment. With those of Bourges Cathedral, the windows of Chartres form the most perfect collection of 13th century stained glass that has come down to us. The aisle windows date from the first quarter of the century, the others mainly from the first half. Under the rose window of the façade there are three windows of about 1250, made in the Chartres workshops, and depicting: the Stem of Jesse, the Childhood of Christ, and the scenes of the Passion. Between 1210 and 1240 the workshops supplied the stained glass for 156 windows. Those of the aisle represent scenes from the Old and New Testaments, scenes from the lives of saints and biblical scenes; in the high ones are figures of prophets, apostles and martyrs. The north rose, given by St. Louis, and known as the Rose of France, features the glorification of the Virgin; the south one shows the glorification of Christ. One of the masterpieces of 12th century stained glass is in Notre-Dame-de-la-Belle-Verrière (Our Lady of the Beautiful Glass) near the south crossing. The whole of Chartres Cathedral forms a perfect harmony due both to its style and to the light flooding through its stained-glass windows.

Chaucer, Geoffrey (c. 1340-1400)

English poet, born in London. He was valet to Edward III and accompanied him on his journeys. In his *Canterbury Tales* he portrayed daily life in 14th century England, while drawing his inspiration from Boccaccio. He is one of the greatest English poets; his style and vocabulary have helped to determine the contemporary English language.

Chevrier, Jean

French illuminator of the first half of the 14th century. In 1343 he decorated, with Jean Pucelle, the *Belleville Breviary*, which is preserved in the National Library, Paris.

Christ-in-Glory

Christ carved on the tympanum of the west door of a church or cathedral and placed at the summit of the composition of subjects represented. The Christ-in-Glory is the high judge of the Last Judgement and is often shown with arms extended.

Cimabue (b. c. 1240, d. after 1302)

Italian painter and architect born in Florence. Little is known of his life. On the other hand, we do know that he was in Rome in 1272, and that in 1301 he worked at Pisa, where the following year he finished the mosaic depicting St. John the Evangelist in the apse of the cathedral

Cimabue
The Sacrifice of Isaac
Upper Church of St. Francis, Assisi

—it had been started by a master called Francesco. Cimabue's principal work is the set of frescoes he painted probably between 1277 and 1281 for the Church of St. Francis at Assisi. In the north arm of the transept of the lower church he painted the Virgin surrounded by angels with St. Francis; in the choir and transept of the upper church, two *Crucifixions* and scenes from the Apocalypse, the life of the Virgin and the lives of St. Peter and St. Paul; on the vault, the four Evangelists. The frescoes are by Cimabue with some assistance from his pupils. While remaining faithful to Byzantine tradition, he gave forms a new dimension; he brought Byzantine monumentality down to earth, making it more massive and therefore less spiritualised. In his *Divine Comedy*, Dante credits him with the great qualities of an historical painter. Among some of his works now in museums are: a *Virgin with Angels* (Louvre), (school work), *Madonna with Angels* (Uffizi).

Cione, Bernado

Italian painter and architect working in the mid-14th century. He was the elder brother of the painter Andrea di Cione, called Orcagna, also his master. Together, about 1355, they painted frescoes in the Strozzi chapel of Santa Maria Novella, Florence: *Paradise*, *Hell*, and the *Last Judgement* with the portrait of Dante.

Cistercian

Pertaining to Citeaux. Near to this village on the Côte-d'Or, Robert de Molesme founded in 1098 a religious community stemming from the Benedictine order. St. Bernard reformed the new order and in 1150 founded in his turn the Abbey of Clairvaux (Aube). The two original monasteries have disappeared; only Clairvaux was reconstructed in the 18th century. In medieval Europe the Cistercian influence was enormous in all fields, political, scientific, economic and cultural. There is a Cistercian style, very sober, breaking with the magnificence of the Benedictine abbeys and well expressing the mysticism of St. Bernard. The Cistercian monks swarmed almost everywhere in France and the rest of Europe. Fontenay Abbey (Côte-d'Or), founded in 1118, represents the model followed by all Cistercian monasteries. While Cistercian houses spread over Europe, an architectural influence could be perceived stretching from Norway to Greece. After some vicissitudes, the Cistercian Order was once more reformed in the 17th century by the Abbot of Rancé, who refounded the monastery of La Trappe, near Soligny (Orne), whence came the name of Trappists given to those Cistercian monks. At present there are seventeen Cistercian abbeys in France.

Clément

French painter-glazier of the 13th century, born at Chartres. Between 1235 and 1240 he made a stained-glass window in the chapel of the Virgin in the Cathedral of Notre-Dame at Rouen and signed it "Clemens vitrarius Carnotensis me fecit". It is probable that Clément worked for the cathedral and the churches of Rouen.

Clermont-Ferrand (Cathedral of)

The building of the Cathedral of Notre-Dame at Clermont-Ferrand was begun in 1248 by the architect Jean Deschamps (also the architect of Narbonne Cathedral) on the site of a Romanesque Cathedral. It was consecrated in 1346, while still unfinished. All the chapels in the lower parts are ornamented with late 13th century windows representing legends of the Saints. St. George's chapel has two 13th century frescoes: *The Martyrdom of St. George*, and a battle scene. In the sacristy of the chapterhouse another 13th century fresco can be seen, depicting *The Crucifixion.*

Clouet, François (1522-72)

French painter attached to the courts of Francis I, Henry II, Francis II and Charles IX. He was a great portraitist. His pictures and drawings are dispersed among the European museums. Clouet's painting is characterised, like that of his father, by considerable gravity, profound psychological study, and a rigorous search for essential likeness, stripped of superfluous detail. The museums of the Louvre and Chantilly possess numerous portraits by this painter.

Cluny Museum

Mansion of the abbots of Cluny Monastery, built in Paris in the 15th century. Converted into a museum, it houses a collection of 14th, 15th and 16th century objets d'art. Its tapestries are famous, particularly *The Lady with the Unicorn*, which dates from the beginning of the 16th century.

Concordance, Biblical

Alphabetical list of all words mentioned in the Bible. The first edition of concordance tables appeared in the times of the Church Fathers.

Conxolus

Romanesque painter who lived in the first half of the 13th century. A number of works signed by him exist, particularly a large *Virgin* in the lower church of Subiaco. In the convent of Sagro Speco, Subiaco, is a picture of St. Francis carried out in 1228 by one of his pupils. This and the one by Berlinghiero are the oldest known pictures of St. Francis.

Council of Trent

The most important of all the ecumenical councils, it lasted eighteen years from 13th December 1545, the date of the first session, to 4th December 1563, the last day of the twenty-fourth and final one. Five popes succeeded one another in the course of its duration. It was dissolved twice because of religious wars which embroiled Europe at that epoch. It can be divided into three periods: the first dealt with the confirmation of the Holy Scriptures, the definition of original sin, and the justification of the Sacraments in general, baptism and confirmation in particular; the second was troubled by the disagreement of the German princes who made light of the council, until finally they rallied to the directives from Trent and the work was able to continue; the third period, in which the Pope was able to offer safe-conduct to Protestants who attended the later sessions. The twenty-first session determined the doctrine on Holy Communion; the twenty-second dealt with the Holy Sacrament of the Mass and left to the Pope the decision about communion in two kinds. Between this session and the next there took place the famous discussion on the relation of the episcopacy with the Roman Primacy: to know whether the bishop derived his authority directly from the Pope or from Christ himself. The Italians upheld the first opinion; the Spaniards the second. Finally, the question was suspended until the last Council of the Second Vatican. The Council of Trent fundamentally reorganised the Catholic Church.

Crusades

Expeditions to the Holy Land patronised by the Church, which took place from the 11th to the 13th centuries. There seem to have been eight. At first, the dominant aim was to liberate the tomb of Christ and enable pilgrims to visit it as in the past. But very quickly the Crusades became more than solely religious enterprises; men "took up the cross", as they said, but were influenced by all the political opinions in Europe and the Mediterranean. Soon it was necessary to take up the Cross to defend the principalities established in the Holy Land, so the Crusades then became permanent military operations. Between the first Crusade (1096-9), which was preached by Peter the Hermit (St. Bernard preached the second at Vezelay in 1147) and the eighth and last (1270), during which St. Louis died, a Christian kingdom was founded in the East. This caused profound repercussions in Jewish and Arab countries and in Europe, and the subsequent relationships between Europeans and Orientals were often fertile in spite of intermittent squabbles. Gothic architecture was "exported" and numerous Gothic churches sprang up in Syria, Lebanon and Cyprus (Notre-Dame of Famagusta); strongholds were built: the Knight's Krack, Sidon Castle, etc. New economic ties were established, and oriental thought made its appearance in European universities. Many feudalists were ruined in the Crusades, which hastened the emancipation of the "communes", and the centralisation of royal power, particularly in France. They had a great effect on the arts: Villehardouin (fourth Crusade) and Joinville were the first French chroniclers.

Miniature
Crusade
National Library, Paris

Bernado Daddi (late 13th century-1350)
Madonna and Child
Thyssen Collection, Lugano

Dante: *The Divine Comedy*
Inferno: The Mysterious Forest
Imola Library

Daddi, Bernardo

Florentine painter born at the end of the 13th century, died about 1350. He was one of Giotto's best pupils. He is credited with the decoration of the Berardi Chapel, where his frescoes recount the stories of St. Lawrence and St. Stephen, and also the great gates of the old town of Florence. With Jacopo Sandini Casentino, he founded St. Luke's Academy, Florence.

Dalmau, Luis

Painter of the Flemish school. He worked at Barcelona between 1428 and 1460. Nothing is known about his youth. He may have held the title of painter to the King of Spain. While carrying out a mission in Flanders for Alphonso V he saw the reredos *The Lamb of God* by the Van Eyck brothers which was placed in the church of St. Bavon, Ghent, in 1432. From 1433 onwards we find Dalmau at Barcelona, where in 1445 he finished his altar screen, *The Virgin of the Councillors of Barcelona*, now in the town's municipal museum. This reredos, which clearly shows the influence of Jan Van Eyck, is the only one of this artist's works to survive.

Dante Alighieri (1265-1321)

The greatest Italian poet, born in Florence. His education was extensive and he very early became interested in philosophy and the sciences of his time. Politically involved, he was a supporter of the Guelphs (for the Pope), who were at war with the Ghibellines (partisans of the German Emperor). His native town entrusted him with several diplomatic missions. When his enemies regained power, they condemned him to death. His house was razed and his property confiscated, so he began a life of exile which took him to Northern Italy, the Tyrol, and Paris, where

he lived for some time. Balzac wrote a portrait of him in one of his philosophical novels, entitled *Les Proscrits*. He returned to Italy and settled in Ravenna, where he died. Dante wrote numerous sonnets and canzoni; he sang of his love for Beatrice Portinari, but he is mainly known for *The Divine Comedy*, a vast poem written in Italian, with three parts: *Inferno*, *Purgatory*, and *Paradise*; *New Life*; and a political treatise, *On Monarchy*, written in Latin. In his *Convivio*, Dante explains the purpose of poetry thus: "It is necessary to know that writings can be understood and should be explicit preferably in four senses. The first can be called literal, and does not go beyond the meaning of the letter; the next can be called allegorical, and hides under the cloak of parables... The third sense is moral, and the readers should pay great attention to seeking this in the writing for their benefit and that of their disciples... The fourth can be called anagogical, in other words super-sense: this is achieved when a writing is explained from a spiritual point of view which represents the things of eternal life both in the literal sense and by what it implies..." *The Divine Comedy* was one of the most popular works of medieval literature.

Del Castagno (c. 1410-57)

Florentine painter, born in Castagno, worked all his life in Florence and died there. He decorated the church of San Miniato fra le Torri, where he painted an *Assumption*; he also painted the nine portraits of famous men and women in the convent of Santa Apollonia, a *St. Andrew* in the cemetery of Santa Maria Novella and a series of small frescoes in the Villa Carducci.

Destorrent, Ramón

Fourteenth century Spanish painter who succeeded Ferrer Bassa as painter appointed to Peter IV the Ceremonious, King of Aragon. He worked in Barcelona. The only surviving work of this painter is the Iravalls reredos dedicated to Martha and Mary. It is at the Tower of Carol in the Eastern Pyrenees. It is a beautiful example of Spanish Gothic painting influenced by the Sienese school.

Dierck Van Delft

Dutch painter who worked at Delft during the 15th century. Practically nothing is known of his life or his work. In 1428 he did a painting of St. Christopher for the Church of St. Ursula.

Dourdin, Jacques

Late 14th century French tapestry-maker who, with Nicolas Bataille and Pierre Beaumetz, made many representations of the life of Du Guesclin.

Druidical

Pertaining to Druids, the ancient Gallic and British priests. The Druidical religion had no temple and the priests assembled the faithful in the forest. The Druids were the repositories of divine power and interpreted the celestial signs. The Druidical religion believed in the immortality and transmigration of the soul. Druids possessed judiciary powers and had great political influence among the clans.

Duccio di Buoninsegna (c. 1260-1318)
The Flight into Egypt
Cathedral Museum, Siena

Duccio di Buoninsegna (d. 1318)

Italian painter of the Sienese school. His birth is estimated around 1260. A document dated 1278 tells us that he was then an established painter in Siena. In his youth he also worked in Florence, Lucca, Pisa and Pistoia. Duccio was one of the greatest Sienese painters. At a time when Siena had not yet formed a "school", Duccio founded his own which had a profound influence on Italian Trecento painting. A great many of the works have disappeared, particularly those from Lucca, Pisa and Pistoia. But his masterpiece, *La Maestà*, painted for Siena Cathedral, has survived. It is now exhibited near the church in the Opera del Duomo Museum. This reredos traces the life of Christ in twenty-six sections and also depicts the enthronement of the Virgin, and when it was finished the town of Siena hailed it as a miracle. A century later it disappeared into oblivion and Ghiberti himself in the 15th century called it, inaccurately, *The Crowning of the Virgin*. Vasari seems to have seen Duccio as the artist who reinstated coloured pavings and mosaics. Finally, *La Maestà* was relegated to a cathedral storehouse in 1506. What remains of Duccio's work is scattered among museums and private collections: *The Nativity* and *Two Prophets* in Berlin; a triptych (*The Annunciation* and *The Transfiguration*) in the National Gallery, London; *The Raising of Lazarus* (New York), a *Madonna* in the Perugia Picture Gallery; several figures of male and female saints at Rome in the Stroganov collection, and, in his native town, *La Maestà* in the Opera del Duomo, and the bust of an angel in the Saracini Palace.

Duecento

Italian for 13th century. This term applied solely to the Italian Gothic period, 1200-1300.

Dupont, Jacques (contemporary)

French art-critic and historian. Author of several works on Gothic Painting, including: *Les Primitifs français*, Paris, 1937, and *La Peinture gothique*, Geneva, 1954.

Durham Cathedral

In 1092 the Bishop William of St. Calais settled the plans for the construction of the cathedral; he built the choir and began the transept and the nave, which were finished in 1140 with the hall of the chapterhouse. The Lady, or Galilee, Chapel was constructed in 1175; the Chapel of the Nine Altars, which forms the east transept, is Early English in style and dates from 1280. The cloister and other parts of the tower were built during the 15th century. Durham Cathedral is a classic example of the first cathedrals in Anglo-Norman style.

Edward III (1312-77)

Son of Edward II; King of England from 1327 until his death in 1377. His mother was regent at the beginning of his reign, but in 1330 he got rid of her and her favourite Mortimer by a coup d'état. He conquered Scotland. He dreamed of uniting his kingdom with France and creating an Anglo-Franco-Norman community. He started the Hundred Years War and was victorious in the battles of Sluys and Crécy. He forced the peace on John the Good (Treaty of Brétigny). Edward III founded the Order of the Garter.

Epinal

The Epinal Museum was the first French museum to make a collection of popular prints, which have since remained famous under the name of Epinal prints. The great period of Epinal prints was the 19th century.

Escorial

Palace built by Philip II about 25 miles from Madrid to fulfil a vow made during the battle of St. Quentin. It was designed in the form of a grille to recall the martyrdom of St. Lawrence. This monastery-palace served as a sepulchre for the Spanish kings. Philip II died there in 1598.

Etigny (Church)

In 1950 the Abbé Boucher, who officiated there, brought some 13th century mural paintings to light. They were devoted to the miracles of St. Martin, recounted by his disciple Sulpicius Severus. They are a good example of Gothic painting with their fresh tonalities and lifelike attitudes.

Saint
Mural painting (c. 1230)
Etigny Church (Yonne)

Evrard of Orleans (c. 1270-c. 1357)

French painter, sculptor and architect. He worked for several nobles at the French court and was appointed to the Countess of Burgundy, Mahout of Artois. He is known to have decorated the abbey of Maubuisson, near to Pontoise. Little else is known about his life or his work.

Ex-voto

Object or inscription placed in a church or chapel in gratitude for a favour obtained.

Jean Fouquet
Virgin and Child
c. 1450
Fine-Arts Museum, Antwerp

Ferrer, Bassa (1290-1348)

Spanish painter and miniaturist who worked in Barcelona for the Kings Alphonso IV and Pedro IV of Aragon. His only surviving work is the set of murals, finished in 1336, in St. Michael's Chapel of the Convent of the Poor Clares at Pedralbes near to Barcelona.

Folio

Page of arbitrary dimensions which, when folded in two, represents four pages of a book. The term is also used to describe a book made up of such pages.

Foliole

Little leaf assembled with others to form a whole, as for the calyx of a flower, or an oak or acacia leaf.

Fouquet, Jean (c. 1420-c. 1480)

French painter and miniaturist, born in Tours, son of a priest and a prostitute. His work emerged from oblivion in 1805, thanks to a German collector, George Brentano-Laroche, who discovered forty miniatures of the *Hours of Etienne Chevalier*. The archives tell us little about Fouquet's activities. A few miniatures of *Judaic Antiquities* in the National Library, Paris, were able to be identified as by his hand. His work also shows the monumental dignity of Dierck Bouts and Piero della Francesca, who were his contemporaries. One of his masterpieces is *The Virgin Surrounded by Red and Blue Angels*, Fine Arts Museum, Antwerp. Jean Fouquet can be considered as one of the creators of French painting.

Fra Angelico (Giovanni da Fiesole) (1387-1455)

Dominican father and painter, born at Vecchio in Tuscany. The grace, freshness of tone and profound religious inspiration of his paintings make him considered one of the greatest artists of the Florentine Quattrocento. He decorated St. Mark's Convent, Florence—*Annunciation, Coro-*

nation of the Virgin and *Descent from the Cross*—and the chapel of St. Stephen and St. Lawrence in the Vatican.

Franco Bolognese

Italian painter and miniaturist working at the beginning of the 14th century. He was probably the pupil of Oderigi de Gubbio. Franco Bolognese was also the founder of a school of painting at Bologna attended by Vitale, Lorenzo, Simone Jacopo and Christoforo, among others.

Frederick II (1194-1250)

Emperor of Germany, born at Iezi, died at Florentino. He was firstly King of Sicily and Germany, then Emperor of the West in 1220. He was excommunicated by Pope Gregory IX. He took part in the sixth Crusade. Italy rose against him. Frederick II was a great lover of art.

Frederick III (1415-93)

Emperor of Germany from 1440 until his death in 1493. Like his ancestor, he was a friend of art, but he was also a pitiful politician. Phlegmatic, apathetic to the point of cowardice, and firmly convinced of the grandeur of his rule, he gave occasion to one of his councillors for this sally: "He would like to conquer the world without moving a muscle". During twenty-seven years he not once left his hereditary province and had himself represented at the Diet by a single ambassador.

Fresco

Method of painting on to a wall so that the colours soak into the lime plaster. This art is delicate and usually involves four basic operations: the preparation of the site, the preparation of the plaster, the application of the cartoon, and the painting itself. Numerous precautions have to be taken, including the degree of dryness of the wall, time of day when the painter must stop because of the sun, polishing of the first layer of colours.

Froment, Nicolas

Fifteenth century French painter, born at Uzès, died at Avignon. Nicolas Froment was one of the most important representatives of the school of French primitive painters, which at the time was undervalued by a public more interested in Italian art. It was Nicolas Froment who, with Enguerrand Quarton, introduced the new Flemish style to the Avignon Papal Court. About 1450, after the Popes had left Avignon, the two artists gathered many pupils who formed the realist stream in the provincial primitive school. We recognise this realist style (of a period considered "crude") in the Avignon *Pietà* and *The Raising of Lazarus*.

Agnolo Gaddi? (c. 1333-96)
Saint Eloy the Goldsmith
Prado Museum, Madrid

G

Gaddi, Agnolo di Taddeo (c. 1333-96)

Florentine painter who spent his youth in Venice. He had a sure talent and a richness of feeling. *The Raising of Lazarus* (San Jacopo tre Fosse, Florence) and eight frescoes on *The Legend of the Cross* in the choir of Santa Croce, Florence, are by him. Berlin possesses a *Virgin and Infant Jesus* and the Louvre has an *Annunciation.*

Gaddi, Giovanni di Taddeo (d. 1383)

Florentine painter, grandson of Gaddo Gaddi, friend of Cimabue, and pupil of his brother Agnolo. He decorated the church of San Spirito, Florence.

Gaibana, Giovanni

Miniaturist of the Italian school working in the 13th century. He is known to have been a priest at Trisigola near Ferrara.

Gener, Gerardo

Painter of the Valencia school. He worked at the end of the 14th and beginning of the 15th century.

Gentile da Fabriano (c. 1370-1427)

Born in Fabriano, a province of Ancona, and died at Rome. According to Vasari, he was a pupil of Fra Angelico. He is recorded as being in Florence in 1420, and as Magister Magistorum among the painters commissioned to decorate Orvieto Cathedral in 1425. He was a great artist, who enjoyed a high reputation in his own lifetime and had numerous pupils. He executed the reredos of the Virgin's altar in St. Nicholas, Florence, and the decorations in St. John Lateran, Rome. Berlin has the *Mary with the Infant Jesus and Two Saints*; Milan has numerous paintings including *The Glorification of the Virgin*; the Louvre, Paris, has a *Presentation in the Temple* and a *Virgin and Child.*

Ghibelline

Name given in Italy to the partisans of the German Emperors of the Holy Roman Empire, in opposition to the partisans of the Pope, the Guelphs. From the 12th to the 15th century these two parties split Italy with their ferocious struggles, which went on right up to the French invasion in 1494.

Giotto (1266-1336)
Noli me tangere (detail)
Fresco (c. 1305)
Scrovegni Chapel, Padua

Ghiberti, Lorenzo (1378-1455)

Italian painter and sculptor, born and died in Florence. It was he who in 1403 began the famous baptistry door in San Giovanni, which numerous critics and authorities agree marks the beginning of the Renaissance as far as sculpture is concerned. This door is divided into twenty-eight medallions and was not finished until twenty years later. Vasari, "a bad critic, but a man who saw through the eyes of the Renaissance" (C. Steiner) did not hesitate to accuse Ghiberti of a certain ingenuousness: "The draperies still retain some of the old style of Giotto", he wrote. Ghiberti carved two more doors; of the last, Michelangelo said that it was worthy to be the door of heaven.

Ghirlandaio (Domenico Currado Bigordi, known as) (1449-94)

One of the most important painters of the Quattrocento, born and died in Florence. He illustrated the life of St. John the Baptist on the chapel walls of Santa Maria Novella, Florence, and painted *The Funeral of St. Francis* at Santa Trinità. He worked in the Sistine Chapel, Rome. He painted numerous portraits.

Giottino

Or Giotto di Maestro Stefano. He lived in the 14th century and was a zealous pupil of Giotto. The frescoes showing scenes from the life of Christ in the crypt chapel of Santa Maria Novella, and the high altar frescoes at Assisi are attributed to him. The Uffizi, Florenze, possesses a *Descent from the Cross.*

Giotto, Ambrogio Bondone (1266 ?-1337)

Born at Colle di Vespignano in Tuscany, he was a remarkable technician, and visionary of genius. Giotto was a peasant's son and himself a shepherd. Cimabue met him guarding his sheep on the road to Bologna, according to Vasari. He must have been astonished at the precocious genius of the child, who was sketching a lamb. He took him with him and made him his pupil. Giotto reset man in the divine creation and reintroduced a taste for truth copied from the heart of nature. He freed art once for all from Byzantine influence. St. Francis of Assisi had brought the Christian religion into natural surroundings; trees, flowers and animals, which only existed as symbols for the people of the Middle Ages, were changed back into realities. This is what Carlo Steiner writes: "The new men, the poets of Dolce Stil Nuovo, perceive the life of

a flower opening its morning petals, the dew glittering on evening branches, the balm of twillight which draws regret from the human heart, and see in them the language of a world entirely renewed. In Umbria, Jacopone da Todi writes his *Stabat Mater*, contemporary with, or only slightly earlier than, the work of Giotto. How can one reconcile this lyric form, so profoundly human and obviously springing from the very soul of the people, this tragedy of the Woman and the Mother, with the Queen of the great Maestà pictures, which are mystic to the point of abstraction? Considered from this angle, Giotto, the former shepherd, is no longer an inexplicable prodigy, but a link in the chain, a fundamental element in one of the most perfect civilisations humanity has ever known." Giotto perfected the art of fresco with incomparable mastery. He passed on his technique to his pupils, who in turn taught the entire world. Dante considered him "the greatest painter of the human race"; Leonardo da Vinci said he was the only one beside Masaccio who remained faithful to truth; Vasari called him "the father of painting". Degas scribbled in one of his notebooks "O Giotto, help me to see Paris!". Giotto decorated the upper basilica at Assisi, and the Arena Chapel at Padua; a remarkable *Madonna* in Florence is attributed to him.

Giovanni da Milano

Painter of the Lombardy school. He was born at Milan in the first half of the 14th century. He executed historical paintings and portraits in several Italian towns. There are some in the Uffizi, Florence, including the *Saints*; in the Metropolitan Museum, New York, *The Virgin and Donors*; at Rome, in the Corsini Gallery, the *Virgin* and the *Life of Christ*.

Giovannino de' Grassi (d. 1398)

Italian painter, sculptor, architect and miniaturist, whose date of birth is unknown. Little remains of his work. He is known to have worked for Milan Cathedral; but only the font in the sacristy decorated by him with *Christ and the Woman of Samaria* has come down to us.

Girard d'Orléans (d. 1361)

French painter known for his *Portrait of John the Good*, preserved in the Louvre. This portrait is painted in distemper. The artist accompanied John the Good into exile in London after his defeat at Poitiers. Girard d'Orléans was also a miniaturist.

Giusto di Menabuoi (d. 1393)

Known as Giusto Padovano. Florentine painter born in the first half of the 14th century, died at Padua. He was very influenced by Giotto and specialised in religious scenes. The National Gallery, London, has a triptych attributed to him

Saint Gregory inspired by the Holy Spirit (993)
State Library, Treviso

representing the *Coronation of the Virgin*. In 1370 he finished the frescoes in the Cortellieri Chapel, Padua.

Gnudi, Cesare (contemporary)

Italian art critic. Of his work we should draw attention to the section on Italian painting in *La Peinture gothique*, Geneva, 1954.

Great Chronicles of France

Manuscript presented to Philip III the Bold, concerning the history of the early Valois. The Chronicles, translated from Latin and published at Saint-Denis in the 13th century, are also known as the *Great Chronicles of Saint-Denis*. The manuscript, ornamented with beautiful miniatures, is preserved in the National Library, Paris. The same library also has the manuscript of *The Great Chronicles of France*, illustrated by Jean Fouquet between 1450 and 1470.

Gregorian

Indicates everything concerning St. Gregory I, 7th century Pope, who effected liturgical changes within the Catholic Church and instituted Gregorian chant, or plain-chant, which suffered a long eclipse during the Renaissance and the classical and post-classical periods, and was only brought back to favour at the end of the 19th century. The Abbot of Solesmes, Dom Guéranger, who died in 1875, was one of those mainly responsible for reinstating Gregorian chant in France.

Grisaille

Monochrome cameo-painting in grey which gives the impression of relief. The range of shades used in grisaille painting can be vast. It was chiefly used for miniatures at the end of the Gothic period. The *Narbonne Frontal*, a painting on silk, is one of the most famous examples of this process.

Grünewald (Mathias Gothart Nithardt, called) (c. 1460-1530)

German painter, famous for the *Issenheim Reredos* preserved in the Colmar Museum. It prefigures modern style but in many ways is still linked to the Primitives and the "Gothic Idea". He was a profoundly original artist, aided by expert technique. He succeeded in incorporating the cosmic element of Christ's message into his painting.

Ridolfo Guariento (known from 1330 to 1365)
Angel
Ceiling panel from the Carraresi Chapel
Civic Museum, Padua

Guariento, Ridolfo

Born in Padua and died before 1370. He is known to have worked on the decoration of the great hall of the Venice Council in 1365. The Eremitani at Padua preserves several frescoes by him. The museum of Bassano possesses a *Crucifixion* with the Virgin and the saints; the Ferdinandeum Museum, Innsbrück, a *Head of a Young Man*; and the Doge's Palace, Venice, the *Paradise*.

Guelphs

Papal partisans in Italy. The Ghibellines rallied to the German Emperor. Their struggles rent Italy from the 12th century until the French invasion of 1494. Dante was a Guelph. The Guelph party was itself split into two parts, the Blacks and the Whites.

Guerau, Antonio

Fifteenth century Spanish painter. He was in Valencia from 1411 to 1439, and in 1425 is mentioned as painter to King Alfonso V of Aragon. He did the paintings in the *Cambra Daurada* in the Valencia Town Hall.

Guild

The guilds were formed in the Middle Ages by artists, artisans and merchants. It was an honour for an artist at that time to be accepted by his town's guild. Most of the great Dutch and Flemish painters were so honoured by the guilds of their towns, which brought them numerous commissions.

Guillaume de Machaut (1300-77)

French poet and musician, Canon of Reims. Principally known for his *Mass of Our Lady*. He was a musician to Charles V.

Hundred Years War

This war between France and England lasted a little over a hundred years, from 1337 to 1453. There were interruptions and long periods of peace. Its causes were dynastic, political and economic. The French lost the early battles, Sluys and Crécy (1346). Ten years later the Black Prince (so-called because he wore black armour) was taken prisoner by John the Good at Poitiers. Anarchy reigned in France and particularly in Paris, where Etienne Marcel attempted to establish a democratic municipality. Then the Treaty of Brittany, 1360, handed half of France to England. With the accession of Charles V there was a reversal. The King was aided by great warriors like Du Guesclin, Clisson and Admiral John of Vienna. By 1380 the English held only five ports in France. There was, however, a further reversal under the reign of Charles VI. After being defeated at Agincourt in 1415, France was once more invaded; but the centre and the south-east remained independent and Charles VII was able to organise a shaky government at Bourges. There, Joan of Arc sought him out and asked his authority to fight. Aided by Dunois, she undertook a successful campaign. After her death in 1431, the English were gradually evicted from the country. They were beaten at Formigny, near Bayeux, in 1450 and at Castillon, on the borders of the Dordogne, in 1453, where the old English Constable Talbot was killed. The Hundred Years War served to consolidate French unity; England, despite brilliant victories early on and in the reign of Charles VI, emerged the poorer, and fell into the civil Wars of the Roses. During this long conflict the arts did not suffer too much. Most of the great cathedrals were finished. This was a period of flamboyant style. Only the Paris school vanished with the Anglo-Burgundian invasion.

Illuminated Capital

Ornamented letter placed at the beginning of a chapter or a paragraph. In medieval manuscripts illuminated capitals usually incorporated a small picture, generally of religious inspiration. The capitals in Irish manuscripts are remarkable for their interlacings.

Illumination

At the height of the Middle Ages the trade of illuminator or calligrapher was the exclusive occupation of monk copyists. The great abbeys like Cluny, Glastonbury and Mont-Saint-Michel, had workrooms, or *scriptoria*, fitted with alcoves where the monks worked. At the start of the Gothic period the art of illumination became secularised and the workrooms of illuminators clustered together in principal towns.

Innocent III (1160-1216)

Pope from 1198-1216. He instigated the fourth Crusade and himself undertook that against the Albigensian heretics. He fought against John the Landless and Philip August. He forced the latter to lay down his arms and seek refuge with the King of England. This Pope had a conception of European unity with the Vatican at its head. The temporal power of the Papacy was never so great as during his reign.

Interlacing

Designs of lines interlaced together. Moorish art offers some beautiful examples (mosques at Córdoba and Granada). For still obscure reasons, interlacing was carried to a high degree of perfection by Irish monks. The Irish "interlace style" inspired sculptors of the great English cathedrals (Winchester, Durham), In France the nave of Bayeux also presents specimens of Irish interlacing. But it is in Romanesque illumination that the examples abound.

J

Jacopino da Bologna

Fifteenth century Italian painter. From 1478 onwards he worked on numerous restorations in Orvieto Cathedral.

Jacopo del Casentino (Landini, known as) (c. 1300-58 ?)

Italian painter and architect, born at Prato Vecchio. He was a pupil of Taddeo Gaddi, whom he followed to Florence in 1349, where they together founded the painters' corporation. We have several works which are dispersed among the important European museums (Florence, London, Budapest, Brussels, Frankfurt).

Jacopo di Paolo

Italian painter who lived in Bologna from the end of the 14th to the middle of the 15th century. Four small pictures are attributed to him, two in the Bologna Picture Gallery and two others in the Di Stefano Museum; the Municipal Museum has an *Annunciation* by him.

Jacquemart de Hesdin

French miniaturist and painter who worked at Hesdin (Pas-de-Calais) in the late 14th and early 15th centuries. He was appointed miniaturist to the town of Paris and painted several miniatures for the *Book of Hours of John Duke of Burgundy*, dating from 1384. In 1400, he also did the illustration for a *Missal for the Duke of Berry*. The *Great Hours of*

Book of Hours of the Duke of Burgundy
St. Mark
Single Combat
15th Century
Condé Museum, Chantilly

the Duke of Berry, preserved in the National Library, Paris, were finished in 1409. The *Very Beautiful Hours of Our Lady* are divided between the Royal Library, Brussels, and the private collection of Maurice Rothschild. The National Library, Paris, also has the *Little Hours of the Duke of Berry* by the same artist.

Jean d'Arbois

Late 14th century French painter working at the court of Philip the Bold, Duke of Burgundy. The Duke engaged him while travelling in Lombardy, and D'Arbois accompanied him to Paris then to Bruges. It was Jean d'Arbois who introduced Melchior Broederlam to the Parisian aesthetic.

Jean de Bruges

See "Bandol, Jean de".

Jean d'Orléans
Fourteenth century French artist. He was court painter to Charles V and valet to Charles VI. He is known to have worked at the castle of Saint-Germain in the 13th century chapel.

Jean Petit de Troyes
Late 14th century French painter attached to the court of Philip the Bold, Duke of Burgundy.

Jeanne of Bourbon (1338-1378)
Born at Vincennes. In 1350 she married Charles V, King of France, who called her "the sun of his kingdom". She died in Paris. Portraits of her and Charles V are shown in profile on the *Narbonne Frontal*, a grisaille on silk, made about 1375 and preserved in the Louvre.

John the Blind (1296-1346)
Or John of Luxembourg. Son of the Emperor Henry VII, he was King of Bohemia from 1310 until his death in 1346. He took part in the Battle of Crécy on the side of Philip VI despite his blindness, and was killed there.

John of Berry
See "Berry, Duke of".

John the Good (1319-64).
John II, the Good, son of Philip VI of Valois, was King of France from 1350 until his death in 1364. Early in his reign he went into battle against Charles the

Funeral Procession of John the Good
14th century miniature
National Library, Paris

Bad, King of Navarre. Many times the estates general had to be convened because of his bad financial management. The struggles between France and England resumed in 1356. John the Good was defeated at Poitiers by the Black Prince. In 1360 he signed the Peace of Brittany and returned to France after a long captivity in London. He was indirectly the founder of the second house of Burgundy by giving the Duchy of Burgundy to his son Philip the Bold. He died in London where he had taken his son's place.

John the Fearless (1371-1419)
Born at Dijon, son of Philip the Bold, he was Duke of Burgundy from 1404 until his death in 1419. In 1407 he had Louis, Duke of Orleans, assassinated. At the head of the Burgundian party, and with the aid of the Cabochiens he seized Paris after the Battle of Agincourt in 1415. Shortly afterwards he tried to reach some agreement with Charles VII, the Dauphin, but he fell into an ambush and was assassinated on the bridge of Montereau by the King's councillors with whom he had come to negotiate. Pol de Limbourg, attached to the court of Burgundy, executed for him the *Breviary of John the Fearless*, preserved in the British Museum, London. Jean Malouel painted his portrait, which was presented to King John II of Portugal.

Joinville, Jean (Master of) (1224-1319)

Joinville Presenting his Memoirs to St. Louis
14th century
National Library, Paris

French chronicler, adviser of St. Louis. He wrote the *Memoirs*, which he finished in 1309, and which dealt with the history of St. Louis and the eighth Crusade. The Joinville *Memoirs* are one of the first great texts of French literature.

Juan I of Aragon (1350-96)
King of Aragon from 1387 to 1396. In 1391 he reconquered Sardinia. His court was an important artistic centre.

Klosterneuburg

Austrian town, near Vienna. It is famous for an abbey of regular canons of St. Augustin founded in 1106.

Laborde, León (Marquis of) (1807-69)

French historian; author of several works including *Les Ducs de Bourgogne.*

Laon (Cathedral of)

Laon cathedral was begun in 1160 and finished in 1220. It was restored in the 19th century with excess and bad taste. The nave, 328 feet long and 88 feet high, is a beautiful example of Gothic style. Several 13th century windows survive in the apse. The two fine towers which frame the portals, frightfully restored in the last century, were drawn by Villard de Honnecourt. In the Middle Ages, the town of Laon harboured some renowned illuminators' workrooms.

Lecoy de la Marche, A.

French art critic and historian of the late 19th century. He is the author of several works on medieval painting, including *Histoire des Miniatures.*

Le Mans (Cathedral of)

The nave of the cathedral of St. Julian is 11th century Romanesque; the choir was built in the Gothic style from 1217 to 1254. The nave is lit by beautiful 12th century stained-glass windows. The façade is Norman-Romanesque. With its 108 feet high choir and double ambulatory, Le Mans cathedral represents Gothic architectural style at its height.

Limbourg Brothers

Illuminators from Limbourg working in the early 15th century. There were three of them: Pol, who died after 1416; Hennequin, or John, and Hermann, both of whom died before 1439. From 1402 onwards, the first two were in the service of Philip the Bold, Duke of Burgundy, at Dijon, and after his death in 1404, they served John the Fearless. The *Breviary of John the Fearless* (British Museum) was probably executed by Pol. From 1405 onwards all three brothers were attached to the court of John of France, Duke of Berry. The *Beautiful Hours,* sometimes called the *Hours of Ailly,* which are now in the Baron Rothschild collection in Paris, were made for the Duke of Berry between 1403 and 1413. Their best work

Limbourg Brothers
The Very Rich Hours of the Duke of Berry
Month of January
The Duke of Berry at Table
Condé Museum, Chantilly

The Very Rich Hours of the Duke of Berry (Condé Museum, Chantilly) dates from about 1415. It was finished between 1485 and 1489 by Jean Colombe of Bourges. The miniatures attributed to the Limbourg brothers comprise twenty-nine large compositions and twenty-four small, representing scenes from the Old and New Testaments and the celebrated *Calendar*. Although of Flemish origin, the Limbourg brothers are linked in style and colour to the early 15th century French miniaturists.

Lippo (c. 1354-1430)

Florentine painter and mosaicist. Of his work all that remains are some frescoes in Arezzo Cathedral. He is not to be confused with Lippo di Benivieni, who, in 1315, painted the doors of the ancient St. John Tabernacle in Florence, nor with Lippo di Corso, who worked in the same town about 1400.

Literature

After the metrical chronicles of the Romanesque era: *The Song of Roland, Lorraine Epics, Legends of King Arthur*, etc., there was in the 13th and 14th centuries the advent of a lyrical and courtly literature, and at the same time the appearance of the great chroniclers: Villehardouin, Joinville and Froissart, then, later in the 15th century, Commynes. Poetry was first represented by Renaud de Coucy, Blondel de Nesles, Colin Muset and Thibaud de Campagne. It developed with Rutebeuf, Guillaume de Lorris and Jean de Meung *(Le Roman de la Rose)*, and ended with Charles d'Orléans and François Villon. Farces, satires and fabliaux *(The Story of Renart against Ysengrin)* form an interesting part of 13th century literature. But it is with the drama that we touch the spring of the medieval expansion of lyric art. Numerous mystery plays were presented in front of cathedrals; the most classic, which is still produced today, is the *Mystery of the Passion* written by Arnoul Greban in the first half of the 15th century. The French theatre owes much to medieval comedies *(The Farce of Master Pathelin, The Mad Mother, The Frank Bowman of Bagnolet)*. Alain Chartier, who has left some mediocre verse, was, however, a great prose writer. Finally, it was in the Middle Ages that women poets first appeared in France: Marie de France and Christine de Pisan. At the same time, in Germany stories and legends were born on the banks of the Rhine, particularly the Cycle of the Grail. England's first great poets were William Langland and Geoffrey Chaucer; Italy had Dante, Boccaccio and Petrarch; Spain had its *romanceros*.

Lochner, Stephen (d. 1451)

German painter, a most important representative of the Cologne school, which developed towards the end of the 14th century. Like Fra Angelico in Italy, Lochner's paintings portray a mystic grace, expressing the quietude of religious souls. His chief work is the triptych *The Adoration of the Magi*, in Cologne Cathedral, but his *Madonna with a Hedge of Flowers* in Cologne Museum is considered his most beautiful and also his earliest work. The museums of Cologne, Berlin, Bonn, Darmstadt, Frankfurt, Munich and London share the pictures of this painter, often called "the last of the Gothics".

Lorenzetti, Ambrogio (d. c 1348)

Ambrogio Lorenzetti
Allegory of Good Government
Detail of fresco
Municipal Palace, Siena

Painter born in Siena at the end of the 13th or beginning of the 14th century, and died in the same town. He and his brother, Pietro, are among the most characteristic painters of the Sienese school. Ambrogio was the younger by five years. The *Madonna of Vico l'Abato* is attributed to him. In 1857 two of his frescoes were discovered under a coat of whitewash in the cloister of St. Francis, Siena: *The Martyrdom of the Franciscan Monks at Ceuta* and *The Obedience of St. Louis of Anjou in the Hands of the Pope*. Both frescoes were transferred to the Church. Ambrogio worked on the restoration of the Siena Cathedral *Madonna* in 1335. We have records of nearly all his work, but much has disappeared. In 1342 he painted *The Presentation in the Temple*, now in the Uffizi, Florence. Vasari sang the praises of Ambrogio Lorenzetti and pronounced him educated, with "manners that were rather those of a gentleman and a philosopher than of an artist". The *Madonna Feeding Her Child* in the Siena Seminary marks a decisive step on the road to realism. But it was with the frescoes of *Good and Bad Government* in the Municipal Palace, Siena, that Ambrogio accomplished a work of profound originality which expressed medieval ideas from their most characteristic angle: that of allegory. Justice, Peace, Temperance and Fortitude appear, themes characterised by a serenity and a superior manner of living which contrasts with the realism of the subjects which surround them. Many European and American museums share his works.

Lorenzetti, Pietro

Pietro Lorenzetti's work is better known than his life, of which our knowledge is scanty. He lived during the first part of the 14th century and, like his brother, was born and died in Siena. Vasari tells us little about his life and work. The first dated work is a polyptych of 1320 for the Archbishop of Arezzo, the *Virgin with Several Saints*, now in Santa Maria della Pieve, Arezzo. We have no information about the dates of the great frescoes at Assisi, *The Crucifixion*, *The Deposition*, *The Laying in the Tomb* and *The Resurrection*. They are among the most beautiful of the Sienese school, and were for a long time attributed to Pietro

Pietro Lorenzetti, sometimes attributed to
Story of the Blessed Umittà
Uffizi, Florence

Cavallini or Puccio Capanna. Pietro's characters express gravity and often sadness, and his genius appears austere and sometimes rough; his Madonnas and his angels rarely smile, but every figure expresses great spiritual strength. Numerous works by Pietro still survive dispersed among museums and collections in Europe and the United States.

Lorenzo di Pietro (c. 1412-80)

Painter, sculptor, architect and bronze caster, born at Castiglione di Val d'Orcia. He followed the tradition of the primitive Sienese masters. In the Spedale della Scala at Siena he painted a set of scenes from the Old and New Testaments, which is classed with his earlier work.

Maci, Jacquet

French 14th century illuminator. With Jean Pucelle and Anciau de Cens, he decorated the *Bible of Robert de Billyng* in 1327, which manuscript is in the National Library, Paris.

Maerlant, Jacob Van (c. 1235-1300)

The "father of Flemish poetry", whose often didactic work was very important. He was opposed to the nobility and severely criticised clerical abuses in his time. His main work is a *History of the World.*

Maïmonides, Moses ben Maïmon (1135-1204)
Born at Córdoba. Jewish doctor, theologian, and philosopher. He wrote *The Book of The Doubtful,* which is both a work of Jewish theology and philosophical treatise inspired by Plato and Aristotle. Maïmonides sought to reconcile faith and reason. Like Averroès, he had a profound influence on Thomas Aquinas.

Mâle, Emile (1862-1954)

French art historian and expert on medieval matters. Member of the Académie Française. His principal publications include: *L'Art religieux du XIII*[e] *siècle en France*, Paris, 1931; *L'Art allemand et l'Art français du Moyen Age*, Paris, 1940, *Rome et ses Vieilles Eglises*, Paris, 1946; *La Cathédrale de Chartres*, Paris, 1948.

Malouel, Jean (d. 1419)

Painter of Flemish origin, working in Dijon from about 1380 onwards. Jean Malouel was the uncle of the Limbourg brothers and greatly influenced them. In 1397 he was appointed court painter to the Dukes of Burgundy, succeeding Jean de Beaumetz. In 1398 he was commissioned to do five altar pictures, including *The Martyrdom of St. Denis*, which on the death of Malouel was completed by Henri Bellechose; it is now in the Louvre. In 1412 he painted the portrait of John the Fearless, which was presented to King John II of Portugal. *The Dead Christ Supported by the Eternal Father*, from the Carthusian convent at Champmol, and now in the Louvre, is attributed to him.

Marmion, Simon (1425-89)

Painter and illuminator, born and died at Valenciennes. He was appointed painter to the Duke of Burgundy. Simon Marmion worked in Valenciennes, Tournai and Amiens. Aix Museum has several pictures by him: *Jesus Meditating on His Passion*, *Portrait of a Young Man*, and *Seascape*. Berlin has *The Life of St. Bertin*; and Nuremburg, *The Coronation of Frederick III by Pope Nicholas V*.

Marsal de Sax

Spanish painter, certainly of German origin, who worked in Valencia during the 14th century. In 1396 he decorated the meeting-hall of the Town Hall, Valencia, and, about 1400, several altars in the cathedral.

Martini, Simone (1284-1344)

Simone Martini
The Virgin
Uffizi, Florence

Painter born in Siena and died at Avignon. Martini was initiated to painting from his childhood and made the acquaintance of Duccio. In 1315, he painted the *Madonna Enthroned* in the Siena Town Hall. He travelled much: in 1320 he was in Naples and earned several commissions; at Pisa, the polyptych in St. Catherine's is signed by him; in 1328 he was back at the Town Hall, Siena, painting *The Equestrian Portrait of Guidoriccio* on the wall op-

Martinus Opifex (c. 1445)
Guido Colonna
History of the Sack of Troy
National Library, Vienna

posite the *Madonna*; the work is remarkable for its abstraction. In 1333 he painted his beautiful *Annunciation* (Uffizi, Florence). Finally, in 1339 he was called to Avignon by Pope Benedict XII, and went there with his wife and his brother Donato. He worked at Notre-Dame-des-Doms. Martini met Petrarch and is said to have painted the portrait of Laura, in gratitude for which the poet wrote in a sonnet, "Surely my Simone was in Paradise; his work is such as one imagines in heaven, but not here where our flesh veils our eyes". He could not have praised him better. The painter died at Avignon in 1344. His nobility of posture, elegance of line, and flexibility of colour ensure for Simone Martini an eminent place in Trecento painting. His surviving works are very numerous.

Martinus Opifex

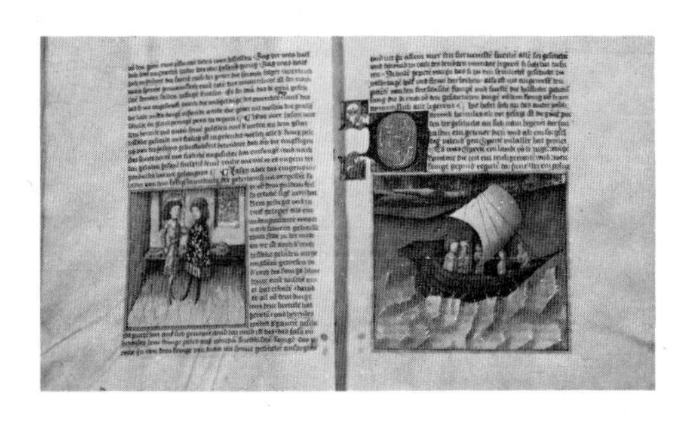

Monk and miniaturist who lived in the monastery of Melk in the first half of the 15th century. He illuminated the *Breviary of Sigismund of Luxemburg*, King of Hungary, and the *Trojan War*, by Guido Colonna.

Martorell, Bernado

Spanish painter, died c. 1453, having worked nearly all his life in Barcelona. He is credited with the decorations of the monastery at Pedralbes in 1439, and works commissioned by the Barcelona Shoemakers' Corporation in 1437.

Masaccio (Tommaso di Giovanni di Simone, called) (1401-28)

An Italian artist of outstanding genius, doubtless inspired by Donatello and Brunellschi. He worked in Florence, where he painted the frescoes in the Brancacci Chapel, and later in Rome. This great artist, lost prematurely at the age of 27, had a profound influence on the Quattrocento. He died in Rome.

Maso

Italian 14th century painter and sculptor. Like Giottino, he was a discipline of Giotto.

Master of Anthony of Burgundy

Flemish illuminator, working in Bruges between 1460 and 1490. He takes his name from the many manuscripts he composed for Anthony of Burgundy: *Valérius Maximus* (Breslau Library); the *Chronicle of Aegidius de Roya* (Meerman Westreenen Museum, The Hague); and his masterpiece, the *Book of Hours for Maria Sforza*, of Milan. In 1466-67 he made a *Black Prayer Book*, written and

Master Bertram
The Creation of the Animals
c. 1380
Kunsthalle, Hamburg

illuminated on black parchment, now in the National Library, Vienna.

Master Bertram (c. 1345-1415)

German painter and sculptor working in Hamburg; a certain number of his works have survived. He can be considered as the best landscape artist and animal painter of his time. He would have painted the altar screens in the Churches of Kiel, Hanover, Doberan and Tempzin. The reredos in St. Peter's, Hamburg, known as

the Grabow reredos, was done about 1379, and is now in the town's museum, which also has the *Buxtehude Altar* of about 1390, a *Coronation of the Virgin*, and the *Harvestehude Altar*, all by the same artist.

Master of Catherine of Cleves

Illuminator working about the mid-15th century, so-called after a book of hours he decorated in 1435 for Catherine of Cleves. He must have known the work of the Master of Flémalle and the Van Eyck brothers. Other manuscripts by this master are preserved in the Meermann Westreenen Museum at The Hague and the Library of Leyden University.

Master of the Copses

French illuminator working in the mid-14th century. He took his name from his habit of including little groves of trees in his illustrations. He is the author of the miniature decorating the *Bible of John of Sy*, the *Poetry of Guillaume de Machaut*, *The City of God* and the *Great Chronicles of France*, all four of which manuscripts are in the National Library, Paris. He also decorated the *Livy of Charles V*, the *Historical Bible of Charles VI*, and the *Golden Legend* of Jacques de Voragine, also several Bibles which are in the British Museum, London, and the Meermann Westreenen Museum at The Hague.

Master Eckhart (c. 1260-c. 1328)

German Dominican and theologian born at Hochheim (Thüringia). Student and afterwards professor of theology at Paris University. Director of the Dominicans in Saxony from 1303 to 1311. Master of theology at Cologne in 1323. His boldest sermons date from that time. On 27th March 1329, Pope John XXII published the Bull *In agrodominico*; the twenty-eight propositions attributed to Eckhart were condemned and the author condemned as a dangerous heretic. It is impossible to summarise the profound and subtle thought of Master Eckhart here. Eckhart was a philosopher (Aristotelian) and a mystic, though neither an anguished nor emotional one. He is an intellectual mystic: "What makes my happiness is not that God is good, but solely that he is intelligence and that I know it". Eckhart's originality resides in his conjunction of the didactic and the mystic, and in that he introduced the notion of immediacy into a revised perspective of scholastic philosophy. He has left us some works in Latin: *Parisian Questions*, and *Sermons*, and some in German: *Discourse on Discernment*, *Book of Consolation*, and *Of Noble Man*.

Master Francke

German 15th century painter, probably a pupil of Master Bertram. Master Francke was a great colourist and represents the height of Hanseatic painting, which was later influenced by the Dutch and Westphalian schools. He was forgotten until the 18th century and many of his works have not yet been identified or rediscovered. One of the oldest, done between 1415 and 1420, is *Christ of the Sorrows*, in the Hamburg Museum, and a small replica is in the Leipzig Museum. Hamburg Museum also has a *Crucifixion*, *The Scourging*, and *The Flight of Thomas of Canterbury*.

Master of the Heart of Smitten Love

Illuminator of the second half of the 15th century. So called after the title of a romantic tale composed by King René of Anjou (Codex No. 2597, National Library, Vienna). The same anonymous artist decorated a French translation of Boccaccio's *Theseid*; this manuscript is also in the National Library, Vienna. This master's miniatures are among the most beautiful of medieval French art in its decline. One tradition maintains that it was King René himself who wrote and illustrated the tale. In any case, it was an excellent artist who painted the characters, lit by a supernatural radiance in a fantastic setting. Sixteen of the forty-one projected miniatures were carried out.

Master of Heiligenkreuz

Early 15th century Austrian painter who carried out the reredos depicting *The Annunciation* and *The Mystic Marriage of St. Catherine* for the Cistercian Abbey of Heiligenkreuz. The panels are in the Vienna Museum.

Master Honoré

French illuminator working in the 13th century. He was the artist of the *Breviary of Philip the Fair* (National Library, Paris). Another breviary in the same library is attributed to him. He was also the author of a *Decree of Gratien* (Tours Library), which he relinquished in 1288 and which was finished in 1323 by Thomas of Wymonduswold. Among the workers in his studio were his daughter and Richard of Verdun, his son-in-law.

Master Martin

See " Martinus Opifex ".

Master of the Middle Rhine

Early 15th century German illuminator. His reredos *The Garden of Paradise*, of

Master of the Middle Rhine
The Garden of Paradise
c. 1420
Staedel Museum, Frankfurt-am-Main

about 1420, is in the Staedel Institute, Frankfurt.

Master of Otto Van Moerdrecht

Early 15th century Dutch illuminator. The manuscript executed for Otto Van Moerdrecht, which is in the library of Thubingen University, is attributed to him. He is also the author of the *Breviary for Duke Reinaud IV of Guelders* of about 1417, now in the Pierpont Morgan Library, New York. Ninety-three miniatures in this manuscript are by his hand; the others are by a contemporary Dutch illuminator known as the Master of Zweder Van Culemborg.

Master of Trebon

Late 14th century painter, born in Bohemia, author of the Trebon reredos, which he painted about 1380; the panels are in the National Gallery, Prague.

Mathieu d'Arras (d. 1352)

French architect, born in Arras, died in Prague. In 1344 he began the Cathedral of St. Guy, Prague, taking his inspiration from Narbonne.

Michel Bernard d'Arras

Late 14th century French tapestry maker, whose sole known work is *The Battle of Roosebeke*, which he made c. 1387 for Philip the Bold.

Monaco, Lorenzo

Late 14th-early 15th century Italian monk of the monastery of the Angels, Florence, and one of the foremost illuminators of his period; he was also a great painter. It is thought that he is the author of the forty-four miniatures which decorate the monastery's celebrated missal. His paintings are distributed among museums in Europe and the United States.

N

Neri da Rimini

Miniaturist working in Rimini about 1305. He probably decorated an antiphonary with figures copied from Giotto.

Notre-Dame

The cathedral of Notre-Dame-de-Paris, built in the 12th century and finished in 1330, is the last church with tribunes but one of the earliest with flying buttresses. The 18th century and the French Revolution destroyed practically all the furnishings and Gothic decoration. Part of the furnishings, frescoes and stained glass were replaced in the 19th century by the workmen of Viollet-le-Duc, who added a spire to the transept crossing. Nearly all the old 12th and 13th century windows were destroyed by the 18th century canons. Although subjected to centuries of restorations the three great rose windows have nevertheless survived practically intact. The west rose still contains a few 13th century panes, so does the south rose, which is devoted to scenes from the New Testament. The north rose, dating from the end of the 13th century, is the best preserved; the general colour is a blaze of azure, and it depicts Old Testament figures surrounding *The Virgin Holding the Infant Jesus.*

Orcagna, Andrea di Cione (after 1308-after 1368)

Italian architect, painter and sculptor. He worked in Florence where he decorated the tabernacle of St. Michael's Church. He painted *Death and Judgement* at the Campo Santo, Pisa. He was a pupil of Giotto.

Paris Psalter (c. 1230)
Nativity; The Announcement to the Shepherds
Arsenal Library, Paris

Pacino di Bonaguida

Italian historical painter of the 14th century, contemporary with Giotto. He illustrated scenes from the life of Christ and the manuscript is in the Pierpont Morgan Library, New York.

Paolo Veneziano (c. 1340-c. 1362)

We know very little about the life of this artist except that he was certainly born in Venice. The Louvre has a triptych, the centre panel of which depicts the Virgin. He decorated numerous Venetian churches.

Paris School

The Paris school denotes a particular style of Gothic illumination which evolved in the Parisian workrooms at the beginning of the 13th century. This style influenced the whole of Europe. Miniatures of the school are distinguished by very fine drawing and delicate colours. It disappeared towards the end of the Hundred Years War.

Pediment

A triangular, or sometimes semi-circular, architectural embellishment over the entrance of a building.

Pedro I

King of Aragon (kingdom north-east of Spain) from 1094 to 1104. His victory at Albocacer is depicted by the painter Marsal de Sax on the reredos of St. George's, now in the Victoria and Albert Museum, London.

Pedro IV

King of Aragon 1336-87. He was nicknamed the Ceremonious. He gave many commissions to painters of the Barcelona school.

Perez, Gonzalo

Spanish painter working in Valencia from 1405 to 1423. He decorated Valencia Cathedral.

Portrait of Philip the Good
15th century
Condé Museum, Chantilly

Petit-Quevilly Church

Seine-Maritime church, near to Rouen, which has one of the rare Gothic frescoes which is practically intact. It decorates a sexpartite vault.

Petrarch (1304-74)

This Italian poet who sang of his hopeless love for Laura di Noves was also a philosopher and a grammarian. He was still a man of the Middle Ages, an unqualified admirer of Aristotle. In 1367 he published a book which rapidly achieved celebrity: *On His Ignorance and That of Many Others.*

Philip II (1527-98)

Son of Charles V and Isabella of Portugal, King of Spain and the Low Countries. Zealous defender of Catholicism. He sent his " Invincible Armada " against England, but the enterprise turned to disaster. He died in the Escorial castle-monastery. His grandiose projects crumbled in his lifetime and Spain emerged enfeebled from his reign.

Philip III the Bold (1245-85)

Born at Poissy, son of St. Louis and Margaret of Provence. He became King of France in 1270. In 1271 he annexed the County of Toulouse to his kingdom. The Pope excommunicated Pedro III of Aragon and gave the kingdom to Charles of Valois, son of Philip the Bold. Philip III died at Perpignan, after being defeated at Catalonia. His first wife was Isabella of Aragon, the second Mary, daughter of Henry III, Duke of Brabant and Lothier.

Philip IV the Fair (1268-1314)

Born at Fontainebleau, son of Philip III and Isabella of Aragon, became King of France in 1285. War between England and France nearly broke out at the beginning of his reign, but conflict was avoided, due to the intervention of the Pope. Philip the Fair had a long disagreement with the Church over the imprisonment of the Bishop of Pamiers. He was reconciled with Rome only after the assumption of Pope Clement V and his installation at Avignon.

Philip III the Good (1396-1467)

Born at Dijon, son of John the Fearless, he became Duke of Burgundy in 1419 and was one of the greatest sovereigns of the period. The House of Burgundy knew magnificence in his reign. He was regent to Charles VI and became reconciled to Charles VII by the Treaty of Arras. In 1429 he created the Order of the Golden Fleece, the primary great European order.

Philip VI of Valois (1293-1350)

Son of Charles of Valois and Margaret of Sicily. He became King of France in 1328, in which year he vanquished the Flemish at Cassel. Early in the Hundred Years War, Philip was beaten in the naval battle of Sluys 1340, and at Crécy in 1346. At the end of his life he bought the Dauphinry and the seigniory of Montpellier. His first marriage was to Jeanne of Burgundy and his second to Blanche of Navarre.

Pierre of Brussels

He worked in Paris from 1318-29. Many of the frescoes in the castle of Conflans are attributed to him, especially those depicting the sea voyage of Robert II of Artois.

Piero della Francesca (c. 1410-92)

Tuscan painter, born at Borgo San Sepolcro, a little town in the Tiber Valley. He was educated at Florence by Domenico Veneziano. His first work, *The Baptism of Christ*, is in the National Gallery, London.

Piero della Francesca (c. 1410-92)
St. John the Baptist and St. Sebastian
Communal Picture Gallery, San Sepolcro

In 1440 he was at the ducal court of Urbino, an important centre of the "first" Italian Renaissance. He worked at Rome for Pope Pius II, and subsequently spent the rest of his life with the Montefeltro court, at Urbino and at Arezzo. In his frescoes he has given us the highest examples of Quattrocento art. He carried out his chief work, *The History of the Holy Cross* (Arezzo), between 1452 and 1460.

Pietro da Rimini

Italian painter who lived during the first half of the 14th century. We should mention his *Crucifixion* in the Church of the Dead, Urbania.

Pisanello (1395-1455)

Painter and medallist, born at Pisa. Pupil of Andrea del Castagno. It is thought he was also an illuminator for some time. He was an artist of extended register and precious poetry, very influenced by Gozzoli and Pinturrichio. Most of the frescoes he painted have perished, except for the *Annunciation* in the Church of San Fermo, Verona, and *St. George Delivering the Princess Trebizond*, in the

Lippo Vanni
Virgin and Child
Centre of a polyptych
Lehman Collection, New York

Church of St. Anastasia, Verona, both fairly dilapidated. But it was in medals that Pisanello revealed a more perfect world of expression. His production was important and his influence in Europe extensive.

Polo, Marco (1254-1324)

Italian explorer who crossed Asia by way of Mongolia and returned via the Philippines and Sumatra. He stayed in Mongolia for seventeen years in the service of the great Kubla Khan. His journeys, described in the *Book of Marco Polo*, constitute a precious geographic and human document.

Polyptych

Term applied to a picture made up of several panels.

Porcher, Jean (contemporary)

Paleographic archivist, member of the school of Rome; member of the Society of Antiquaries of London and the Pierpont Morgan Library, New York; honorary chief keeper of the manuscript room in the National Library, Paris; author of numerous works on medieval painting and miniatures.

Poussin, Nicholas (1594-1665)

French painter and engraver born at Villers near to Les Andelys. He spent a great part of his life in Rome. He is one of the most illustrious representatives of French painting in the 17th century.

Printing

From the 6th century the Chinese had carried out a process of engraving letters on wood and printing them on leaves. In the Middle Ages, about the 12th century, a crude method of printing letters on parchment was also known. But it was not until 1436 that Gutenberg, in Mayence, invented the movable metal letter and the hand press which enabled him to produce a book in several copies. There followed some great 15th century European printers, such as Henri Estienne, Elzévir, Plantin, Froben and Alde.

Pucelle, Jean

French miniaturist of the first half of the 14th century. Influenced by Master Honoré. We read on one of the two illuminated pages in the National Library, Paris: "Jean Pucelle, Anciau de Cens and Jacquet Maci, they have illuminated this book... the year of grace one thousand CCC and XXVIII, on a Thursday, the last day of April, on the eve of May the Vth month". It is one of the oldest signatures of illuminators. In 1325 and 1328 Pucelle illuminated the prayer book of Jeanne d'Evreux. His work was important. He was one of the greatest painters and illuminators of the Gothic period.

Quattrocento

In English: fourteen hundreds, the years of the 15th century. It has been convenient to use this name for the Italian artistic movement of the "first Renaissance".

Reformation

Religious and political movement in Europe, which, in the early 16th century, came into conflict with the Roman Catholic Church. It enjoyed unequal fortunes: its following was fairly weak in the Latin countries, but German and Scandinavian countries provided a large welcome. A new "reformed" church was instigated in France by Jean Calvin, and in Germany by Martin Luther, and in England Queen Elizabeth I became head of a new established religion: Anglicanism. The consequences for the political and religious unity of Europe were immense. The Reformation had an influence on the arts throughout the 16th century.

Reims (Cathedral of)

Begun in the early 13th century, possibly by the master workman Jean d'Orbais. The nave and the towers date from the end of the 13th and the first half of the 14th century. It still has some beautiful stained glass of the flamboyant Gothic era. But it is its 15th century sculptures and tapestries, in particular the sculptures on its portals, that make Reims Cathedral one of the most beautiful showplaces of Gothic statuary.

Reliquary

A coffer, ampulla or case holding the relics of a saint. Many were made in the Middle Ages. The art of the reliquary

Reliquary of the Holy Thorn
Cathedral Treasury, Reims

reached its height in the 14th and 15th centuries. The Treasury of Reims Cathedral contains the reliquary of the Holy Thorn in rock crystal, gold-enamel, pearls and rubies. This beautiful example of the art was made about 1460 by Guillaume Lemaistre, a Parisian goldsmith.

Renaissance

Word designating the artistic, literary and scientific movement which occurred during the 15th and 16th centuries. This movement was primarily based on the arts, literature and sciences of antiquity. The Italian Renaissance is divided into two parts: the first Renaissance in the 15th century (Quattrocento) with Masaccio, Brunelleschi, Botticelli, Donatello, Leonardo da Vinci, etc., and the second dominated by Michelangelo and Raphaël. Francis I attracted several Italian Renaissance artists: Leonardo da Vinci, Primaticcio and Benvenuto Cellini, who in their turn inspired such French artists as Pierre Lescot, Philibert Delorme, Jean Goujon, François Clouet and Germain Pilon.

René I (1409-80)

Born at Angers, son of Louis II and Yolanda of Aragon, Duke of Anjou, Bar and Lorraine. From 1434 he was King of Aragon and Sicily. His first wife was Isabelle of Lorraine and his second Jeanne of Laval. René I remained popular for his taste in arts and letters. He was familiarly called King René.

Renoir, Auguste (1841-1919)

An Impressionist Master; painter of *Ball at the Moulin Rouge*, *The Gipsy*, *The Boaters' Picnic*, etc.

Reredos

Painted or sculpted panel which is raised behind an altar. Also known as an altar-screen. One of the most famous is in St. Mark's, Venice. Numerous altar screens were erected by Gothic painters in Spain, particularly in the Valencia and Barcelona schools. In France, there is a beautiful 14th century sculpted reredos in the Basilica of Saint-Denis.

Ribbed Vaulting

Vault supported by an 'ogive' or diagonal groin or rib. The pointed arch formed by ribs makes the vault easier to construct and much stronger. The ribbed vault was one of the great discoveries of Gothic master builders; it enabled them to enlarge the surface of the vaulting and raise the height of the buildings. The reception hall of the Abbey of Mont-Saint-Michel offers a fine series of early Gothic ribbed vaults.

Richard II (1367-1400)

Born at Bordeaux, son of the Black Prince, King of England from 1377 to 1399. In 1382 he married Anne of Bohemia, daughter of Charles IV. He was in perpetual conflict with Parliament, and abdicated in 1399.

Richard I the Lionheart (1157-99)

King of England from 1189-99. He went on the third Crusade and on his way home was captured by the German Emperor, who released him only on payment of a huge ransom.

Richard of Verdun

Early 14th century French painter and miniaturist. He collaborated with Jean de la Mare to decorate the three lost antiphonaries of the Sainte-Chapelle.

Rosace

In architecture this term indicates a round-shaped ornament of symmetrical foliage or petals. The term is also applied to a circular assembly of stained glass in a church, otherwise called a rose-window. The most beautiful rosaces of the Gothic era are in the cathedrals of Paris, Chartres and Bourges.

Roussillon

Province in south-east France bordering on Spain. Ancient capital, Perpignan. In the Middle Ages Roussillon was the connecting link between the culture of the North and the Catalan and Spanish artists, many of whom worked in Perpignan. Roussillon came under the French crown in 1659.

Rutebeuf (died c. 1258)

One of the greatest French medieval poets, with François Villon and Charles d'Orléans. He wrote numerous plays of which a few survive including *The Miracle of Theophilus*. He also wrote laments and satirical poems. He was often poverty-stricken.

Ruysbroek, Jan Van (1294-1381)

Nicknamed the Ecstatic Doctor. Celebrated Dutch theologian and mystic, born in Ruysbroek and died at the convent of Groenendaal, of which he was prior. He was the master of Jean Tauler and Gerard de Groote. He wrote many works, of which the two most famous are *The Treatise on Christian Faith* and *The Twelve Virtues.*

St. Bernard (1091-1153)

Monk. Born at Château de Fontaine, near Dijon. As Abelard was the master of the art of thinking, so St. Bernard appears as the enemy of all dialectic, although his mysticism was not lacking in intellectual rigour. He was primarily the furtherer of a monastic tradition which had its roots in the earliest apostolic times and carried on through the Church Fathers: Origen, Gregory of Nysse, Maxime and St. Augustin. All St. Bernard's doctrine, one might say, originates in direct line from the Old and New Testaments, built up by Catholic dogma and rigorous observance of the Rule. The problem posed by St. Bernard was that of the restoration of man. As against the schools where Aristotle and Plato were taught, the monastery readopted "the school of the early church", of which Christ was the master. The emphasis was no longer philosophic but mystic, and its ultimate aim was the comprehension of the supernatural through love. St. Bernard was a man of action, and preached the second Crusade. His work is known to us from his treatises, and his life from the important collection of his letters. He reformed the Cistercian Order and founded Clairvaux Abbey. From the artistic point of view, his reforms had profound effects on religious art.

Saint-Denis, Basilica of, Paris

This Basilica, which served as a mausoleum for the French kings, was the first great

Gothic edifice built in France. The façade and the first two bays of the nave were erected by Sugar between 1136 and 1140; the choir and the crypt followed between 1140 and 1144. It was enlarged and rebuilt from 1231 but successive hindrances slowed it down. The abbey was not finished until 1281. The choir still has several beautiful 12th and 13th century windows.

Sainte-Chapelle

Mitre for mourning ceremonies
Former treasure of Sainte-Chapelle
Mid-14th century
Louvre, Paris

In Paris. St. Louis had it built to house the crown of thorns he brought back from the Holy Land. It was constructed between 1242 and 1248. It comprises two chapels, an upper and a lower. Fifteen remarkable 13th century stained-glass windows decorate the upper chapel.

St. Francis of Assisi (1182-1226)

Francesco Bernadone was born at Assisi. His father was a rich cloth merchant.

Bonaventura di Berlinghiero
Story of the Life of St. Francis
Church of St. Francis, Pescia

After a fairly gay youth, he began in 1205 to lead a strict religious life. Two years later, hearing the words of the Evangelist on the mission of the apostles, he was deeply impressed and became "engaged to Lady Poverty" there and then. His first companion was a gentleman of Assisi, Bernardo di Quintavalle; the next was Pietro di Cataneo, also of Assisi. Together they founded on 12th April, 1208, the Brotherhood of the Penitents of Assisi, which several years later took the name of the Little Brothers. The movement spread rapidly and very soon the Pope was obliged to nominate a prelate to protect the order, Cardinal Ugolino. An excess of asceticism on the one hand and certain relaxations on the other gave the founder some anxiety. But finally unity was respected. St. Francis went to Egypt, where he was welcomed with great honours. He received the stigmata on Mount La Verna two years before his death (*St. Francis Receiving the Stigmata*, by Giotto, Louvre). St. Francis had an immense influence in his lifetime; after his death the Franciscan message strongly coloured medieval thinking. Poets celebrated it, Dante foremost. But it was

Life of St. Louis, King of France
Scenes from the King's childhood
National Library, Paris

principally in the field of art and painting that his influence was to leave its deepest mark. The Franciscan spirit inspired numerous Trecento painters, particularly Giotto, and later, during the Quattrocento, Piero della Francesca and Fra Angelico, to name only the greatest.

St. Louis (1214-70)

Born at Poissy, son of Louis VIII and Blanche of Castille, Louis IX, or St. Louis, was King of France from 1226 until his death in 1270. From 1226 to 1236 he reigned under the regency of his mother, who suppressed a vassals revolt and ended the war against the Albigensians by the Treaty of Meaux, 1229. In 1234, Louis IX married Marguerite of Provence. In 1242, he uncovered a plot against him by the Count of Marche and the English, but the struggle was not finally settled until the Treaty of Paris, 1259, which gave Louis IX Normandy, Anjou, Maine and Poitou. He went on the seventh Crusade to liberate Palestine from the Sultan of Egypt. He was taken prisoner and bought his freedom, but prolonged his stay in Palestine until 1254, returning to France on the death of his mother. After a reorganisation of the provinces, the construction of the Sainte-Chapelle, and the Sorbonne, among other buildings, and the enlargement of the St. Denis Basilica, he set off on the eighth Crusade in 1270, during which he died of the plague in Tunis. His exemplary life, his charity and his high sense of justice earned him great esteem. Joinville wrote his life-story. He was canonised by Pope Boniface VIII in 1297. In his reign Gothic style attained its height in architecture, painting, stained glass and miniatures.

St. Paul

Born at Tarsus in Asia-Minor, martyred in Rome in the year 67. The Acts of the Apostles tell us that he had a celestial vision on the road to Damascus and was converted, consequently preaching Christ in Jerusalem, Ephesus, Corinth, Rome, etc. His epistles form part of the New Testament.

St. Thomas Aquinas (1225-74)

Nicknamed the Angelic Doctor, born at the Castle of Roccasecca. His father, Landulf Aquinas, sent him to the Faculty of Arts of Naples University from 1236 to 1239. To the despair of his family, who would have preferred to see him a bishop, he entered the Dominican Order. From vocation and also from the ardent desire to create, Thomas Aquinas threw himself into the study of antiquities and the philosophies of the time. He worked at Cologne from 1248-52 under the guidance of Albert the Great. Then he studied in Paris. In 1272 he returned to Naples. He died two years later while going to attend the Council of Lyons. The work of St.

Beato Angelico
St. Thomas Aquinas
St. Nicholas Chapel, Vatican, Rome

Thomas is very important. He was a religious philosopher but above all a theologian, and it is a mistake that his *Doctrine Against the Gentiles* is sometimes called a "philosophical doctrine". Thomist thought is a process of revealing God in man; it is a science, a methodology. William of Auxerre had already written: "If theology did not admit principles it would be neither an art nor a science". St. Thomas evolved a new process of reasoning. His influence was very great in all fields of thought and art in the Middle Ages. Dante placed him in the fourth heaven, that of the sun, in his "Paradise" (*Divine Comedy:* "Paradise", Canto X). The Trecento artists knew his work and were influenced by it. Andrea da Firenze painted a monumental picture: *The Triumph of St. Thomas Aquinas.*

Sano di Pietro (1406-81)

Painter and illuminator born in Siena. He was of profoundly religious temperament, and his work is entirely concerned with the Virgin and the lives of certain saints. He painted many pictures of St. Bernardin and St. Catherine of Siena. The Chantilly Museum has his *Mystic Marriage of St. Francis with Lady Poverty*, the National Gallery, London, has a *Coronation of the Virgin*, and the Louvre has several scenes from the life of St. Jerome.

Sano di Pietro
The Virgin appearing to Callisto III (1456)
Picture Gallery, Siena

Scholastic

Of knowledge that was taught through the schools. Principal method of teaching in the Middle Ages. Scholastic philosophy was a dialectic, but unfortunately lacking the counterweight of a rigorous critique.

Scotus, Duns (c. 1270-1308)

Franciscan priest of Scottish origin, ordained at Northampton in 1291. Worked in Paris and taught at Oxford and Cambridge. His subtle and profound thought was qualified by liberality, in the sense that he was guided by the concern to found a rational theology.

Scriptorium

Workroom of an illuminator. In the Romanesque period the scriptorium was in the monastery itself, but from the end of the 12th century, scriptoria were set up in important towns. Those in the rue Boutebrie and the rue de la Parcheminerie in Paris were renowned.

Sens (Cathedral of)

Prototype of the Gothic cathedrals. The principal work was carried out between 1130 and 1160, and consecrated by Pope Alexander III in 1164. The façade is 13th century; the building was completed at the end of the 15th century. The nave prefigures that of Canterbury, which was built by William of Sens in 1175. The treasury, one of the richest in all France, holds some gorgeous fabrics and tapestries. Despite mutilations a lovely assemblage of Gothic stained glass can still be seen: the high windows of the apse representing the life of the Virgin, the Passion and the life of St. Stephen (13th century) and the set of windows in the north ambulatory (14th century).

Serra Brothers

Pedro and Jaime, Spanish painters who worked in Catalonia during the second half of the 14th century. Pedro was the artist of the celebrated reredos of Holy Spirit (1394) which is in the Church of Our Lady, Manresa.

Shaw, George Bernard (1856-1950)

Dublin-born writer and dramatist. Author of *Candida*, *Caesar and Cleopatra*, *Man and Superman*, etc. Writer full of paradoxes, imaginative and trenchant. Nobel prize, 1925.

Shrine

Coffer in which the relics of a saint are kept. The following are some of the most characteristic Gothic shrines: St. Firmin, Amiens Cathedral Treasury, mid-13th century; that said to be of St. Rémi, Châlons-sur-Marne Cathedral Treasury, also mid-13th century; St. Romain, Rouen Cathedral Treasury, late 13th century; St. Stephen of Muret, Ambazac Church, Haute-Vienne, c. 1200. The Rhenish and Mosan arts produced some beautiful shrines in the 13th and 14th centuries, so did Flemish art, of which one of the most prestigious is that of St. Ursula at Bruges, decorated by Memlinc. Most English Gothic shrines were destroyed at the time of the Reformation, among others, that of Thomas à Becket, at Canterbury.

Sigismund of Luxembourg (1368-1437)

King of Hungary and of Bohemia in 1387 and 1419. German Emperor in 1411. Defeated at Nicopolis. Marred his reign by burning the reformer John Huss despite the safe-conduct he had granted him to attend the council of Basle.

Signorelli, Luca (1441-1523)

Painter of the celebrated frescoes in Orvieto Cathedral: *The Antichrist*, *Hell*, *The Resurrection*, *Paradise*, powerful works displaying remarkable technique and anatomical knowledge. Michelangelo was influenced by Signorelli's work.

Simone Camaldolese (Don)

Italian monk and illuminator, also known as Simone of Siena, working in Florence at the end of the 14th and beginning of the 15th century. Apart from the missal he illuminated for Santa Croce, Florence, no other work can be attributed to him with certainty. All the same, there did exist a school of Camaldolese which produced several illuminated manuscripts.

Simone dei Crocefissi (c. 1330-99)

Italian painter, born and died in Bologna. He was a pupil of Vitale da Bologna. In his native town he carried out numerous frescoes and religious paintings, of which many have disappeared.

Soest, Konrad Von

Early 15th century German painter and miniaturist. He is thought to have illustrated numerous manuscripts and painted a religious picture at Niederwildungen.

Spandrel

Masonry of the angle at the intersection of two walls or between two arches. In the Romanesque nave of Bayeux Cathedral there are some interesting carved spandrels sculpted with Irish-inspired interlacings.

Spinello Aretino (c. 1346-1410)

Italian painter born in Arezzo. Pupil of Jacopo del Casentino. His chief work, dating from about 1400, is the celebrated fresco he did in Santa Maria, Arezzo, representing *The Fall of the Rebel Angels*, the fragments of which are preserved in the National Gallery, London. Towards the end of his life he decorated a hall in the Palazzo Publico, Siena, with frescoes depicting *The Venetian Campaign against Frederick Barbarossa*. Much of this artist's work is dispersed among museums.

Stefano da Zevio (c. 1375-c. 1451)

Painter born in Verona. Specialist in historical and religious scenes. He worked in Mantua, Verona and Castel Romano. Few of his paintings survive. Budapest Museum has a *Virgin and Infant Jesus* and the Brera Gallery, Milan, an *Adoration of the Magi*.

Stigmata

Marks resembling the five wounds of Christ Jesus Crucified. They appeared on certain saints of the catholic church including St. Francis of Assisi, of which Giotto's workshop painted a picture—*St. Francis Receiving the Stigmata*, now in the Louvre.

Suger (1081-1151)

Abbot and minister in the reigns of Louis VI and Louis VII. It was he who undertook the construction of the St. Denis Basilica, of which he was the Abbot. During the second Crusade, which took place from 1147-9, he was regent of France in the absence of Louis VII, and earned the nickname "Father of the Country". He wrote a *Life of Louis VI* and was an enlightened patron of the arts.

Tapestry

Work of wool or silk composed on a loom. There are three distinct types of tapestry: high warp, low warp, and needleloom. Tapestry flourished in England from the Romanesque period, but it was primarily in the 13th century that the art spread through Europe. The influence of the Crusades was instrumental in bringing this about. In the 14th century Flemish manufacture underwent a great development, to such an extent that Italy started calling tapestries *arazzi*, a corruption derived from Arras. Many tapestries have disappeared, others have badly deteriorated with time. Among the most remarkable and best preserved from the Gothic period are the *Apocalypse*, of Angers, *The Legend of St. Stephen* (Cluny Museum) and those in the treasury of Sens Cathedral.

15th century Arras Tapestry
Story of St. Stephen
Cluny Museum, Paris

Paolo Ucello (1396-1475)
Battle of San Romano
Louvre, Paris

Tempera

Method of using water and a fixative to bind pigments for painting. The best is egg tempera. Medieval painters used this process widely. Egg in fact fixes the pigments better than a simple water medium. White of egg is insoluble in water and gives the colours brilliance as well as rendering them more transparent. Cennini has left us the best recipes for tempera.

Theoderich

Czech painter working in Prague between 1359 and 1381. He was attached to the court of the Emperor Charles IV for whom he made the paintings in the royal chapel at Karlstein. He was president of the Prague painters' corporation. The museum there has his *Virgin and Infant Jesus Adored by Charles IV*. In the Vienna Museum is a *Christ on the Cross*, *The Virgin and St. John*, and *St. Ambrose and St. Augustin*. His painting was strongly influenced by the work of the Italian painter Tomaso da Modena, who had settled in Prague.

Tomaso da Modena (c. 1325-c. 1379)

This artist worked in Modena from 1350. He also lived in Prague. Most museums of the large towns in Northern Italy possess work by him. The Vienna Museum has a *Virgin and Infant Jesus*.

Trecento

Italian for three hundred, meaning all dates beginning one thousand, three hundred, i.e. 1300-99. Artists of this period are often referred to as Trecentisti.

Tympanum

Term applied to the triangular space formed between the doorway and the top of its containing arch. Those of Gothic cathedrals were very rich in sculpture, generally illustrating scenes from the New Testament: *The Last Judgement*, *Christ in Glory*, or *The Life of the Virgin*; among the most famous are those of Chartres, Reims, Amiens and Bourges.

Uccello (Paolo di Dono, called) (c. 1396-1475)

One of the great Florentine painters of the Quattrocento. He started as a goldsmith, then he studied painting in Florence and Padua. His chief work is the series of frescoes which decorate the cloister of Santa Maria Novella, Florence. He is also known for battle scenes. *The Battle of San Romano* is in the Louvre, and the National Gallery, London, and Uffizi, Florence, each have a work on the same subject.

Roger Van der Weyden (1399-1464)
Pietà
Burgos Museum

Vagaggini, Sandra (contemporary)

Italian art critic. She is the author of works on medieval Italian painting, including a book on *The Florentine Miniature in the 14th and 15th Centuries.*

Van der Weyden, Roger (1399-1464)

Also known as Roger of the Pasture. Flemish painter born in Tournai and died in Brussels. He was the pupil of Robert Campin in 1427; five years later he was received as a master painter in Tournai. Apart from a few portraits his work is almost entirely religious. After 1443 he was commissioned to decorate the chapel of the Beaune asylum, where he painted *The Last Judgement.* Although of unequal value, his work is, with *The Adoration of the Lamb* by the Van Eyck brothers, the most notable in Flemish Gothic art. Bouts and Memlinc were influenced by his painting.

Van Eyck Brothers

Hubert, born c. 1370, d. 1426?; Jan, born c. 1385, died in Bruges in 1441. The two celebrated "primitive" Flemish painters, authors of the reredos of Saint-Bavon, Ghent, *The Mystic Lamb. The Virgin and the Chancellor Rolin* in the Louvre is attributed to Jan Van Eyck, so is the portrait of Arnolfini and his wife in the National Gallery, and the triptych of *Canon Van der Paele* in the Communal Museum of Bruges.

Vasari, Giorgio (1511-74)

Painter, architect and historian of Italian art. He is best known for his work *Lives of the Best Painters, Sculptors and Architects*, which is a valuable document containing much information on 14th, 15th and 16th century painting. Without Vasari we probably would have none of this information.

Villon, François (1431-c. 1465)

One of the great French poets. He led an adventurous life and was even condemned to be hanged, but was reprieved by Louis XI. He is the author of the *Little Testament* and the *Great Testament* and an odd collection of poems in incomprehensible criminal jargon, or medieval slang.

Vincent de Beauvais (c. 1190-c. 1264)

French Dominican, theologian, philosopher and counsellor of St. Louis. We owe to him many works, religious, artistic and scientific, but his major work is the *Speculum Majus*, or Superior Mirror, which contains a good part of all the general knowledge of the time.

Vitale da Bologna

Italian painter and sculptor, born at Bologna between 1289 and 1309, and died between 1359 and 1369. Founder of the Bologna School. He produced the polyptych in St. Saviour's, Bologna. The *Madonna of the Battuti* (a flagellant order), one of his principal works, is in the Vatican Museum.

Voragine, Jacques de (Jacopo da Varezze) (c. 1228-98)

Italian hagiographer and poet. Author of *The Golden Legend*, a collection of lives of saints, which he wrote about 1260, but which did not acquire its title until the 15th century. He inspired numerous painters and illuminators.

Winchester Bible (1160-70)
Scenes from the Reign of David
Cathedral Library, Winchester

Westminster Abbey

Beautiful Gothic edifice erected from 1245 on the site of a Benedictine Abbey dating from the year 740. It is a national sanctuary where the sovereigns of England are crowned and illustrious people are buried. The choir is ornamented with a fine 14th century tapestry and late Gothic stained-glass windows.

Winchester

One of the most ancient towns in England. For a long time it was the capital of the Kingdom of Wessex and long-standing rival of London. It possesses the largest medieval cathedral—second only in size to St. Peter's, Rome. William Rufus, son of William the Conqueror, is buried there. Winchester was a very active artistic centre at the height of the Middle Ages. The workshops of its illuminators were renowned even on the Continent. For political and economic reasons, the importance of Winchester declined after the Hundred Years War.

Printed in Italy

List of Illustrations

Maps

Dictionary

Bibliography

Marcel Aubert: *Vitraux des Cathédrales de France: XIIe-XIIIe Siècle*, Paris, 1937.
Marcel Aubert: *Le Vitrail en France*, Paris, 1946.
Marcel Aubert: *La France glorieuse au Moyen Age*, Paris, 1948.
J. Baker: *English Stained Glass*, London, 1960.
F. Baumgart: *Das Kunstgeschichtbuch*, Frankfurt-am-Main, 1962.
B. Berenson: *Essay in the Study of Sienese Painting*, New York, 1918.
Anna Maria Cetto: *Miniatures du Moyen Age*, Lausanne, 1950.
P. Deschamps and M. Thibout: *La Peinture murale en France au Début de l'Epoque gothique*, Paris, 1964.
B. Dorival: *La Peinture française*, Paris, 1946.
W. Dräyer: *Giotto – Die Geschichte Christi*, Munich, 1960.
Jacques Dupont: *Les Primitifs français*, Paris, 1937.
Jacques Dupont and Cesare Gnudi: *La Peinture gothique*, Geneva, 1954.
Elie Faure: *L'Art médiéval*, Paris, 1964.
H. Focillon: *L'Art en Occident*, Paris, 1938.
P. Gay: *Giotto*, Paris, 1949.
René Huyghe: *Dialogue avec le Visible*, Paris, 1955.
E. Lambert: *Le Style gothique*, Paris, 1943.
J. Lanz: *Les Tapisseries gothiques*, Lausanne, undated.
Jacques Lassaigne: *La Peinture espagnole: Des Fresques romanes au Greco*, Geneva, 1952.
A. Lecoy de la Marche: *Les Manuscrits et la Miniature*, Paris, 1884.
L. Lefrançois-Pillion and J. Lafond: *L'Art du XIVe Siècle en France*, Paris, 1954.
Emile Mâle: *L'Art religieux du XIIIe Siècle en France*, Paris, 1931.
Emile Mâle: *L'Art allemand et l'Art français du Moyen Age*, Paris, 1940.
Emile Mâle: *Art et Artistes au Moyen Age*, Paris, 1947.
André Malraux: *Les Voix du Silence*, Paris, 1951. English translation by Stuart Gilbert: *The Voices of Silence*, London, 1954.
E. Newton: *European Painting and Sculpture*, London, 1961.
Régine Pernoud: *Histoire du Peuple français: Des Origines au Moyen Age*, Paris, 1951.
J. Pirenne: *Les Grands Courants de l'Histoire universelle*, volume II, Paris, 1944.
J. Porcher: *L'Enluminure française*, Paris, 1959.
L. Reau: *Les Primitifs allemands*, Paris, 1910.
D. E. Saunders: *English Illumination*, Florence, 1930.
F. Unterkircher: *La Miniatura Austriaca*, Milan/Florence, 1954.
S. Vagaggini: *La Miniatura Fiorentina*, Milan/Florence, 1952.
G. Vitzhum: *Die Pariser Miniaturmalerei*, Leipzig, 1907.
G. Westlake: *History of Design in Painted Glass*, London, 1894.
Wilhelm Worringer: *L'Art gothique*, Paris, 1941.

PRODUCTION
EDITO-SERVICE S.A., GENEVA

PRINTED IN ITALY

03 015 013 (30)